# WE DID PORN

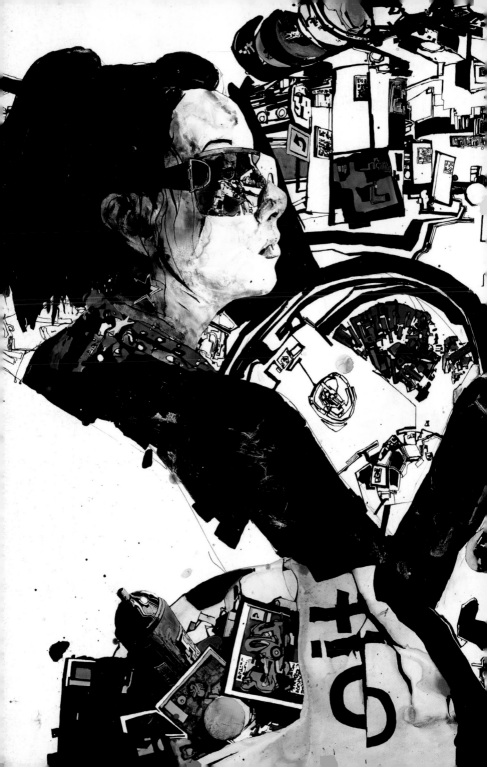

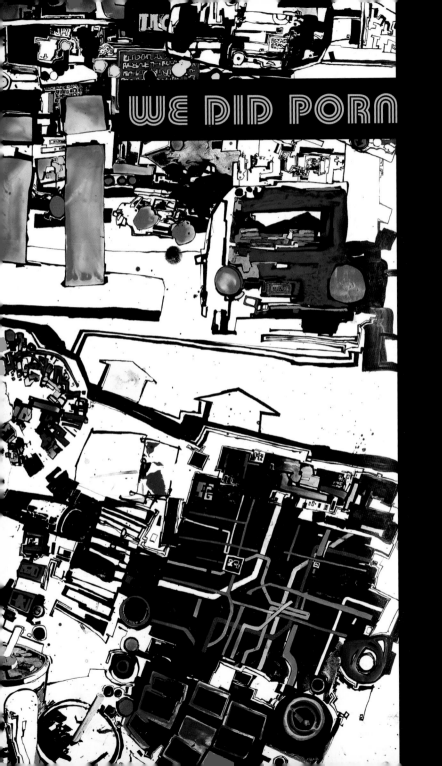

Published by Tin House Books, Portland, Oregon, and New York, New York
Distributed to the trade by Publishers Group West, 1700 Fourth St., Berkeley, CA 94710,
www.pgw.com

Library of Congress Cataloging-in-Publication Data

Smith, Zak, 1976-
  We did porn : memoir and drawings / by Zak Smith (Zak Sabbath). — 1st ed.
   p. cm.
  ISBN 978-0-9802436-8-0
  1. Smith, Zak, 1976- 2. Artists—United States—Biography. 3. Motion picture actors and
actresses—United States—Biography. 4. Pornography—United States—Case studies. I.
Title.
  NX650.E7S64 2009
  709.2—dc22
  [B]                                            2009006673

First U.S. edition 2009
Design by Laura Shaw Design, Inc.
Printed in Korea


www.tinhouse.com

# DEDICATION

*To Cathy S. and Grady S. III*

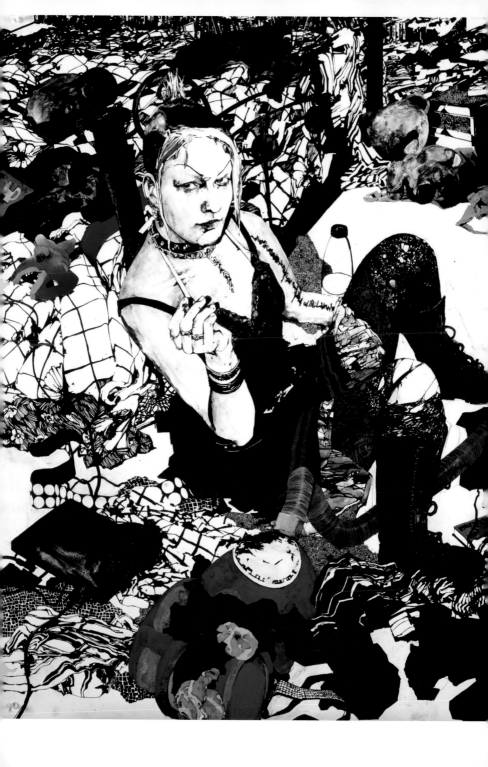

# CONTENTS

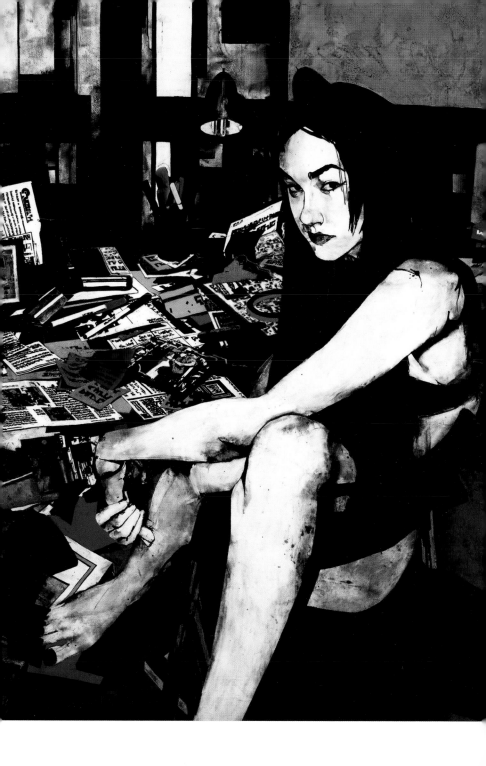

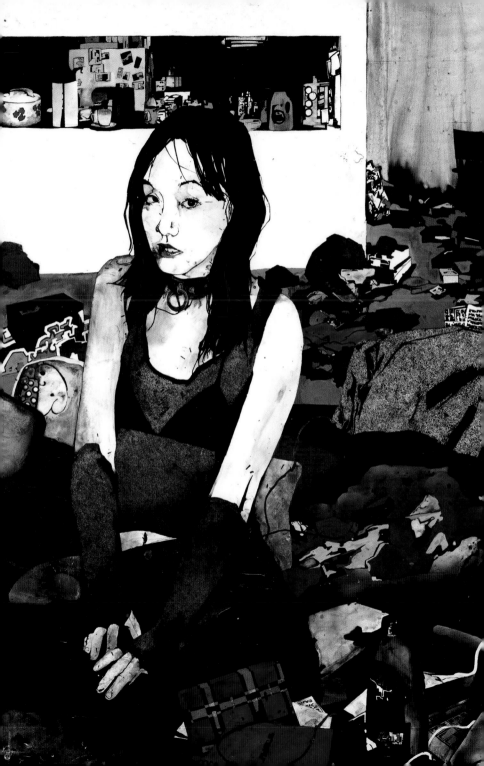

# Author's Note

**There are drawings and** paintings in this book, and there are words. The pictures and the words do not go together in any consistent relationship; although they feature many of the same places, ideas, and people, the order of the pictures has no particular meaning.

This is nonfiction—both parts record what things looked like from where I was standing. However, in the text, I consciously distort reality in three ways:

1. I have changed people's names, along with the names of film companies and movies. This is not so much to disguise people (obsessives will be able to trace all the main characters back to their actual stage names) as to remind readers—and myself—that there is probably more to them than I managed to see or record.

2. In *very* rare cases involving physical danger, I have altered inessential details (names of birthplaces, et cetera) and divided people in half (for example, splitting characteristics and adventures of Diana from Austin between "Lisa" from Austin and "Carla" from Jersey City) in order to protect them from their enemies.

3. Since very famous people who aren't in porn, or at least gossip about them, is essential to the texture of life in Los Angeles in general and the adult industry in particular, realism demands I include them. For legal, artistic, and humanitarian reasons, it's important to disguise the very famous people while still making it clear to the reader that the people being referred to *are* very famous, all without interrupting the flow of the story. How famous? About as famous as Dwight Eisenhower. Therefore, unless there is some reason to be specific, whenever any very famous person comes up in this book, I refer to him or her as "Dwight Eisenhower." Needless to say, the actual Dwight Eisenhower is not directly responsible for any of the events or behaviors discussed in this book.

# Valentine's Day

**At first,** the only noise is coming from trucks washing over a nearby road, and this sounds like it does at night—like enormous things going on underwater. I feel small. I'm in a car parked on a nowhere corner where no one lives and what light there is, from the gas station, wedges itself in around the air pockets where the tinting hasn't stuck to the windows, making shapes. My knuckles are cold. All of this is normal for people on Valentine's Day.

This is years ago—before I had done porn, or ever thought I would.

At eight o'clock on every Valentine's Day there are people who wait, and who don't know what's going to happen. In Europe there's a time difference, so it's already happening, whatever it is. In Japan, it's called a "chocolate obligation" and they are now sleeping off, or waking up next to, whatever it's done for them. I hope it does something for them—you hear things can be hard, romantically speaking, for the Japanese. In Brooklyn, people are still waiting in the backseats of cars.

Some are tired, scared, or bored. Some think they're going to ruin everything—some are right. Some have flowers or headaches or both, some are going to cry, some are taking pills or rehearsing what they'll say, some have skin problems that have just gotten started, some don't care but are doing it anyway and don't think much about it, some are doing it but don't think it'll work, some will never do it again but don't know that yet, some will go home on a train and swear into the reflection on the other side of the train car that they will spend every night from now on alone in front of a TV flipping to any show where anyone is talking about anything as long as it isn't them or maybe just watching static. And they'll eat whatever they want from a bowl and drink tea even after it gets cold and not care forever until everyone forgets that they ever lived. Some want to call ahead and ask the Japanese how it'd gone.

I'm in the backseat of a car. Punks are not supposed to have to do this kind of thing, and, maybe because I never have before, now that I'm here I feel hyperaware of all the other lone people who must also be waiting in the dark all over the rest of the hemisphere. "I never *realized*," I say to them in my head, at the beginning of my date. "The conditions here are awful. You all should unionize or something—collectively *bargain*, like."

The hired driver of the hired car had stopped and gotten out without saying why. Is this what happens when you pay people to drive you around? Thinking how things sometimes are over faster if you don't ask questions, I didn't ask questions. For a while, there is just the noise of traffic and dead air from a road I can't see and the usual blinking in the black and in the distance, like we're in the electronics deparment after hours—but at some point something in the car begins *breathing*.

When you're strangely dressed and worrying, it feels like anything—*any*thing—might be a big cold night-snake ready to ambush and fuck you. So what's this breathing? Is it just a sound made by this kind of car? Did he go to get it fixed? Isn't the Rumblers' garage just over . . . No, it's *breathing*. Someone's mouth is valving gas around this car for sure. This isn't a *limo*, there isn't room for some *secret* person. Is a person in the trunk? Why did the driver leave me alone on Valentine's Day with a person in the trunk? That isn't normal. Will I have to solve this? Fuck this *Day*.

The driver comes back, opens a bag of chips, gives them to a totally unexpected Puerto Rican boy in the passenger seat in front of me, gets back behind his wheel, and pulls back onto the road. The driver says, "Thank you." I say, "No problem." Then no one says anything.

Brooklyn spins around us, windows reflecting intersections and storefronts and forty-year-old abandoned cars. We almost kill someone on a bicycle.

My instructions are, basically, to act stupid. My porno date wants to be taken someplace where she might see Puff Daddy. This is our first date, so I have to try to act like someone who someone who would want to go somewhere where she might see Puffy would want to be at that place with—until I figure out how she really is and can act some other way. I'm scared. I'm also happy and lucky. I breathe and hear my own breathing and am glad to hear it still sounds like me. Trying not to overprepare, I watch the Brooklyn usual go by to the tune of Godflesh songs I'm playing in my head: an ad for gum; capsized strollers; the grease-smeared hotbox of a shallow-fronted take-out place full of fizzing Chinese; tiny kids in coats alone outside delis; bikes chained with every kind of lock and missing every conceivable combination of parts like a forensic display on methods of bicycle decomposition; the tags of world-famous street-art geniuses and of people who never tagged again; the stoic, eaten globe of a broken subway-stop pole casually decapitated for the thousandth time; JMZ trestles casting piano-key shadows; Fat Albert's Warehouse; whole blocks that haven't heard English in decades; a restaurant that used to be a hat shop; a church that used to be a furniture store; a nothing that used to be a theater; dogs tied to anything vertical; stained buses like rotten fridges shoving themselves up the lane from red light to red light; a pile of televisions and fans half covered in plastic—expecting rain; and pizza places painted the colors—red, yellow, green—of the pizza version of the Italian flag. These things feel good and familiar. Tonight, nothing else will be both. I'm starting to think the kid in the front seat might somehow work against me on my date, so I'm relieved when we get to the girl's place—on a warehousily empty street—and she says—through the speaker—to let the car go while she finishes getting ready.

So none of that mattered. Breathe some more. Move smart in your embarrassing black Valentine's getup. Good-bye, car and kid. You were okay. You got me this far.

∞∞∞∞∞∞∞∞

The first sign is good—Tina DiVine is more nervous than you'd think a porn girl about to go on a date with *some painter* would be. The dark dots in her eyes roll all over their twin whites, pushing her nose and mouth around, as if she's just gotten her beautiful face and is trying to discreetly test it out. She is a little person with a vanilla-and-butter complexion. She has a big loft whose nonoffice end has almost nothing in it except a titanic television that turns on with a sound like a sucking rupture in space-time and a chair shaped like a big, sexy shoe. She asks me to sit in the sexy shoe while she goes off to a corner that's leaking pink plastic and accessories into the main room and gets dressed. I try to look casual in the shoe and try to use the remote casually. Shiites won the Iraqi elections; we have a new attorney general; and Arthur Miller is dead. In a window behind the TV, the city now seems frozen and quiet.

She comes out in something black that looks like it tried as hard as it could to crawl over her but gave up halfway across her chest, and she says how exciting it is to get to wear it somewhere other than a strip club. It *is* exciting. There are swollen and then falling and then swelling-again curves and spaces between them that the dress has clearly and promisingly been totally unable to negotiate. I call us a cab.

∞∞∞∞∞∞∞∞

The place we go, in Manhattan, is—well just know for now none of this is my fault, I mean: the thing had been multiple choice and the options hadn't been . . . Okay, more later, *anyway—*

The place is glowing and foam-colored, with everybody crisply looking—or trying very hard to look—as if they always drank in a piece of cheap rendering software's idea of a room.

It is like one of those pitiful goal-less games where you have an *account* and are represented by a gliding, hard-haired humunculus and click and chat as your hours devour themselves. They click and chat. It's not my fault.

We have to spend some time at the bar before we get to eat. *One* of the bars. The bars have names. One is called "The Amuse Bar." No one there explains it, it's just that way. Tina asks me about wine and I don't know.

She says, "A red? Okay, a red," and begins to runway-walk, on stripper heels, away toward the bar. I watch. But then she slows and shrivels and shrinks and swivels and puzzling and trouble creep onto her face.

"You saw someone you fucked," I say.

She nods as if she's just suddenly realized that she only has one nerve left, and that it's been stretched out like gum or pizza-mozzarella, and that when it snaps she'll just bolt away and leave you looking at a screenful of static. (She looks that way a lot. She doesn't when she smiles, or makes porn, or talks about making porn, but often otherwise she does. Not like she's not all there—just like she's extremely ready to leave.)

Then this Someone walks over and so probably things I never see or know anything about start happening on *my* face, because I know him.

◦◦◦◦◦◦◦◦◦

Artists' reputations are based on lines half read in doctors' offices by bored people, written on deadlines by distracted

freelancers, and commissioned by editors who don't necessarily care.

All artists have detractors—mine like to send letters. A lot
of them are older artists who make paintings that are different than mine. One appears to be French, one does a comic
book about being sad, one is a very persistent and angry stop-
motion animator. There usually doesn't seem to be any point
in writing back to them or reading their mail closely, but now
that I am here at the Amuse Bar I begin to wish I'd paid more
attention.

Here's why: The only thing the French or sad-comic-book
or other letter writers have in common is that, because they've
read, while waiting for their aunt's blood test or bypass, about
how I once went to an expensive school, and they are, I guess,
themselves too wealthy to have heard that, despite everything,
this country still keeps routinely loaning its citizens money
for that kind of thing, and because they also know they don't
like what I do, they deduce fictional pasts for me. They're
usually made of movies where people overdose or episodes
of detective shows where it turns out the artist did it and the
perp had an upper-middle-class childhood, sunny with sub-
urbs, and bullies, and proms, and white people smiling and
waving from parade floats (all of which bears, unsurprisingly,
not a lot of resemblance to life growing up next door to a Sal-
vadoran street-gang hangout in Langley Park and otherwise
in and around Washington DC, the murder capital of the U.S.
during the era of Fugazi, "Da Butt," and crack-addict mayor
Marion Barry) who encourage and somehow shape him into
a casually druggy, bratty, *clearly troubled*, Amuse-Bar-frequent-
ing young painter.

This Photoshopped picture is exhibit A in the early para-
graphs of elaborate letters—often physical letters, written

with pens—where they explain to me how I am bad at my job. They are all bitter lunatics, but they seem to have influence here tonight. The night's programmers might have used them as a focus group when putting together their platonic, vector-drawn restaurant/club/trap.

"So what do you think this *rival* should look like?" "Tall, with black tattoos, and maybe a little linked chain around his neck." And then they put him there, with his walnutlike head and pebbly eyes.

Shouldery and guyish like all 3-D-rendered men—and with the same tiltless back-and-forth head movements and skin-tight, crewneck, plain black T-shirt and tastefully tribal ink— he starts smiling and talking. I keep thinking there should be some way to restart the date without him. Or that he should give me an excuse to punch him until he's unconscious.

But no, that would look *crazy*.

I had a girlfriend once who kept taking me to a bar on Avenue B that was a kind of filing cabinet or support group for everyone she'd ever slept with. He was one of them, down at the far end, next to the peanut machine. He is the manager *here*. Maybe also a medical student, he is widely disliked in and out of New York City and he will eventually go to Europe and take up Eastern religion. My date is completely infatuated with him, but no one else knows this now, and she likes to say disgusting, true things about him when he isn't there.

He wants to give us shots. I don't want him to, but I don't say that, and we have them.

He seems very excited about the shots. Although this is clearly a *reason* to punch him, and I will know later that the prudent thing to do would have been to hurt him as much as possible very quickly, since he hasn't actually done anything but give us free liquor so far, I'm having a difficult time imagining a situation where I punch him and then still have sex with Tina DiVine.

He asks us how we found the place, and although he pretends—with that CG smile that unhinges the bottom of the face—he doesn't care and is just making conversation, he *does* want to know. The walnut-head is wondering if there is a *reason* why the girl whose underwear he fed to a dog last week is suddenly here where he works along with someone who looks like he would very much like to punch him until he is unconscious.

"My dealer," I say—so there is no reason. There is no reason, barring the demigodlike-computer-programmers-in-Valentine's-league-with-heckler-focus-group hypothesis, that this has to be happening. It's coincidence.

Anyway, he thinks this about a "dealer" is very funny.

"No" (people sometimes make this mistake), "I mean the guy who sells my paintings."

This can't ruffle a man with a new favorite thing. "This guy's *dealer*," he says, pointing me out to anybody, friendly-like, "recommended us." LOL.

Talking, electronic beats, and ice. The awful walnut-head keeps saying things about Dwight Eisenhower, and also about how he has a lot of money. It is stupid in here and he is the biggest fuck ever. I repeat something about vodka I read in a book. Everyone agrees.

After a lot of despising and pretending, our bed is ready—you eat on beds here, simple, white block beds that make things seem that much more virtual. The waiters start bringing dinner courses, each with wine, and it's hard to say what they are.

# I Crawl Like a Pig

**The first time** I met Tina DiVine it'd been for work. I was a painter who painted girls in the sex industry and she was a girl in the sex industry. I lived in Brooklyn, she lived in Brooklyn. She had one of those places you reach through a sealed stairwell with one-way locks that you have to free your visitors from after examining them through a little reinforced window in the door—as if they were radioactive or crazy. As soon as she did—Hello, Doctor, do you think I'm well enough to go out today?—I had the unprofessional, atypical, deflating feeling that I was going to have to try to have sex with her.

So, while working, I talked and tried.

She was a confusing person from the beginning—she wasn't working any of the familiar angles.

The most common one is *You Really Think I'm Beautiful? Oh, Thanks, I've Never Heard of Sex or Maybe It's Something I Do Once a Month for Three Minutes in the Dark with My Boyfriend Mostly for Health Reasons and in Europe.* This is the angle that *Playboy* invented and that is still popular among fashion models to this day. When done right, it can make you want to vomit blood. She also was not doing fetish-model favorite *I Know You Want to Fuck Me, So Does Everybody, I Don't Care, No One Looking at Me Could Possibly Fulfill My Unbelievably Sophisticated Sexual Demands and So I'm Bored,* or the only briefly amusing *I Am Going to Flirt with You Mercilessly But Don't Feel Special Because I Do It with Everyone for Purposes That Have Nothing to Do with My Personal Sexual Desire and Are Obscure Even to Me, Here's My Butt.*

Standing, lightly tattooed, with her hands together, looking up from under a curtain of expensive fake black bangs, what was Tina doing? She was doing Brigid O'Shaughnessy from *The Maltese Falcon.* She wasn't the then-aspiring-but-as-of-this-writing-now-actual Queen of Punk Porn who wrote the wildly extroverted copy for DiVinethings.com. No, she was biting her knuckle and shiftily saying, "I've done some things I'm . . . not . . . very . . . proud of . . . " with the clear implication that she'll be doing these things at least three more times before lunch.

She had a way of moving that suggested her apartment was full of water and that she had to bend and shove through the currents you were carving through her tank as you Godzilla'ed around it. She also had cherry-candy-pink transparent heels and red Spider-Man-web underwear and tits like toys and eyes that always went all around the room and a charmingly unsubtle way of bending over her shoe chair, and these and other things distracted me and I made mistakes that Sam Spade would never have made and so, instead of just having a beer somewhere and then coming right back to the apartment or, better yet, playing the balance of the already sort-of-dodgy situation until it seamlessly pornografied itself, I found myself agreeing to go on a *date*.

She had recently made a list for her fans of things not to do on dates, one of which was, if your sweater looked like, but wasn't, a very expensive sweater, you shouldn't say it. Was this the way she was or was this just drugs?

During this time, people trying to have civilian sex with Tina DiVine often succeeded, but only after efforts and humiliations that made everyone involved look bad. The cautiously unironic image of a perfect date for Valentine's Day was much on her mind that season. She said to me she wanted to be treated nice and she wanted to go on a date and she said she wanted it to be on Valentine's Day. So I bit in.

I told her it would be unfuckingbelievably romantic and that she'd have no idea what hit her.

Now in art school, people argue about what "romantic" is, but on Valentine's Day, "romantic" is a very simple concept. Valentine's Day romantic means you are seamlessly surrounded by things suggesting to your senses that

A) God likes you

 or

B) so much money and/or attention is being directed your way that it doesn't matter if God likes you.

Or, as Tina put it: "I'm a princess, I want to go somewhere where I might see Puff Daddy—and dress nice! And I want to not be able to pronounce the food."

Now, dates are always excruciating and anyone who *chooses* them—who thinks of them as a source of *entertainment*— is definitely not someone you should be dating. This is not an extreme or minority position. Consider how eager people are to get married, regardless of whether they know anyone worth marrying. People regularly marry some rube and then pay a psychiatrist to listen to all the person's essentially rube-generated problems and then tell the person *anything* besides *Well, then get divorced*, which they like because if they did get divorced then they'd have to start dating again. They figure if an apparently sane, well-educated, high-income white person can hear all their problems and not just say, "Well, then fuck-ing get divorced," then they don't have to seriously consider it.

So, many Americans are willing to spend half their lives paying someone with a doctorate to help them to not even *think* about the possibility of dating ever again. To not even *ideate* dating. That's how bad dates are.

Not to mention that Tina's entire livelihood depends on many of these same victims also being willing to pay money to secretly watch movies to help them just *imagine for a few minutes* that they had sex without going on a date.

Which is all to say that the fact that Tina *chose* to date when not dating was a clear possibility should have set off as many alarm bells as all the other stuff. And did, frankly.

But then, okay, every girl, no matter how sweet she turns out to be, is terrifying at first. And, hey—Pussy. Fuck alarm bells.

Maybe you know what it's like to just look at someone you don't know and decide that you would, truly, actually do the stupidest thing to get to fondle and suck on all their surfaces and curves. Maybe you know what it's like when they go ahead and ask you to do it. *You know, I have this idea that you should act stupid . . . Oh really? Please do tell me all about it. Please do tell me all about it because I am eager to do it in light of your spectacular* pussy. *Which I would like to* eat. *Soon.* Maybe you know what it's like to know that the real reason you are acting and dressing and spending like James Bond is because really you are a groveling groveling failure busying yourself with naught but groveling. Do you know what it's like to crawl like a pig?

I wanted some Tina DiVine.

So I crawl like a pig.

I had four days' notice. I called the people who sold my paintings for me, my art dealers, because they knew fancy restaurants—because it was their job—and explained the situation.

It eventually worked out there were three top-dollar posh places that still had openings for Valentine's Day. One used to be full of famous people at all hours until it was on a popular TV show about old women trying to decide who to have sex with, which had ruined it, but it was still there, somewhere in midtown and taking reservations. One had excellent food, roses, and a moat—it came recommended. And one had jellyfish in the walls and you ate on beds. Thinking the bed thing seemed promising, and fucking myself, I picked the third one. My dealers used their platinum card to make us a reservation.

I didn't bring flowers, but I did do a little painting of Tina, and I gave it to her. She probably still has it. There. That's the most embarassing thing in this book. Anyway . . .

◦◦◦◦◦◦◦◦◦

Who does this? Well, for starters, all the other people looking at us. A lot of them are in *groups*. Who brings handfuls of friends out for four hundred dollars' worth of food on

St. Valentine's Day? Maybe bankers? Are they bankers? Are they burglars? Are they here talking mergers? Are they just here to watch me screw with the fish eggs on my lap? Are they rotating rings of lovers? Do they do this every year? Do they have to do it on beds? They wear minimalist clothes and glasses on their noses and have spit curls and gold and every kind of mixed drink. They keep chatting and clicking. Some dance in that rigid standing-while-riding-an-invisible-vertical-rowing-machine-and-exercise-bike-simultaneously way you expect in 3-D games. They are amused, it looks like.

They are watching someone with green hair and someone stunning with unbelievable tits on an island in the middle of a restaurant, in bare feet and in white socks, trying to figure caviar out and it is probably funny.

These two—facing cryptic goos in piles, colored, one of which is definitely just onions cut in chunks, warned in advance by art people to avoid the steel spoons and that the waiters'll bring pearl ones, scooping the goos onto pancakes the size of dollar coins when it turns out the waiters don't, spilling it all, licking it off each other, getting more pancakes and also new yellow wine in flutes, all on an unstable, candled cylinder in the center of the bed, which is mostly clean—look cute.

They're not fooling themselves. The guy is moving through an overdetailed hour of cutlery noise, wet salt, glass, and words as if it has land mines in it, and she's semicalmly talking over a mental paste of drug reactions and half decisions.[*]

ooooooooo

---

[*] I also suspect, looking back, that she had temporary saline injections inflating her tits, so she may also have been dealing with increased blood-sodium levels, which can cause dizziness, weakness, and confusion.

We didn't *choose* caviar—there are no choices on the menu, you get what you get. This is either because this is the way things are at the bed restaurant or because it's Valentine's Day and so probably half the people coming in tonight will be women and women can find these decisions not just difficult but actually stressful and mood-alteringly taxing. The simplest thing, someone decided, was to just give everyone all the food in the world in staged courses, like at a wedding, reasoning also, perhaps, that a woman who is pro–Valentine's Day is probably also pro-wedding.

The stressful and taxing What do I want today? problem, incidentally, is probably why girls typically don't ask guys out. If you're walking down the street and you're Tina DiVine, how many of these men you're walking past can you fuck? (The guy unloading the truck, the bent Jewish pensioner in suspenders . . . ) All of them. So going to the grocery store, that's maybe seventy times you have to decide *not* to have sex with people. ( . . . the one with the frozen dinner, the pie man . . . ) Go see some band—maybe a thousand. ( . . . the one in the red hat, the one with the bag . . . ) Go see the Mets play—maybe forty thousand people you have to decide not to fuck ( . . . the one selling drinks, the one with the giant finger, the pitcher, the catcher, the right fielder . . . )—forty thousand decisions. Taxing. No wonder they don't like sports.

Meanwhile, smoove music oozes into everything, and gorgeous, ignored jellyfish finish up the next in a series of totally identical days, and we talk.

She's slept with lots of famous bad musicians (and with these musicians, there *were* decisions—middle-of-the-night-watching-the-lemon-juice-squeezed-onto-a-red-carapace-Red-Lobster-commercials-on-TV-oh-fuck-now-I-want-some-of-*that* cravings). One she says is a genius, though not musically, and his penis is small. She doesn't mention sleeping with any good ones, but she has gotten into an argument with the same good one my last date argued with. There is one who likes stockings, one who is supposed to help judge a beauty contest and doesn't, one I mention who she hasn't heard of but who will be there the next time I see her, one she likes to fuck while listening to, and one who was good once but now does embarrassing things to music for money and keeps it a secret and likes to do them.

She talks about her expensive hair (it's hard to understand how it got expensive—it's just a few white streaks through the long black), her unsummarizable and I am pretty sure unusual kind of feminism ("I contemplated fucking a guy with a strap-on simply because I considered that degrading to men. But the gender inequality is mental, not physical. It's more degrading to change the carburetor in your boyfriend's car than to fuck him with a strap-on."), and her efforts to start being on less cocaine than she usually is. I cut parts of my food off and look at them on the tip of my fork before putting them in my mouth and nod a lot. Her skin is the color of the skin of certain very good cheesecakes. There are a *million* courses. She and the jellyfish and the food are the only things in the room that aren't frightening. She tries to drink all the wine but they keep bringing more. It all tastes the same but it isn't; it is all different places and different years because that's how they do it on Valentine's Day. Also we talk about the small fish that cleans the teeth of other fish, about how she wants to buy things all the time, and about why the walnut-head keeps coming over and talking to us and how we wish he'd stop and go somewhere else and not ever come back.

Then she puts on her shoes and then walks over the flower petals they've spread on the dining room floor, and then has sex with him.

Yeah. This is the date that Tina is talking about during the intro to that movie *Do Me in the Bathroom*. Meanwhile and clueless, I sit on the bed with my date shoes in a geisha-house cubby-grid and eat whatever while other employees bring me more of it and I talk with the voices in my head.

"Houston, it's Zak, I'm at the place."

"What's it like?"

"I'm on a *bed*, there's fucking rose petals on the floor—it's fucked. My shoes are in a *cubbyhole*."

"Wow. You couldn't just take her to a bar?"

"Fuck off, man, long story. I'm here now—guh, I don't know what part of a fish I just ate. I don't know why I'm eating a fish at all, actually. I think maybe I thought it's more romantic to eat a fish than let it be dead on your plate looking at you until they bring you something better."

"Maybe. You could hide it."

"There's nowhere to hide a fish in here."

"Whatever—how you making out there?"

"Mmmm . . . "

"Did you try 'I'm-a-punk-you're-a-punk'?"

"Fuck yeah, first thing off—no go, I think."

"What about 'Hey!—*Smarter than I look!*"

"'Cause I look pretty stupid."

"Yeah, especially if 'I'm-a-punk-you're-a-punk' isn't working."

"Yeah—um, what else we got?"

"I think that's about *it*."

"Fuck. Oh, she's coming back . . . "

After that the walnut-head comes by once in a while, again all friendly-like, with more trivia about the champagnes and cooks, because, well—because if someone gave you an opportunity to see something that you knew for certain would be the most pathetic thing you would ever see, you would take it. See this rube!—with his hand still compulsively scratching at his green head! In his new clothes! Still squirming and grinning in the grip of a date he thinks he's on! Hello, Rube! Still shoeless, he munches he-knows-not-what and drinks, too! Still dying to fuck the slut. What a goofy rube! "Oh yes I did, and there was this *rube*, he had a tattoo on his *head* and . . . "

While I am not yet guessing that things have gone quite that gruesome, I had figured out I was not on a good date before that long trip (which she explained away by saying she and the manager had quietly gotten into a fight). In conversation, Tina and I constantly meet at intersections and, given a green light, immediately speed off in different directions.

But really: I had no fucking clue. I didn't *care* so much that I had no fucking clue—since if you're the guy you're used to that feeling—you *never* really have a fucking clue. Not until it's actually *in*.

One time, in another country, I heard this *thunk* and I looked over—the girl I'd met, and just brought home, and who was just then climbing up to the loft bed had fallen off and was facedown in a pool of her own blood. Cracked jaw. In need of serious medical and dental. Through broken English and teeth she asked me to immediately fuck her anyway. So I did. And, like everyone else, in a dozen normaler and more legible and more promising circumstances, nothing happened and I didn't. With all the physics and women going on you *never* have a fucking clue.

However, I had seen and heard about definitively good dates before, in real life and on TV, and they went like this:

At a certain point, very early, English stops meaning what it means, and you get the impression you are unbelievably and unexpectedly fluent in a coded language that your date *also* seems to know, and you keep using it in order to hide what you both know from all the people around you while the sexual tension just lies there off to the side like a fat, over-filled, birthday-cake-green, bloated and sausagey water balloon that either of you could just reach out and fork all over the carpet whenever you want. The date and the obligations of dates become a harmless formality. The night gets to be like the fortune-cookie game where the words *in bed* are added at the end of whatever future or advice the cookie has. "You will take a long and rewarding journey." "All your hard work will eventually pay off." "Your family will be a source of strength." "What do you wanna do now?" "What do you want for dessert?" "What's your major?" This was not the thing happening here tonight.

For example: now she is crying (in bed). About this: she has gravely disappointed her weird mom by choosing a career in porno movies. However, she has a stupid plan: in six years she'll have children and raise them all to believe all the things her mother did even though she doesn't think any of them are true. She's said so much by this point that is not sane that it is hard to believe she (or the focus-group team of date-night-programming gods) isn't just feeding me lines, but now she is really crying. On me. In a bed. Limp, trembling, and all wet, like a warm amphibian trapped in a stocking. You couldn't call her boring.

I am nice about this crying and I try to make her comfortable while she cries and I stare out at all the pricey, blurry, apathetic geometry while the simuloids in our local bed cluster try not to see her. I realize I am not doing what I inevitably do in this kind of situation, which is bring up the children of the Lobster Boy, Grady Stiles Jr.

At birth, the son and daughter of the famous American traveling-circus freak inherited not only a childhood's worth of abuse at the ectrodactylic hands of their murderous and eventually murdered alcoholic lobster-father but also his condition. "Just think," I usually say, "you could have all the problems you have now, *plus* have lobster claws instead of hands."

I'm not bringing it up because there isn't the right level of trust between us for this to seem funny instead of just evil. Plus I'm not sure she has a sense of humor.

It is not good to have someone who doesn't have the right level of trust or a sense of humor crying on you. In a bed.

"We often forgive those who bore us, but we cannot forgive those whom we bore"—the original French is less ambiguous and ambitious than in our language. The way we read it in English, it might attempt to map the situation between me and Tina *or* Tina and her mother.

Read any way around, it leaves Tina at the intersection of two one-way streets, forgiving everybody.

In the middle of all this somewhere—but after the crying— she agrees that after dessert, we'll fuck at my place, so I hit my brakes and, trying to look casual, make a wide psychological three-point U-turn. Cruising now in the other direction, with the top down, I think, *Ahh, I was on a good date after all.* Clearly, cause and effect have just quietly untied themselves, and I have stopped being an important influence on whatever is going on and it doesn't matter: it's over and now I just have to stay alive until she isn't wearing any more clothes. Also, according to the menu, I still have a steak and a piece of strawberry cake coming to me.

Tina asks about sex. About sex and me. I say I am generally flexible and not very particular. She says she likes to be spit on, hit, choked, and called a whore. I pay the large bill, and we leave, and we sink into the dark, roaming quiet of a taxi and the smeared, multicolored layers of signs over the cheap shops on Delancey for people with kids or who want donuts pass, pinned in the window under the pattern of rain behind her head like something she's dreaming. She says it's the best date she's ever been on. The raindrops quiver, join, grow, and drool away behind her.

She says she never sleeps places; she says she never kisses people. She is as skittish and unintelligible with her dress off as she had been when it was on.

I actually cleaned the apartment before this date—I realize I missed three bottle caps.

# The Sex Scene

**Obviously something cut**
together in the editing room at the last minute by a drunk
radical feminist with a distinctly avant-garde sensibility. It
starts with a female orgasm after a few seconds of exploratory
fingering—for which the female talent, clearly too high to
remember her lines, actually *apologizes*. Their skin is pale, but
lighting skews toward a plasticky nighttime-interior orange.
In some shots, there's a half-finished abstract painting in the

foreground. The action moves on to a blowjob (male POV), which is a very thorough piece of work during which, unfortunately, someone is leaning heavily on the fast-forward. Then a listless titfuck, a few more positions, and some light S&M. Like someone spare-changing who knows she'll die without that next quarter and knows this next prick won't give it to her, with the pinkly split and creamily round halves of her award-winning ass—the papery, bug-wing texture of chronic meth abuse—up and out, she asks, with murky eyes and from under the margin of a complex, unfinished back piece of girl-angels and girl-devils, to be choked and spanked and you can barely hear it. Even the sound in this thing is bad.

The male talent—clearly caught at the end of some kind of very long day that has left him more up for playing dazed than angry (someone should show him the whole script)—isn't used to not leaving marks. The pop is internal, and they use condoms.

The next week, she starts very seriously going out with the walnut-head.

# Wolves

**The most hideous thing**
about pornography, of course, is that it works. On you. Excellent, witty, urbane writers can and do fly in from somewhere and visit pornography and write about it wittily and urbanely and make it all seem funny or make it all seem sad because it is *always* funny, and it is *always* sad. But it also works. On them. On you.

If *this* thing doesn't work, then *that* thing does and if *that* thing doesn't and *most* things don't, then *some*thing else *some-*

where does. Maybe it's not called pornography but it's just some voice you know, or something someone wears—who knows but you? But *something* works on you. Whatever that thing is, think of that thing—keep it to yourself, but think of it now. Don't just name it to yourself, put this book down, close your eyes, and totally imagine the thing. Make it twist and move against the nothing. Now think of what a wreck it makes of you. Because whatever it is, it is a fiction and a lie and a product—and someone without your best interests in mind made it, hoping it would interest you best. And it worked. A dose of it, dropped in at the right moment, metastasizes and hisses and breeds until it seems more compelling than anything real and practical left clinging to life in the spiked pool.

Tina worked on me. If we are going to find out something that we don't already know, something that hasn't already been covered over the course of someone's witty weekend, then we'll have to spend some time here—in the part of the brain where porn isn't just a joke or a disaster but is also the product of someone's successful attempt to go to work on your mind—and to make $3,075.64 every second doing it.

In this quiet, greedy continent, pornography is big business, and big lives of big numbers of real people really living are affected in big ways, and it's a place where economics, politics, ethics, philosophy, and reason have no say. Because pornography is selling things people want a lot. It made enough to keep someone housed and fed for twenty years while you were reading this paragraph.

Tina once said that she was much more comfortable around creepy guys than nice guys. This is perhaps because she—ex-stripper, sexual-assault-survivor, pornographer—knows what men so often want, and the creepy guy has no talent for pretending he wants anything else. She knows where she stands with the creepy guy. The creepy want their creepy piece. On my bed, which was a mattress on the floor, she stood unsteadily and held her temporarily oversized tits in her hands. "Well, this is me," she'd said—she seemed ashamed. Like she was doing something she was not . . . very . . . proud of. I had been doing "nice guy" all night—and that was even before she cried. Crying tends to really bring out the nice guy in people. It's the point of crying.

I knew a childlike virgin once, and, sex-wise, she was a type: a twentyish Asian girl who seemed perfectly happy doing nothing but baking cupcakes in Hello Kitty tins and getting excited about buying furniture with polka dots on it and rubber place mats in solid colors with rounded edges. She told me once that she had a recurring dream set in a glass elevator. Inside there was a tickling dog as tall as her, or taller—hairless, hog-skinned. It stood on its hind legs and leaned into her and tickled her with its front paws so hard it hurt. It leaned and tickled and it was terrible and it was a nightmare and made her wake up into a sweat-stained bed exhausted and relieved she wasn't being tickled by the dreamed dog.

Rather than pretending they don't exist, or ascribing them to some chakra or plan, it's good to remember that the real differences between boys and girls are the differences between what you'd do if you were little and got sick a lot and what you'd do if you were a little bigger and didn't.

I think men must seem really like dogs to women—hungry and large, often slobbering—as a species, unpredictable and sometimes dangerous (the dogs of war, the dogs of doom) but as individuals, predictable and clockwork and cute (like puppies, like hounds), and, if you spend enough time with them, each with a different personality (babe hounds, faithful hounds). Some are tiny and harmless, some are harmless and big as bears, but all have predatory, long-boned bodies with teeth and claws essentially made to hunt and hurt smaller things. To deliver yourself sexually to an unknown one must be like putting yourself at the mercy of a strange, large, imprecise, and hairy animal that you can just only hope is well-trained. Straight men should imagine how much differently they'd behave if their lovers were—to scale up—wolves.

From the point of view of men, sex does not automatically or ordinarily have the radioactive glow of risk, of pleasure-snatched-from-danger. Because for us, sex has no downside. Going from making out with a stranger to fucking her involves no more trust or psychophysical commitment than eating a melon. Men all bitch to each other about the complications— things get slippery, things get sticky, you get juice everywhere and seeds on the floor, *She keeps saying I should . . . Oh I was in the middle of checking it when she calls wanting . . . She gave me this frikkin'* . . . but really they are just bitching about life. That's the horrible downside—having to walk around and be *alive* all the time. Life is the horrible downside to sex. We'd rather be dead all day and then come up for a few hours to eat and fuck and maybe fight someone (preferably simultaneously) and then be dead again. Like Dracula.

But we aren't Dracula, and we feel much more like wolfmen. Wolfmen lose all sense at night and wish they could hide from the world but can't because they are too hungry to sleep.

I don't get very much sleep in the dry weeks after my date, and I work mostly to distract and exhaust myself. Since I have no other post-humiliation/enigmatic-glamour-date-trauma experience to compare it to, I don't know how well this plan works, but I get a lot of work done. The painting comes out very nice.

# Nothing Unimportant

"Nothing unimportant ever happens at the Plaza."

—*New York society saying*

**I live with another artist** and, after a long stretch of wretched (she doesn't call) that gets worse when someone mails me the date postmortem she's published online (revealing a lot of opinions that she later went back on and, of course, what the hell had taken her so long in the bathroom) (and confirming the general aura of "Why? Because drugs" surrounding the whole deal), life goes on pretty much as it had before:

Roommate: "Mmmmm . . . gubleguhWhat? Come innn . . ."

Zak: "Sorry, I didn't mean to wake you up."

"You're up earrrrly."

"Yeah, I guess, y'know, you're still on winter break time so you're sleeping late so I'm up before you."

"It is a horrible reversal."

"Uh . . . I just wanted to see if you wanted chicken."

"I should . . . I should eat chicken, um, yeah, gimme ten minutes."

"Look at this fucking rain, it's like a fucking . . . "

"It's fucked."

"It *is* fucked, it's the worst possible thing. I don't want to even think about going out in this fucking rain to the godforsaken Nokia Center."

"Aren't they playing tomorrow, too?"

"Tomorrow I have some thing."

"A thing?"

"Yeah, there's art."

"What thing?"

"Oh there's some people with Andy and Jess . . . "

"Some collectors?"

"Yeah, they have a barn."

"A barn? What are you talking about?"

"Yeah, they have all this art in a barn and they want us to look at it."

"It can't be in the *city*. Where are you going?"

"It's in some *rural* place, like the *country*. They have a barn there and my art is *in* it."

"You're going to go to the country to see your art in a barn?"

"From what I understand, yes. They invite people up once a year to look at their art in a barn. I have to drive up with Andy and Jess."

"That's weird."

"It *is* weird. It's my art and it's in a *barn*."

"Why do they do that?"

"I don't know."

"Is it some kind of farm? Will there be pigs there?"

"Maybe."

"Pigs . . . "

"Pigs."

ooooooooo

Casual observers sometimes have the impression that "the art world" is a place where artists live—it isn't. Artists—who are often no less surprised, and more upset, than civilians to find this out—spend a lot of time doing things everyone else has to do.

We take the subway and buy mousetraps; we go see Today Is the Day and Against Me at the spiteful benefits CBGB's keeps throwing for itself until the landlord closes it; we give our friend a birthday cake and make a cheerleader riding an alligator out of frosting. We live in Bushwick next door to a whorehouse. We eat takeout and bitch.

The art world is a place artists visit. They stay until everyone's too drunk to remember who they are and then they take the train home. Often the more successful they are, the less they are required to visit it. After seeing the barn, the next time I get called to visit is for a ceremony at the Plaza Hotel.

So, about the Plaza: Whoever built the Plaza Hotel was not fucking around. They may have had no way of knowing there was going to be a Truman Capote, but they went to every length to ensure that if there was, and he threw a fucking ball, it was sure as fuck going to be thrown *here*. Nevertheless, they did decide to close it for renovations in 2005, and this ceremony I'm going to is going to be the last anything at the Plaza for three years.

They're honoring, among other people, the most famous and well-respected artist at the gallery that represents me-I'm asked to come because he probably won't. My job is to be a sort of consolation prize for all those helpful curators and collectors who are eager to eat dinner near the great pop artist.

While waiting for the conversation to scintillate, art collectors talk about nannies, home repairs, Prada, pre-K, the appeal of various minimalists, shrinks, and whether or not to pay a hundred thousand dollars for a drawing. Like the bed restaurant, events in the Plaza feel plutocratically pseudoreal, but in a more traditional style: at the Plaza, you look down and see your legs have unexpectedly gone *squiggly* and you try to pull oozing food off a sketchy oval using an indistinct fork and you realize you've become part of a *New Yorker* cartoon.

"Hi! It's so nice to meet you—we just loved your piece about that Thomas Pynchon book at the Whitney!"

"Thanks!"

"So, what are you working on these days?"

"Oh, um, a bunch of paintings of girls in the naked-girl business. Strippers and porn girls and stuff."

Things take on a sort of Oh-rrreally? kind of tone.

"Well I bet that'll be interesting. Is there some *narrative*?"

"You mean is there a story? No, it's just portraits, y'know—though someone wants me to write an article about the girls and it hardly seems like there's a point since like almost every girl I know is naked on the Internet and so I think, y'know, what's the point of even making a thing of it because it's really normal and it seems like I might as well do an article about, like, People Are *Blow-Drying* Their Hair These Days! What's Up With That? Let's Explore This Trend!"

Everyone simultaneously and silently responds to the private image of themselves naked on the Internet.

"Well, I can sure tell you *I'm* not naked on the Internet!" There's some mirth.

"Okay, so alright," I say. "Help me here, help me write my thing—why not?"

"Well I'd have to get a few things *done* first . . ." More mirth.

"Okay, but, is it just, like, about how you *look*?"

"Well, no, I mean, I would pose, say, for *you*, it wouldn't be a problem . . . "—suppressed giggle from the lady's next friend over—"but if it was a photograph then . . . well if it was on the Internet, then I'd be afraid of what it might be *used* for."

Everyone simultaneously and silently responds to the image of a nude photo of the woman talking being *used* in some way. One of them changes the subject.

"What else are you up to?"

"Well, there's a hundred paintings of a hundred girls and a hundred octopuses."

"Isn't it 'octopi'?"

"It can be both, actually, or 'octopodes'—but I like to say 'octopuses' . . . "

"Well that sounds very interesting, is there some *narrative*?"

"No, it's just a hundred girls and a hundred octopuses."

"Well you're obviously totally fucked up."

(No one says this, really, but there are a few mouths and pairs of eyes—slitting like cracks in leather soles down and away—thinking it—and dreaming of some other, better party, or some Greek video artist.) "Anything else . . . ?"

"And a big semiabstract painting of, uh, this villain robot—Unicron."

"A unicorn? Did you see [other young artist]'s painting of a unicorn? At Zwirner, I think . . . "

"No, Unicron. He was this giant planet-eating machine-world from the original, animated Transformers movie."

"I see—does the painting have some kind of . . . narrative?"

"Well, no, but—it's like an image of . . . Well—when I was a kid and the first Transformers movie came out in the theaters, everything was so *huge* and, though I could tell, like, the animation was pretty uneven, the sequences with Unicron were deliberately paced and majestic and bright and dark and, like, just *terrible*—in the old sense of the word 'terrible'—like *godlike* terrible. Old animation-cel animation on a big screen is so *bright*—like it was like the horrible bigness of the most big and horrible thing that a fourth grader could imagine. Unicron was, like, massive, just grinding across space like that bent note from the beginning of 'Iron Man' that makes you want to, like, curl up on the carpet with your head between two big black leather headphones and just *disappear*—like, just . . . *salient* and eating whole worlds with this mandibled mouth/eye thing it had and it had the voice of dying Orson Welles. It was the last thing he ever did. It was like what all those philosophers talk about, like the Sublime, the Abyss Staring Back, the Impossibility of Death in the Mind of Someone Living—I wanted to make a painting that looked like how I remember that felt . . . you know?"

"Orson Welles broadcast *War of the Worlds* from here," says someone.

"So there's no narrative?" says someone else.

"No."

I remember (from doctors' offices) that, when trapped on the unstable line supporting a drawn drawing-room in the *New Yorker*, there is always, on the opposite bank of the margin, the inviting and dry and firm ground of some Seymour Hersh thing about Abu Ghraib. I steer the topic of conversation toward how the president is going to kill us all, and things get light again.

The ceremony takes place in front of fifty round dinner tables, each big enough to seat ten people in front of mediocre dinner and then excellent dessert, under a Second Empire baroque barrel-vaulted ceiling wearing a chain of decatiered chandeliers that is at least two buses away from us on the floor. It's all lavish and big as money and the women seated all around in their Bushwick-corner-girl-sized bracelets of gold nuggets all look as if dollhouse replicas of that ornamented room have melted onto them. They own things that own things that own Puff Daddy.

There are some very nice helium balloons: white, more spherical than usual, one for each ten-guest table, anchored by lines to cube-shaped centerpieces and spectacularly overgrown—as large around as the tables they're over. Big enough to hold a hockey team. You could reach and tug on the ribbons and the balloons would bob like drunks drowning overhead in their reverse world, against the imaginary, undulating plane defined by the common length of their leashes.

The show starts, and there are unfamiliar introducers speaking ecstatically and at length from a podium, with eager cheeks and rehearsed descriptions. A man who apparently once, in the 1970s, created or hired someone to create a sculpture that *made a statement about the issues of resistance and bondage and others that blurred the notions of private and public space* shuffles onto the stage in a tan overcoat, publicly trades some inside jokes about basketball with his introducer— clearly some friend—to anxious, tentative laughter from the crowd, then shuffles back into private space with his ribbon. A woman in mighty shoulder pads hands an identical thing to another woman as a reward for creating works perfectly matching the range of bewildering behaviors you imagine whenever someone says the words *performance art*. And then comes our pop artist.

After each introduction, and before each august talent strides to the stage, there are projected videos of the artist's works and studio and of interviews with the artist and his or her champions with slow pans and floating typography and critics offering glowing glosses (occasionally someone gets to say *narrative*) and humanistic sentiments from pals and unprofessional video fades and jazz *everywhere*. In the briny pond distilled from an eighty-year river of living and ideas and artwork, I see the man's face swim up to the surface, make some comment about as laconic as his work ("I just like blue, I guess"), and then sink under the image of one of his own paintings trapezoidalized by perspective against a museum wall.

Our guy's adult son and daughter go up to accept the award on his behalf, pretending Pop is too sick to come. And as they go up, I see the worst thing—or rather, begin to *notice* it, because it takes a moment to dawn, but then comes on like the irresistible gravity of the Transformers' transcendent villain-world beginning to rip into the real estate of a new and more innocent globe. What I notice is that all the women who work at my gallery are *crying*—and not from boredom, or even because the video has made them miss my stablemate's easy-going octogenarian company, but crying *tears of joy* because this actually is *not*, as I had casually assumed, one more in a continuous cycle of socioprofessional engagements with one more group of uptown cultural well-wishers to be notched on behalf of one of their artists but rather a crowning and consummating oh-my-God-it-was-all-worth-it moment after a lifetime of dedicated labor.

This has quite an effect on me.

I see a future inflating in front of me, like a corporate varmint for the Macy's parade growing and gaining shape in time-lapse while it expands to a wild size that blocks the sky: If I am very *very* good, if I work hard and keep on the good side of all these kind people, with their dinner jackets and chokers, and all their art-collecting children, and am *very* lucky and things go as well as they can go for a contemporary artist in the zeros, then a half century from now some young people will come to make a little holovid or trideo of me bent over my table with my pencil-sized brush, and ask me about green, and splice what I say in with melancholy footage of my ex-models—buried under layers of grandchildren and plastic surgery, talking from armchairs and from under emphysema, eerie gray-and-magenta hairdos, and broad black layers of lace and fishnet the fishermen were no longer bothering to empty out spread across the liver-spotted beaches of their sandy skin, about how nice it'd been to know me—back at the turn of the century, with its automobiles and charming clockwork-unreliable electrical computers—and then into the awed and deskbound speculations of the full-grown academics waiting to manifest themselves from inside one or other of the three-foot cute-tuxedoed offspring chasing each other under the oak table legs of the Plaza's Terrace Room here and now. And I will mount the three steps over there in my overcoat, trade a knowing aside with Shawn Cheng about grindcore, bask in the bold glamour of my cyber-ribbon, and then maunder back home to "investigate the potential realities of post-naturalistic depiction" or "undermine normalizing assumptions about the rhetoric of signs" until at some point I die.

No wonder Pop stayed away. Things immediately get more humiliating—from the point of view of Art. The fourth and final presentation, the one that inspires the finest and longest video (breaking the fifteen-minute mark) and the most effusive and tear-filled and stage-packed and *genuine* drama on the little stage—and the only one that seems to evoke the empathically responding two-way performance of emotional recognition between audience and players familiar to people who perform onstage—does not award any long-cherished but underappreciated radical idol or broadly respected and consulted eminence of creative thought but a happy couple (jacket, pearls) who are being commended for having bought a lot of things and pictures and other art and having put them in their large house.

And now, as if the spirits of the Plaza (perhaps I'd embarrassed Orson Welles) feel I am so dim I need to be warned by both example *and* parable, another thing happens.

At least since the performance artist, I'd been distractedly stabbing my table's balloon string with a bread knife and, just as the couple are handed their prize, our balloon breaks free. It sails elegantly ceilingward and then hits with a voluminous and ominously prolonged hippopotamus-bounce I realize, along with dozens and possibly hundreds of other people who'd looked up, that that trembling, tumbling ball is, though filled with gas lighter than air, definitely massive and otherwise physically meaningful enough to do very expensive damage to and, thanks to the parabolic arc of that particular ceiling, clearly on a bounding path toward colliding with one of human civilization's most delicately constructed lighting fixtures. Is this the *not* unimportant thing meant to emerge from this evening at the Plaza? Young Artist Ruins and Is Ruined by Having Ruined Priceless Crystal Copy of Versailles Chandelier. After another bump and a roll, the round fiend looks about to pounce but then, maybe aware that it has gone as far and high as it will ever go, loudly and abruptly suicides itself on some unseen and jagged French Renaissance detail of the inverted plasterwork. Its immortal and insubstantial insides rise to join whatever society of gasses and old exhalations congregates near the ceiling of the mezzanine level, and its rubber ghost falls out of the sky, smacking our table in the form of a cold, poncho-sized latex sac.

Gone pop.

ooooooooo

The zeros keep going all over and I live in them with everybody else. Things happen. The source once known as "Deep Throat" is finally revealed. The Pentagon announces it will investigate reports that soldiers are posting photos of dead Iraqis on the Internet in exchange for free porn. One of the better American cities is annihilated by a hurricane.

In Chelsea, New York City's art neighborhood, the art dealers and critics are stirred by a series of simple yellow or orange post-and-lintel doorways hung with rectangular pieces of identical fabric in a park that one dissentingly calls "nothing less than an unforgivable defacement of a public treasure" and says that "everyone responsible for promoting it—including our publicity-seeking mayor—should be held accountable, not only for supporting bad taste but for violating the public trust," and they continue to be exercised and intrigued, as they have been for decades, by people, many of whom seem to know each other, who make art—and speak, in interviews, at length—about doing coke. One museum causes a scandal by acquiring, with public money and at great cost, works of art made by one of its own directors, while many others acquire smug and depleted works in all styles and media entirely without incident. Artwork critical of the government is regularly protested by small citizens groups who cause it to be forcibly removed or defunded, and editors of magazines encourage writers to pretend it doesn't exist.

Hardly anyone who doesn't buy, sell, write about, or make art notices any of these things. I continue making what a popular and eccentrically edited coffee-table book published that year refers to as "studies in contemporary American horror vacui." I do well.

I'm not sure future generations, comfortable with all the names in their history books, will appreciate the degree to which, in the mid-zeros, everything even remotely resembling public life in America felt like a crudely mounted shadow-puppet play smoke-screening some unspeakable underlying soul-death. Unusually crudely mounted. Especially. Worse than usual.

The best news sources were mostly just jokes. All the futures offered seemed equally inconceivable, and a version of reality willing to indulge any one of them seemed totally incompatible with any version willing to indulge the others.

For example: Who would be the most powerful person in the world next? The ice-queen veteran of human history's most humiliating marriage? Another actor? A grinning skull with dying hair? A black guy? No one knew. None of the choices were not weird. The winner would be, it seemed, less the candidate who convinced America that s/he would rule wisely, and more the one who convinced America that s/he was not actually a fictional character and that his or her election to the presidency would not make the country and the lives of the people living in it and everywhere else seem even more unreal than they seemed at the time.

And W, what the hell was he? The explanation offered at the time—that our president was somehow simultaneously a religious nut and a rich aristocrat and a drunk hick and a dumb jock and a warmongering draft dodger—was obviously some kind of lame cover story, a crude amalgam of every available caricature of right-leaning Americans, no matter how mutually exclusive, designed to throw everyone off the trail. You have the benefit of hindsight—tell us. Was he a robot? A mistake? Some kind of ruiner—only that was certain then.

But this is not about him, really. The point is, it was a cynical time. A cynical cynical time, made for cynics and full of cynicism.

The Internet didn't help; we were still getting used to it. Everyone argued about what was being fucked and how fast. Antifacts were manufactured until every truth had a twin across the line of scrimmage. Entirely alternate realities were posed and men and women were bribed into talking them into being. Crimes and their evidence were covered up so continuously and so callowly that anyone admitting to having noticed the universe of fingerprints papering every surface sounded paranoid and tastelessly earnest.

If "the times" ever feel like anything to real people, they felt like that. The condition that emerged, that we all felt then, was not a sense of opposing factions but rather of a life that was all slippery, in a total conflict of definition, where you could cross a street in front of your house and then expect to be rewarded or assaulted for taking the bold and ballsy stand that, yeah, the street was actually there and was crossable, and, yeah, citizens had the right to cross it.

Even the dullest people were affected—they began to spend their time with puzzles of numbers instead of puzzles of words, so awful was the shadow of meaning. People who read the Bible every day on the way to work couldn't remember anything in it. People on buses repeated simple sentences over and over into their cell phones.

Most products and services appealed only to the insane or to the chronically confused but made them comfortable enough that their conditions became difficult to diagnose. Everyone smart wanted to get rich making one.

The most popular magazine among young people was called *Vice* and it was the most cynical thing yet made by human hand—it even came out against threesomes, explaining that they could come to naught but awkwardness and defeat. People's essential hopelessness made everything seem boring and they only talked about a topic if everyone could agree that it was stupid. Wit consisted in coming off as the least bitter complainer. A great trade in openly pseudodemocratic TV shows arose, where vast voting audiences eagerly waited for the weekly results of talent contests between warring morons that viewers doubted they'd actually participated in. These offered the thrill of finding yourself a victim of electoral fraud without the disappointment of realizing it might matter.

Likewise, there were new, lavish shows whose essential fascination was that they claimed to be "real" but transparently weren't, offering viewers a sort of harmless equivalent to their everyday humiliations—the Sherlockian joy of sorting truth from fiction accompanied by the unusual comfort of knowing that no one would die if you were wrong.

As usual, shows about police were popular, and addressed strange needs: one of them came in three varieties—a version where a violent, irrational, terrified husband and a skeptical, childless, unmarried, terrified woman came together to defeat sex crimes; a version where a smart man came and tricked felons into telling the truth; and a version where it was usually someone's mother's fault. On the most popular police show, machines solved everything (in a spin-off, machines solved everything and there were bikinis). The best shows were like the worst ones only more complicated and the crimes almost never got solved or took so long to get solved that the perpetrators were already dead for some other reason.

In music, the proportion of songs about the sex appeal of not trying very hard or of possessing vast wealth increased exponentially.

In movies, zombies were the most popular monster.

They are unusual, among monsters, for being inferior to their victims and winning only by weight of numbers, and for having no brains, but wanting to eat them. Their popularity extended to porno movies, and those were good years for zombie porn—Tina DiVine's first role, for instance, was as a zombie.

So this was the zeros. This is the time we're talking about.

oooooooooo

During this time, an ambitious young filmmaker who went to art school decides to start making porno movies. Either cynically or uncynically, he names himself Leom McFrei, after a famously uncynical artist from a generation earlier. Cynically *and* uncynically, he markets his movies in such a way as to emphasize their unusual lack of cynicism. His movies are ambitious for porno movies, but they are always porny enough to be distributed in the American commercial-porn distribution system, meaning the characters keep having sex for twenty minutes at semiroutine intervals whether or not it can be made interesting in the nonmasturbatory sense of the word. However, Leom has talent, and sometimes his movies. especially when they fail and fall apart in their overt job as pornography, are caught in the net of his talent, and they become some other and more telling thing.

The first sex scene in his cynically titled *Girls Are Liars*, while being for me, and most people with any other options, probably a total failure as pornography—that is, as a thing that would turn you on—is one of the most fascinating sequences ever committed to film, if a bit too long. It could only have been done exactly when it was done—it is not zombie porn, but it is close.

The soundtrack is basically built around a monologue by actress Sunny Carmichael that starts with her lip-synching up with some rhythmic porn moans on a flickering TV, then turning it off and wondering aloud to John Wood* why he's looking at *it* instead of *her* while epic music—"Queen of the Borrowed Light" by Wolves in the Throne Room—dawns. Mostly, Sunny doesn't stop, and John's few lines, all just agreeing to get her to go on with whatever it is she thinks she's doing, come like the mumbles of some lazy, arguably trainable, pet. He is, in this scene, somewhere between there and a corpse—with the gauntness and long beard of a Civil War prisoner, the lines of his knuckles standing out vinelike—a long-dried-up

---

* Porn's John Wood, not the somewhat well-known painter John Wood, or the colonel who died in Iraq, or the suicidal millionaire, or the clergyman/botanist/activist, or the historian, or any of the four sportsmen, ten government and political figures, or the relative of famous ghost Pearl Bryan of the same name. There is, as far as I know, only one Sunny Carmichael.

and retired demon-man, stranded now in a realistic and small Southern Californian apartment with sour light and a box fan, unmoved by any offering—even freckly, cream-colored Sunny. Everything in the scene seems to be pretending to be something else offscreen. More than usual.

There is a hollow static-type sound that the ear can detect but that doesn't really sound like anything—sound engineers call it "room tone"—and the music in the scene is somehow mixed in *under* the room tone, on purpose, so that "Queen of the Borrowed Light"—dense, impressive, orchestral black metal, full of shrieking—isn't broadcasting the characters' mood or pretending to be something playing in the room or even in the next room but instead comes on like a radioed-in commentary from unseen parties who are contemptuous of—and murderously enraged by—what they're watching. Meanwhile, Sunny, when Wood's utterly massive snake cock isn't rubbing around inside her dark-speckled face, keeps up the scene talking titties and pussies with the condescending rhythm of a brat who knows she doesn't get to go to recess until she turns in a convincingly cute version of "Itsy-Bitsy-Spider" to some teacher or otherwise useless grown-up. She becomes uncanny. Here, with a curtain of straight hair that's the pale yellows of a freshly used condom, and in green tennis shoes, something in her half-consciously parted lips and stoned, lined eyes has the unhealthy gleaming of Wonder Bread–clean things with some absolutely essential ingredient blasphemously absent. At one moment, while sucking cock, her dead doll-baby eyes fix with an obedient intensity on a stray, shapeless tattoo up Wood's leg for an unwholesomely long three seconds, as if waiting for it to tell her when to stop sucking and breathe. In another shot, with her head somehow blearily appearing on the far right of a penetration close-up with Wood's wrinkled equipment and Sunny's smooth-curved cunt and thigh all in the sliding white-and-chocolate-and-strawberry color of ice cream—only drier—she desperately squeaks, between snotty moans, "Oh—I love it when we do things together!" Relentlessly antiathletic, almost antipornographic, they sit and shift on one another in positions that show off almost nothing and shove the body's curves down into the dirty white lard of listless furniture, and, for the cum shot, she waits, face upturned under him, with all her features twitching and wincing separately in a wind-up rhythm the way old Walt Disney animatronics do when they're giving speeches.

# I Go to Los Angeles to Be in Porn

**I just now** looked up the name of the song in Sunny's scene. Google initially finds only one other use of the phrase (outside the title of the song) "Queen of the Borrowed Light." It's on one of those vain, totally disordered pages with cryptic display fonts and a lot of purple that's obviously the work of some fanatic. It's about tarot cards, and it's cribbed from the article on the High Priestess card from A. E. Waite's 1910 *Pictorial Key to the Tarot* (from which so much later lunacy has flowed, usually west): " . . . the mantle suggests light—a shimmering radiance. She has been called occult Science on the threshold of the Sanctuary of Isis, but she is really the Secret Church, the House which is of God and man. She represents also the Second Marriage of the Prince who is no longer of this world; she is the spiritual Bride and Mother, the daughter of the stars and the Higher Garden of Eden. She is, in fine, the Queen of the borrowed light, but this is the light of all."

In the entertainment business, ideas are important, especially dumb and primitive ones with no basis in reality. The cards are really just cards, old playing cards that people later found and thought meant something more than they meant because of the freakish pictures. The pictures were freakish because it used to be that when people wanted entertainment they used to have to get someone to draw cards with their hands. It was usually the same nearsighted girl who these days they get to write the specials and the soup of the day on the coffee-shop chalkboard and who always adds a smiling cup with a curlicue of steam coming out of its head. So all the kings and all the queens in all the decks of anyone anywhere in the world who felt like playing cards were different and it made each wrong and weird. This is what happens when a medium expresses itself through the constant use of whatever real people happen to be convenient. You get things that seem to be telling you things—like "Queen of the Borrowed Light."

That's a phrase that seems to be trying to tell you something. I might've named this book "Queens of the Borrowed Light" if I thought anyone but Wolves in the Throne Room and a few hippies would've got it.

⊙⊙⊙⊙⊙⊙⊙⊙⊙

The card described—the High Priestess—is, upside down, the root of all my troubles, according to a reading I once had. If you know enough strippers or Californians, sooner or later one of them will ask to read your cards. Although I felt safe and more or less content with my last fortune ("You will receive something good in the mail" and some lucky numbers), I agreed, knowing it was best to keep on the reader's good side. Also, I was inclined to humor the cards, since it was their fault I was in Hollywood and sitting on a sleeping bag on the girl's floor.

How? Basically: I write that article I was talking about at the Plaza. To do it, I find and meet for the first time and talk very briefly to Leom McFrei. Leom tells me about this other director named Osbie Feel, who does "pirate porn" and distributes it himself. Osbie is named after a guy in a Thomas Pynchon novel, so I call and ask about that, figuring I can maybe use it in the article. We talk on the phone about the enigmatic Pynchon/alternative-porn connection (Pynchon's niece was in porn, the director of the influential alt-pinup Web site SuicideGirls has the symbol from The *Crying of Lot 49* tattooed on his bicep, etc.) and I send him JPEGs of my drawings for Pynchon's *Gravity's Rainbow*.

That's that. Nearly a year after that one phone conversation, I get this:

*Hi, Osbie here, long time no talk. I'm in preproduction on a porn movie for Hustler/GSP, tentatively titled* Far Gone and Out. *It is centered around the theme of Tarot cards and mysticism as they relate to a man trying to make sense of his sexual history and love life . . .*

He goes on politely and uncertainly to say it would mean a lot to him if he could use my pictures in the movie. I say it's no problem and that it'd mean a lot to me if I could fuck some girls in the movie. He writes, "Well we need a punk and there aren't any, send photos."

So: I ended up in porn because one day I sat down and decided to draw one picture for every page of a very thick book no one I knew had read and then made a joke.

I was going to be naked and at the mercy of total strangers. In Los Angeles. My best and—other than the girl who wants to read my fortune—only friend in Los Angeles is an ex-crack-whore named Charlie who'd become a reality-TV producer and lives in Koreatown. I call him when I land to figure out where exactly that is.

"Hey Charlie!"

"Hey! How's the pussy?"

"Fucked. How's being an insane fuckup all the time?"

"So far, so good."

"Listen, hey, I just landed and . . . "

"Oh fuuuuuuuck . . . "

"What?"

It turns out that because he is an insane fuckup all the time, he's gone to Dallas to visit his mother and forgot I was coming. Though this turns out later to be actually true, I still have no place to stay so I call Alice—stripper, pinup girl, Californian, amateur cartomancer, and one-time model of mine. She says no problem and that it'd be fifty kinds of rad.

It is Valentine's Day again. I haven't spent much time in LA since I was a teenager.

Alice's small single-room apartment, on the banks of a six-lane road in Hollywood, is half taken up by a mattress on a rug with a single long window over it. Other things—mostly unattached to any furniture, like in a lot of people's rooms in cities, like in mine—drift around the room like clusters of islands: amplifiers; piles of cosmetics and shoes; a lazy cat named Birch on top of the VCR; an old, yellowing, deeply infected computer; a city of VHS tapes with white sidewalk cracks in their cardboard shells, and a thin resurfacing of DVDs on top.

We eat Italian food, play air hockey, and talk about the cat and our jobs. I don't know anything and I don't know anyone and I don't know what is going to happen. I am glad to be away from home. Amazed at the ordinary sunshine of Los Angeles in February, I lie on an itchy once-blond carpet in front of the long window on my borrowed piece of floor and bathe with Birch in the borrowed light.

ooooooooo

Max Clamm used to be in the music business. One day, a porno company gave him a stack of porno movies and told him to put together a collection of the best porno music—perhaps because they detected the veil of 1970s-ness that hangs from Clamm like a Foghat.

Clamm then claimed that he couldn't because the music in the movies was too *bad*—and added as an afterthought (afterthoughts being the kind of thoughts most likely to land men jobs in porn) that the movies sucked too. They said, "Oh you think you can do better?" And he said, "Yes." Now Clamm produces pornos.

He is loud and huge. He drives out to Alice's to get me on a sunny Hollywood morning wearing a vast shirt that's all orange. "Hey man, good to meet you, you like Mexican food?" I do. Climbing into whatever car (I am not from here,

I don't have the car-sense), I become slowly aware that I am sitting next to a straight man who is trying to piece together, in the course of normal, conversational eye contact and driverly mirror-checking, what I will look like naked. He likes to talk, which seems good, because I don't know anything.

My dad had been an extremely unlucky screenwriter (one episode of *Who's The Boss?*), and I'd visited him in LA during the summers. But a kid in a place where he only knows adults lives in a tight, tiny world, so I am not used to any of the things that remind you you're in Los Angeles: constant genuine lines of palm trees—taller than buildings but with trunks so thin you want to call them "stems"; the Hollywood sign really, actually visible out the car window from almost anywhere; telephones shaped like pieces of Xtreme sports equipment; strip clubs on every commercial block; hillside homes like fortified jewelry boxes; cracked parking lots repeating in every shape with their edges rotting off like continents of hamburger; Scientology centers; sitting through turn signals and then having the person driving say, "Oh, man, I totally forgot to turn 'cause I was thinking about rolling blunts"; jungle plants growing out of residential sidewalks; dead skunks in the road; the everyday atmosphere of bleaching and burning; video stores consisting mostly of hand-labeled shipping boxes and sun-damaged posters for things you've never heard of; fat ladies selling hot dogs wrapped in bacon out of carts; roads coming in from halfway to Chicago that refuse to die; a clean, glassy incompleteness built into the taller buildings that always seems to need to remind you about the sky, the ocean, the future.

Clamm, likewise, is from somewhere else—down South— and clearly is used to a more elastic and forgiving moral order. "Hey man! Are you talent?" he says to a young guy walking out of Adult Industry Medical (AIM)—the place where you go to get your STD test—while standing precisely under a sign telling people precisely not to do precisely what he's doing—that is, solicit talent on the premises.

It looks like an ordinary doctor's office, only the abstract pictures on the walls are even more '80s—and, like the title that changes the meaning of the picture, you know everyone who's there reading a pamphlet, or staring at the wall, or flirting with the desk nurse, is a porn star. The title actually *does* change the meaning of a picture in the otherwise normal bathroom. At first it looks like an ordinary Japanese kanji ink drawing—the kind of thing baby boomers aspiring to middle-class home-dom who have decided not to go Impressionist might hang on their walls. But then, where the red maker—or ownership—seal would be in a real ink drawing, it says, in legible English, "John Cassavetes."

At this stage, everything is a puzzle. Was it *by* the amazing independent director? Could this be important?

(I would realize two years later—there are only two AIMs in LA—that it was actually a subtle *portrait* of the man, drawn to disguise itself as calligraphy. But still—why? Maybe this is just what you get at yard sales in North Hollywood. Anyway . . . )

While people get my blood, urine, and signature, Clamm's on the phone asking someone for a hundred thousand dollars for another movie in a pinched twang I recognize, from an ex-Hell's-Angel-cum-math-teacher I used to have, as North Carolina: "See it's never been done before, man, a *porn* version of a *main*stream movie done by the same people who did the *original* movie."

Clamm is somewhere deep in his fourth decade, has glasses set in thick black plastic, long brown hair, and is as wide as an oven, but apparently he and I would both be "perfect" for a series of movies being cast by a wizened, leathery, dying-spark-eyed, and leather-wearing bright orange producer—accompanied by what appears to be a very *ex*-Playmate—we run into on our way out of AIM who speaks to us in the rich, ashy, gin-worn voice of the kind of blazered man-bat you might see late at night on cable, hosting a cruel and forgotten game show. We take his totally unforgivable business card and tell him we'll call him.

(Free idea for conceptual artists: collect and display as many adult industry business cards as you possibly can—in Plexiglas so that people can see the wide range of fucked-up and full-frontal graphics on both sides. Like as a comment on something.)

The modeling agency we visit next, likewise, is time-displaced. It has the wide, dark-wood desks, painted lamps, matte blacks, tweedy textures, gunmetal knicknacks, and midafternoon liquid-lunch slowdown of a much earlier era of office evolution. Only the rows of photos—of curving, oiled, fuckable young girls, full body, only in heels and standing identically in poses, tacked glossily to the worn corkboards, seemingly made more alive by the ossified context—look new, and the sections of the wall they line seethe with a silent, hyp-notizing snatch-force that increases exponentially when you aren't looking their way.

At the biggest desk, across from a black girl in an apple-red dress, the white-moustached, gray-jacketed agent (also from the past) says into the phone:

"Yes, the African Am . . . ah . . . black perform . . . "

"The term is 'nigga'!" jokes Clamm. The words drop fatly out of his face like vended soda cans. And the features col-lected in the small office writhe on their respective indulgent faces like mealworms on petri dishes.

A woman in a corner across from our couch, with a gold Star of David, who turns out *not* to be a mousy secretary but is actually talent, asks, nervously, about whether I'm Jewish too.

"Half."

"Do you everrrrr go to temple?"

"Not since I was like thirteen."

"I, um, well, when I go, then there's *wine* and I always get really *drunk*," and she deflates in around her own neck. She is a little nature special.

"Well, y'know, when you're *bored* then . . . "

"I don't think it's borrrring, it's rrrrreally funnnn. I really like going to temple. I like the *wine*."

During this, Clamm negotiates with the agent about Lotus Lee, who I am supposed to be in a scene with. I ask, "Is she, like, alright? Is she a nice girl? 'Cause I gotta fuck her." Everyone freezes. After scanning the room, as if to establish that no one's wounded, the agent behind the desk goes, "Shhhh," and says that the girl in red is new, as if I were not just stupid but drunk and unruly. And as if, on other days, he had not, in his drawl that corrals and sweeps the sounds into the phone and relaxes again like broom bristles, said things like, "It's just a little choking, honey, just a little like that," to a girl across the desk when she told him she didn't do choking, and one of the two men flanking her with pistols shoved in their waistbands told him that she did. I sincerely hope that whoever Lotus Lee is, she's heard the word *fuck* before.

Lunch:

"We need Tina. She'll take it in the can," says Clamm.

"Plus she has boobs," says Osbie Feel. Osbie is an intermittent addict—aggressively mutton-chopped, pale—but with the blood always struggling up toward the surface, younger than Clamm, and half Mexican, half Irish.

"Tina DiVine?" I say.

"You know her?"

"Sort of."

I tell Osbie and Clamm the whole story over a chicken quesadilla with beans and rice in a strip mall somewhere off Vermont Avenue. The next day Clamm, ever apposite, sends me an e-mail linking to Tina DiVine's most recent public blog entry on DiVinethings.com—the one from this year's Valentine's Day. It's a generous and sympathetic message to anyone reading who might be spending Valentine's Day alone by way of a reminder that no matter how bad their Valentine's Day is, it could not possibly be worse than the Valentine's Day of this guy she went on a date with last year.

°°°°°°°°°

It's not easy to tell what's going on in California. The very first person to mention it said it was an island "very close to the side of the Terrestrial Paradise; and it is peopled by black women, without any man among them, for they live in the manner of Amazons." It has always been a long name at the edge of the map in a language nobody knows. The people in charge are often trained actors, and two of its biggest businesses are aerospace—which is secret—and movies—which is lies.

Luckily, there *is* an accurate survival manual, and it is a Bad Religion album called *Suffer*. I gave it to my much littler brother, who grew up there, for his thirteenth or fourteenth birthday—one year it was Legos, the next it was *Suffer*.

After the title track and "You Are (The Government)" (*1000 points of light and a black reflecting pool*), it moves into: "1000 More Fools"; "How Much Is Enough?" (*Tell me is there any-*

*thing so sure? Rapacity, tenacity, capacity for more*); "When?";
"Give You Nothing"; "Land of Competition"; etc. until it finishes up with "Pessimistic Lines."

Between Alice's small apartment and Hollywood Boulevard there's the spare-changing territory of a homeless girl
with long, dirty-blonde hair who I keep thinking is like a
totally failed version of Alice—she wears a sweatshirt advertising *Suffer*. I keep giving her tens and twenties, thinking if
she's heard *Suffer* and still can't handle LA she must be in *very*
serious trouble. She also makes me think of an early Bad Religion song about trying to cross the street in LA—"Frogger."

Bad Religion thrived in Los Angeles, putting together a
company that sometimes put out good bands and making
deals with shoe manufacturers and generally doing business
in the two decades following *Suffer*. Not long ago you could
see advertisements for their recent and entirely embarassing
album *New Maps of Hell* all over bus-stop benches in the city.

They are still surprisingly good live for some reason no
one can figure out, though they play in places that are much
too big now. At one point, at a show I saw at Irving Plaza,
the sound guy did something or failed to do something or
*kept* doing something and, after some subtle but clearly hos-
tile cues and mimes going literally and figuratively over the
heads of the whopping crowd between the band and the difficult little man on his audio island, their bass player, who
had drifted toward a mike, leaned in and said, smirkingly but
distinctly, so we could all catch it—"Oh yeah, buddy? How's
*your* band doing?"

It seemed like one more piece of Southern California survival advice.

I'm from DC. DC punk bands are known for refusing to
play ball. In New York, they're known for trying to play ball

and failing and then going back to not playing ball. SoCal bands are known for playing ball and being good at it and liking it and laughing at you. And then being on cable TV shows where they get tattooed. I felt I would have to make some adjustments if I was going to survive in Southern California.

Before leaving New York, I'd listened to all twenty-five minutes and thirty-two seconds of *Suffer* while standing in the bathtub and inexpertly shaving everything under my eyebrows as per Industry standard. I nicked my toes.

Then I tried to put together some kind of passable California style. I wanted to give the impression I was someone who had some business putting his dick in people for money. I wondered if such an impression was possible to give. I found a pair of aviator sunglasses—although the frames had gone hopelessly asymmetrical in the junk drawer under the flashlight and the cave troll and the rainbow Slinky, they looked like the right kind of thing to have.

I also packed Hawaiian shirts—a sun-faded traditional red-with-orange-palm-tree-topped-island one and a far more ambitious and enigmatic half-sleeve polyester one with overlapping dye-transferred purple-tinted photos of snowcapped peaks and skiing men and wooden buttons that was, and still is, essentially indescribable in print, from a flea market in Miami Beach. I listened to *Suffer* again and went to the airport.

ᴏᴏᴏᴏᴏᴏᴏᴏᴏ

Los Angeles, early in the morning, sleeps like Alice: like a blonde who is going to wake up hungover, like a half-broken stripper. At night she's all curves in the footlights and the cracks in her face are filled in with makeup, but in the daylight she lies still on a bare mattress, with all her tattoos looking earnest and random, unself-consciously grubby and reduced to undecorated, earthy surfaces the color of use. And so you feel like you have to tiptoe around her while she shifts in response to things happening in her sleep.

Clamm is unusually quiet when he picks me up for the first day of shooting and stays that way until we get the doughnuts.

"You ever fuck uh Asian girl?" he says, ruminating over a jelly, with the wheel in his other hand.

"Yeah."

"Well, I just don't want you to be surprised about Lotus Lee, because when you open her legs . . . "

"All I know is whatever you're about to say is going to be stupid."

"Instead of horizontal it'll be vert—I mean, umm—instead of vertical it's horizontal, man . . . "

I never did find out if it was true. Lotus Lee never showed up and I don't have the energy to Google it and look. It seems unlikely.

We have one of those low-energy workweek mornings where everyone is up about three hours before they should be and where the sun has been switched on but hasn't burned the desert cold off the buildings yet. Everybody holds their coffee close to them and some have doughnuts. I very much have doughnuts. The warehouse, in downtown LA, has never been used for porn and there are the usual hundred thousand things that have to get done before shooting. Since, unlike everyone else, I don't have a life in Los Angeles to go back to when I'm not shooting, they pay me extra to help. This is good because it cuts down on the amount of time I spend feeling like a paralyzed idiot with scabs on his toes waiting around to take off his clothes.

I shiver and hold my doughnut close. I look at everything.

There are bowls and pans of snacks surrounded by a couch of soft, swallowing squared cushions. There's a camera on a low dolly clearly rigged from skateboard parts, and a red-headed Cockney fetish photographer telling legally actionable stories about working on a music video for Dwight Eisenhower—who they lost track of and eventually found in a car shooting heroin with his dad. There are coolers full of drinks too cold to drink, huge lips and breasts on a production assistant making cue cards with a sharpie, and an aging, bitching, helpful thief in a white wifebeater with a moustache like a misplaced eyebrow. There are sandbags, lights on tripods with translucent filtering gels in acid colors pinned with forceps to the matte-black open fins around the cauldrons of their steaming white eyes, and coils of extension cords in different oranges at their feet scattered across every room and floor like a race of spider-legged cyclops gingerly invading a corn-snake hatchery. And: black flights of iron stairs; the owner (an Asian photographer) and his girl (a Playmate); a careful desk with attached shelf supporting rows of *Playboys*; the director with an elephant-god mask and other props; another, strictly decorative, elephant near the couch (I would have sex on one in another movie—an elephant—elephants *everywhere*) and (speaking of paired elephants:) a computer where, each time someone bored checks his or her e-mail, there are more clips and there is more news about the vice president having tried to shoot a bird and instead shooting an old person and good friend in his face. There's exposed plumbing and exposed wiring, text messages from a girl telling me to come see her band play that night, news about record snowfall in New York, and a *Washington Post* story about the Spotsylvania County sheriff saying there was no way to destroy a certain suspected prostitution ring without patronizing it. There are clips of *The Daily Show* with the host writhing in wide-eyed ecstatic revelation and attempting to contain and balance and not waste the fate-ordained privilege of being the comedian-of-record on the week Dick Cheney shot his hunting buddy in the face. There are individual walls with different colors or patterns on them that, through a camera, will, with a few props, look like whole different places, and there is Max Clamm, tense and squinting on a phone that looks like a toothpick in his rump-roast fist. There is the tall porn journalist, Monte Pentagram, and butt jokes, and Lotus Lee nowhere to be found, and pieces of sets left over from commercials, and Hustler/Gary Slynt Productions' very thorough, imaginative, and somewhat science-fictional standard performers' contract allowing them to distribute or modify the images captured of the signatory over the next few days in any way and using any technologies currently extant or yet-to-exist and warning him or her that "your performance may result in possibly being subject to mockery, derision and public verbal degradation." There's production manager Shadrach Meshach saying, from the depths of his navy blue hood, in his theatrically low voice and in his unplaceable islander accent, that he's never seen anyone *read* the contract before. There are mismatched copies of the script, there's me blacking out part of my T-shirt in accordance with film-business rules about product names so that instead of "Born Dead" it says "Porn," and there is everyone and everything being photographed at high speed by Jorge Paz, the Argentinian/Inuit photographer who always talks and knows all the girls and makes them laugh in a way that makes you think he must have cheerfully screwed every single one of them over mai tais on a roof just a couple of days ago and not called yet. And all of these things are doubled in time and rewatched on screens on small, cabled televisions on folding plastic tables and on the littler screens folded out from the side panels of the behind-the-scenes video cameras, and all of this in a warehouse at a quiet, wide-sidewalked end of the garment district scattered with bus stops and rusting newspaper machines, which warm slowly as the new and as-yet-undifferentiated dough of the day bakes in the broad, long oven of downtown Los Angeles.

∞∞∞∞∞∞∞∞

"I don't know if you've ever done heroin before," says Osbie Feel, standing in a bathtub and holding out a fishnet stocking and a syringe full of flat Coca-Cola, "but the thing is—it feels really good. So I need you to imagine the best thing ever is happening and just like lie there with this look in your eyes like it's the best thing ever."

So I'm filmed doing that, and photographed standing next to a girl playing my pregnant wife (people are always getting pregnant in Feel's movies—but never in a usual way. In this one it's a miscarriage, in the next it's a pig, in the one after it's a gory scam for money), and then looking down with her into a grave, and holding my passport next to my face for the production's records, and also just standing around and sitting in a swivel chair, and with my face in breasts. Then it's time for sex.

∞∞∞∞∞∞∞∞

There was once this girl—a sociology student in Madison, Wisconsin—who did not trust herself. She worried that her taste in men was sociologically determined—that it was pressed on her by the dominant culture and the patriarchy. So she resolved only to date men she was not attracted to. She found one.

He was a sexual radical too: he insisted on, at all times, following an extreme version of the Sexual Abuse Prevention Policy protocols invented at Antioch College, Ohio, whereby every ascending level of sexual contact requires a verbal assent. Weeks after they started dating, he would still get very angry if she held his hand or messed up his hair without asking first.

Although they did eventually break up, it is remarkable to consider the medieval precision of the Hell on Earth they briefly created for themselves. Between them, they managed to identify the two ingredients most responsible for sexual pleasure, isolate them away from those responsible for any other kind of interpersonal attraction, and strangle them.

We all know about attractiveness—good looks—and how it's a big deal. The other thing gets slightly less play, but it's just as much a big deal. That's the idea that the other person *knows what to do*. You look at them and you *know* that they *know* and it's filthy and disgusting and excellent. We look at people and we see their rhythms and their tricks.

Of course, really, you *guess* and then they *guess* and pretty soon you're *guess*ing all over each other and then maybe after you smoke a cigarette and sort it all out. Or you guess wrong and cry.

Meanwhile, it's essential to pretend all the guessing isn't stressing you out even though it is.

Osbie Feel is earnestly hoping for "chemistry" between his performers. In a porn context, "chemistry" is a condition exactly the opposite of the Hell on Earth created by the young couple in Madison. There is attractiveness and *knowing what to do*-ness and nothing else.

Porno sex makes all the guessing more and less compli-cated. It is easy to know whether you are going to have sex, but hard to know anything else.

There is only one time in porn—or indeed, in the whole of human behavior—when you can be utterly confident that you can see what someone on film is thinking. In the human catalog, there is only one *visible* emotion: male sexual ecstasy. Tears can be "of sadness" or "of joy" or totally fake, people can make themselves blush, and the swelling and reddening of cunt lips is always relative, sometimes subtle, and usually simultaneous with all kinds of distractions. But you will have to dig deep into the lonely margins of French literature and undergraduate poetry before you find the phrase "he ejacu-lated gloomily."

This puts the male performer at a disadvantage in the on-set guessing game. If he doesn't get happy at some point, there's no movie. The female talent always has the option of acting, plus, she doesn't get to go home until the male talent gets happy, so the incentives point to making him think all his guesses are good. Especially if it's his first day.

There *are* rules: Before the scene, you say to the girl, "What are your rules?" Sometimes the female talent will ask you if you have rules. The only person's rules I can remember well at the moment are Gina Giles's rules, which were "Don't grab me by my head like this and look at me and go, 'I fucking *hate* you!' and then spit in my eye." So, you know, the rules don't tell you all the things you might like to know.

So you have to guess. Or there is also always the option of deciding you're just going to do your job and you don't care. Throughout the first day of shooting, I keep noticing I'm not taking this option.

⊙⊙⊙⊙⊙⊙⊙⊙⊙

Walking toward the set, now totally dressed and lit, puts me in mind of a piece of information about women given to me by Claire LeJense, a model/actress/bartender who, despite being essentially the diametric opposite kind of feminist from the Wisconsinian sociology student, once arrived at a strangely parallel decision. She decided she was going to have sex with this one guy because he was the ugliest person she'd ever seen. When I asked what you would have asked, she said—as if she was glad because she'd been thinking about just how to put it: "Sometimes you fuck the person and sometimes you fuck the situation."

So here's the situation:

At the bottom of the stairs, in a large, high-ceilinged Situation Room that was originally a loading dock, most of the things, forces, and people on the set mentioned so far are arrayed in a wiry, insectile darkness relieved only by the local glow of monitors and a half-red/half-green lighting scheme otherwise used only in the panic-inducing scenes in low-budget Italian horror movies and also around a huge, dead, and mostly gutted yellow Lincoln Continental with suicide doors. It is Osbie Feel's and it had stopped working right before the production's first shooting day and had to be towed in and then raked into place by every male hand present, as well as jacked up and knocked off the standing jack to correct its position so it could be slid into place in front of a wall, where rear-window night footage of the streetlights and twilit signs of Los Angeles being endlessly sucked toward a vanishing point on a black and invisible horizon is now being projected in a loop.

Aside from the small work it takes to get the still photos (pregnant, looking into the grave, etc.), I never see Rebecca Black, the girl who showed up on short notice to replace Lotus

Lee, outside the situation. A big part of it was a your-first-day-at-work-and-we're-sure-you'll-do-fine situation. You've been there.

It's quickly obvious that, from the point of view of Rebecca Black, my job is to be a dildo, and that as long as I behave essentially like a dildo and I do only that which dildos do, she is capable of having toward me any of the surprisingly broad and subtle array of emotions a woman might reserve for dildos in her life, corrected for style, size, color, and consistency. The only way to move into riskier territory would be by doing things dildos don't do. And this I do not do, though Rebecca Black has long, dark, brassy eyes and a fantastic ass. A very narrow range of signals is being broadcast from Rebecca Black. The voices in my head are a whole other story:

"What the hell are we doing?"

"Well, we're sitting on leather upholstery spilling foam the color of crack and getting our cock sucked by a porn star named Rebecca Black in leopard skin while staring into blinding lights coming through the streaks and pits in the windshield behind which the crew is watching on monitors and through the windows and from a balcony and trying not to make any noise stepping over cables and around counterbalancing rods in the nightlike dark. For money."

"That's completely insane. This is the most insane thing we've ever done."

"Oh come on, this is a job—people have this job, people do this. Is it that insane?"

"Yeah I think maybe it is. I mean look at this . . . isn't that guy in the Horrorpops? This is insane."

"Okay, *yes*. But there *is* a blowjob."

"Oh yeah, look at that . . . *yeah*, she's . . . um . . . Forgive me here, but why aren't you . . . "

"*Because I'm too busy answering your stupid questions.*"

"Sorry. Jesus . . ."

" . . . "

" . . . "

"This is so *weird*, what's that guy over there . . . "

"Fuck off! I'm trying to . . . "

"Well maybe, you could, like, grab her ass or something and that'd get you going."

"It *is* a really nice ass."

"It is."

"But I can barely see it, it's all the way . . . "

"Well why don't you move?"

"I can't *move*, it's a fucking movie! I have to sit here and pretend to drive this . . . "

"Christ, why don't you make out or something first?"

"Because if . . . Just fuck *off*, okay?"

And it goes like that until the director decides to stop the blowjob and tells Rebecca and me to get onto the hood of the car. The redheaded Cockney gets behind me with one camera and the Swede—a drummer—who is shooting penetration and liquid-free footage for the cable TV version of the scene, gets inside the car, and I put my face in Rebecca's shaved crotch. This arrangement finally smothers all distraction and dissent and is very very fun—and then we have sex in several ways on the car while the car hood buckles with drumlike echoing sounds when we move, and I keep slowing down worrying that Rebecca, who feels like she might snap in half at any second, will crack her face open on the glass against which it is mashed so Werner can get shots of her in extreme perspective and through the streaks, and people keep mulling and staring and the PA with the tits and the lips keeps circling the car slowly while looking up like she wants a piece (which helps), and Feel keeps wanting more footage from more angles and it's hot and Clamm says GSP will want more softcore and it goes and it goes for two hours or four hours and it stops and it starts and sometimes it's not fun but at all times it's sex so it's always more fun than anything else I could be doing and we do the "fake internal pop" for cable and they say *whenever you're ready* and we fuck more and then I say okay and the people with the cameras clatter in around to catch me shooting two weeks' worth of white load at Rebecca's waiting ass. Then Jorge, talking very fast, has Rebecca hold very still while he photographs the pale lake of evaporating genes from every angle and possible lighting condition as it dries into her and dies in the halogen.

"Jesus, that's an awful lot of cum," I think.

"See? That wasn't so bad," a voice in my head says.

"Once you shut up."

"Well fuck me for trying to keep abreast of the situation."

"What*ever*. Jeez—she *is* a dish isn't she?"

"Yeah, maybe we should . . . "

"We should *not*. Where are my socks?"

"Yeah, okay. But I really wanna fuck someone."

"*Yeah*, me too. What's up with that?"

What's up with that is porno sex—where you have to stay in shot and not knock things over and keep the girl between you and the camera and not move to that nice and very soft-looking pile of sandbags over there—is exactly like being starving hungry and then being hog-tied and picked up and winched into the middle of a buffet table with someone occasionally telling you things like "Hey, only chew the ravioli *three times* before you swallow." It's not exactly unsatisfying, but you do suddenly get the urge for a proper meal.

Speaking of which, my sandwich doesn't show up.

My lunch, for some reason, doesn't come with everyone else's. I lie on a couch like a rubber band finally allowed to snap until someone brings in a provolone-and-meatball sandwich from Subway. A friend, a painter from back home, calls me for some totally other reason and then asks why I'm in LA and I say and he asks me how big the load was. It was unusually big. I eat my sandwich.

ooooooooo

A long and complicated weekend in Hollywood follows. I argue with a four-hundred-pound man and a magician; I have to explain—in the middle of a date—why I have no body hair and razor nicks on my toes; I see Mulholland Drive; Max Clamm says to me, "You're a pat of butter on a sea of grits," which I don't understand; the girl I'm supposed to have anal sex with doesn't pass her test; and Tina won't be on the movie either.

When she comes up, Shadrach Meshach says, "Tina thinks you hate her." I write a short message to an e-mail address I haven't used in a year, telling Tina it was all a long time ago and whatever.

ooooooooo

"Do you want to fuck me?"

"Yes."

"Good, because I want you to fuck me. They told me you are new, and that's okay. If you need lube just spit on my ass, and when you are about to cum just say you're going to cum, and I will cum too—it always works for me like that."

Natalia Dionni is whispering all of this in a vampire accent while we stand behind a curtain at stage left waiting for someone to say "action."

Natalia, a small girl with, that day, black hair in pigtails, would've been just "cute" if it weren't for a certain nastiness in her features like you see in photos of Stalin where the mouth smiles and the eyes smile, but they smile different smiles. The mother of a Polish girl I used to date blamed her own daughter's similar chronic-decapitator look on genes passed down from Genghis Khan. Population geneticists say that either he or Muhammed was the most prolific human progenitor, but thanks partially to ritual taboos about portrait painting, no one knows what either man looked like—and Stalin hardly ever fucked anyone. So who can say? The main thing right now: on Natalia it's hot. Thank god.

Osbie says, "Action." We come out from behind the curtain and the voices in my head start going.

"Okay, let's make out."

"We're not making out, remember? We said we're not making out."

"Why not?"

"Because we didn't want to deal with the possibility of her maybe *faking* making out."

"Okay, great then, but what do we do now?"

"Tits?"

"Tits."

"I like this thing, this red-and-white-striped top-thing with the skull in the middle."

"The director made it himself, I think."

"Really? He's got good taste. I like *these*, too . . . "

"Okay, take your shoes off and *don't fall over*."

" . . . "

"*Jesus.* You want training wheels?"

"You think they'll leave that in?"

"Whatever, this is alright."

"And it's nice how we're not kneeling on rusty metal."

"Yeah, couches are good."

"This couch is kind of disgusting, actually. What is this? Velvet?"

"Yeah, Louis XIV I think."

"I think it's supposed to be bad, it's like she's a rich goth and this is her parents' house."

"This plastic cover is getting all sweaty."

"Yeah, but at least we don't have to worry about accidentally putting her head through a windshield."

"Yeah. I think we're doing a much better job this time. What's that on the back of her neck?"

"*Property of Wally.*"

"Huh."

"This is fun."

"Hey, that whole wall is a big mirror."

"Oh yeah, if I do *this* then I can see *her* but not *me.*"

"Yeah, it's—*Fuck!*"

"What the hell was that?"

"You knocked her in the chin with the top of your head and now her teeth are bleeding."

"She does not appear to give a fuck."

"The director gives a fuck."

"The fetish-photographer guy *seriously* gives a fuck."

"I think he wants to take that bit home with him."

"Okay, break."

"Break."

"We're all sticky. Get one of those things."

"Robe."

"Robe."

"What's going on over there?"

"Clamm is explaining to Natalia that when he said we passed our AIM test with 'flying colors' that this was *not* a nickname for an STD."

"What's she doing?"

"She is standing, smoking, smile-sneering, in pigtails, wearing only stockings and candy-striped socks and telling harrowing stories about mutilations and violent crimes committed by, and against, her immediate circle of friends."

"She's a little weird, isn't she?"

"I like her."

"But she's a little condescending—like, 'Do this, it'll keep your leg from cramping up.'"

"No, she's cool. It's like 'kinky foreign girl satisfying obscure cravings on the nearest available breathing male.'"

"I think she's doing 'maternal whore from a bad coming-of-age movie.'"

"She can't be, she's younger than us. Besides, if she was it'd feel creepy and wrong and it doesn't feel creepy and wrong."

"The only reason it doesn't feel creepy and wrong is because you just got off that date with that cute guitar player who doesn't care that you're in porn and so today just feels like extra bonus sex."

"Good point. Oh, time to go again . . . O . . . K . . . and . . . here . . . and . . . there we *go* . . . "

" . . . "

"So what do they . . . ?"

"Ass-fuck to cum shot."

"Okay, that shouldn't be . . . "

"Remember what she said about the scar tissue in her ass, you have to go down first, *then* up and in."

"Right, okay . . . What the fuck was *that*?"

"That was the producer on the phone with someone in the next room saying, 'Our bowa Zak Sabbath went ta Yale!' and then everyone in here including you simultaneously telling him to shut up."

"Oh. Okay. Just give me a second here. Where am I supposed to pop?"

"Ass."

"Osbie doesn't go in for the whole cum-on-face thing, huh?"

"I think that's like level two stuff. I think Osbie's trying to make it easy on you."

"He's a nice guy."

"Yeah, he's—*Fuck!*"

"What?"

"Look!"

"*Jesus.*"

"Look at her—she doesn't give a fuck. She's got a tissue."

"That is seriously gory. The fetish photographer is cracking up—what's he saying?"

"*Thas two outta three holes, mate! Gonna try for the triple crown?*"

"He is a vulgar, vulgar man."

"I like him."

"You like everybody."

"Guess you hit that scar tissue."

"Yep."

"Break."

"Break."

# Pretend Your Task Is Not Degrading

**One of my favorite books**
is *The Biographical Dictionary of Film*. It was written by a lunatic. You can tell right away because he *wrote* it—he didn't *edit* it or *compile* it—he *wrote* it. Bud Abbot to Catherine Zeta-Jones. It's a throwback to the Victorian era, when ambitious lone individuals regularly went quietly mad and attempted to collate whole categories of creation in print without benefit of

any wiki or editorial commitee or secondary sources, and it is as eccentrically thorough and thoroughly eccentric as any dead white monomaniac's *Survey of Tides and Ocean Currents of the Atlantic, Pacific, and Indian Oceans* or *Guide to the Etiology and Morphology of Horns and Antlers in Odd-Toed Ungulates and Ruminant Artiodactyls.*

Despite giving the impression of having seen nearly every commercially released movie ever made in, or translated into, the English language (as well as having somehow also found time to read a few books and get out to interview people on occasion), the author—one David Thomson—has not, to my knowledge, ever written much about porn. However, know that I would not have brought him up here if I didn't need him or someone very much like him to illustrate things about the place where porn is made and the lives of people in it.

Imagine this situation: you are David Thomson.

You are a British film critic and you have to watch all the movies—if it's made, you *have* to watch it. It's your job. *Stop! Or My Mom Will Shoot, Babe: Pig in the City*, every new screen version of every Jane Austen novel, *The Confessions of Winifred Wagner, Norbit*. Imagine how fucked you would be in your mind.

So, here is Thomson on Adam Sandler:

"All I mean to say is that a very talented actor is hiding away in *Reign Over Me*, testing us. And the test is: is it worth trying this kind of thing again, or is the public so dumb they might as well be rich and stay rich? Sandler's face has grown up. He now listens to what is being said and he watches like someone determined to believe there's a way home. He's going to need help, and he's going to need us."

I don't think this is *pure* lunacy talking—I think that this is actually an intelligent person attempting to stay sane by writing about "the films of Adam Sandler" as if that *weren't* a degrading task for a university professor and author of twenty-five books to be assigned and might actually matter somehow. And, further, this is a man who believes that if he writes this seriously and perceptively about Adam Sandler films for long enough, then maybe that will help the process of the films of Adam Sandler mattering along a little. Because it has to or else Thomson knows he's alone and insane. Because the quality of Adam Sandler films does matter to *him*—and if every time there was a new Adam Sandler film *you* had a professional obligation to watch it as soon as—or even before—it came out and *you* were David Thomson and *your* mind was a database that included about a thousand other things you'd rather be watching and *you* kept telling yourself you'd write a novel one day and *you* had two kids you'd only ever seen in silhouette when you had to review a Pixar movie, then it'd matter to *you*, too, and your wife would not be surprised to find you on your knees in the center of a bloody pentagram sacrificing your next-born in the hope that the next two hours of your life would be more like *Punch-Drunk Love* than *Big Daddy*.

So if you extend this sort of parapsychotic anxiety and commitment to assessing the realness of the fake over five area codes, you will begin to appreciate one of the dominant mental climates of Los Angeles, California.

Right now, for example, as I write, the writer's strike of 2007 is on, and when I walk to Allie's at 3:00 p.m. for lunch, there are screenwriters in packs—in sunglasses, and sometimes corduroy sport coats or new beards. If you were one of them, whether Eddie Murphy is in the mood to play the *Shrek* donkey again or whether he thinks maybe *Norbit 2* has legs is a thing that might actually affect and change your actual and entire life.

This is not a question of selling out—most people in Los Angeles' dearest wish is to be worth enough to someone else to sell out—it is about trying to create a personality for yourself that can *handle* living in an environment where it actually matters whether Dane Cook is moving in a more mature, character-actor-type direction or not, and where people sign binding contracts saying they won't tell anyone that they're making a cartoon about talking bugs because then someone else might steal the idea of a cartoon about talking bugs and make another cartoon about talking bugs first and eat into your profits by saturating the market for cartoons about talking bugs, and where someone wants to do an Incredible Hulk TV show but insists that the Hulk be red instead of green because red is the color of anger. That is the business.

And then the other thing about LA, of course, is there's always things like what you see around, like these things that if you stop and really think, you realize you see almost *nowhere* else—like this personalized license plate on this shiny-as-new dull-emerald Rav 4 here that says, "I DEMON."

*Oh, I've got a great idea! I'll buy a dark green Rav 4 and get a personalized license plate on it that says, "I DEMON," and then I'll drive all around, and everyone will know I am like as unto a demon! In my Rav!*

In other words, a lot of people here are on drugs.

A great deal has been written about the very entertaining conduct of people on drugs and about the desolate consequences of drug addiction—but I have something to add. Drugs have very serious long-term consequences—and I don't mean like on your career or marriage or family or whatever (though that's all true), I mean, even *long* after people stop doing them, on their *heads*. I mean like John liking Yoko, and late Metallica, and Scientology. You think one day someone will think you're cool if you do this thing with them and next thing you know you're driving around Los Feliz in a corporate-colored cookie box with a license plate saying, "I DEMON."

This doesn't just affect the people *on* the drugs. The learning curve for properly grasping human behavior and therefore the world's workings is that much more difficult in any environment where the answer half the time is "Why? Because drugs."

And so, yes, the people who make porn movies are in Los Angeles too (and the forces to be reckoned with aren't *Shrek* or *Norbit* or Dane Cook, they're *Cousin Stevie's Pussy Party* and *Big Slippery White Butts 4* and how long it'll be before Natalia Dionni's scar tissue is healed up enough to do another anal movie) and even, in a few cases, grew up here and have had to breathe LA air since childhood. So it can be a bit of a thing.

◦◦◦◦◦◦◦◦◦◦

The director of this movie grew up in Los Angeles and lives there still. Let's take a look at his script. It starts:

> *Int: Tarot Parlour. The tarot parlour is a dingy, mildewed room cluttered with occult ephemera, statues of Baphomet, and dusty bottles filled halfway with rancid purple syrups.*

Who is Baphomet? Today, Wikipedia says:

> *On Friday, October 13, 1307, King Philip had many French Templars simultaneously arrested, and then tortured into confessions. The name Baphomet comes up in several of these confessions, in reference to an idol of some type that the Templars were said to have been worshipping. The description of the object changed from confession to confession. Some*

*Templars denied any knowledge of it. Others, under torture, described it as being either a severed head, a cat, or a head with three faces.*

So that's him. The script then goes on to mention that the room has my drawings in it, and an octopus, and then a gypsy reads Osbie Feel's cards. It's not clear where the tarot spread comes from—whether it, historically, actually came up at some point in Osbie's complicated life (which the script is based on) or is an artificial spread that serves some dramatic or erotic necessity. It suggests, in six cards, someone beset by a life of self-loathing and epic ruin, surrounded by bottom-scraping losers and problems of his own making, about to meet a Fool.

Rather than dwell on this, as the gypsy begins to explain it, Osbie (playing himself) elects to instead fondle her and tell her the story of his life, which begins with him (played now in the script by me with my hair dyed red and black) having sex with his ex-wife (played by Rebecca Black). Then Osbie's ex-wife becomes pregnant and then the baby dies and also Osbie's mom dies and then he becomes a heroin addict. The fortune-teller tells Osbie, while being fucked, that this is depressing. The octopus is written into the background of this scene, with its slow limbs peeling stretching shadows out of a bath of blue light from underneath its tank all during the fucking (and the script notes that his—the octopus's—expression should be, here, unreadable). There is a joke about Chinese food, and Osbie, now black, fucks a lesbian kleptomaniac and before that, while still me, a rich goth.

Next there's a scene in which Osbie, now entirely a porn actor—and entirely Mexican—has sex with a porn actress (played, of course, by an altogether other porn actress). During this scene the characters—as written—are working on a scene for a movie and having a genuine actual *moment* that is interrupted by the cameragirl saying her battery is dying and when the scene is filmed, an *actual* cameraman, who had either not read or not remembered the script, interrupts the scene to rush over and help with the dead battery, which, of course, is *not* dead because it is not an actual production problem, but a scene *portraying* a production problem, but then, of course, it is *actually* a production problem because he (the cameraguy) has interrupted filming by reacting to the unreal problem as if it is real, which seems hilarious after several maybe eighteen-hour days of filming to the crew and me, but which to Osbie— a sensitive soul who has spent great stretches of time on a lot of drugs—seems like an Escher-ish spiral of competing realities and which may be even in some way moreso if, as some people on the set suspect, Annie Beam and Carlos Most, the actually interrupted actors, were actually having a moment, fucking and making out on that bed in that dressed set with its two tall toy robots raising their dark and hollow plastic fists as if commanded by the brilliant yellow wall that looms over the room like an abstraction of a lurid sun.

The porn girl character's later emotional and professional difficulties, and their discouraging implications, are then summed up in a scene in which she sucks a zombie cock in a zombie porn. This the tarot card reader counters with some sort of allegory I don't feel I've ever properly understood involving the elephant-headed Hindu god of obstacles, Ganesh, getting a blowjob, and then there's a cum shot and the script ends.

○○○○○○○○○

Unlike Osbie's earlier work, the film is produced and funded and distributed and (with the exception of me) cast in all ways as if it is a normal pornographic film, but obviously it isn't.

Seeing Osbie, in a gray cap and a Pirate Booty Productions T-shirt, standing, trying to explain these elaborate things to nobly gleaming actors and beautiful women in their garter belts and their makeup, has something of the feeling of scratchy still photos of short Japanese men in glasses uncynically explaining dramatic or choreographic details into the latex eyes of a staring magma-mutant in the middle of a tiny, handmade Tokyo. It is the disquieting feeling of watching a man humbly in conversation with the contents of his own dreams.

Trying to construct a cheap but watchable movie that includes convincing scenes of real people actually having sex presents many of the same problems as trying to construct a cheap but watchable movie that includes convincing scenes of towering radioactive monsters annihilating a city. The construction of such a scene requires the cooperation of enough relatively rare and relatively expensive talents (in the latter case, because it is so unreal, in the former, because it is so real) that whatever entity has to pay for all of it will want the scenes to be long—in order to get their money's worth in footage. However, the idea of sitting through a twenty-minute scene of underfunded rubber freaks destroying homes, places of business, and public works is objectionable enough to certain parts of the filmgoing public that the only way for the film to be viable is if it is marketed and constructed *entirely* around the theme of building-smashing and therefore makes itself seem so absolutely essential and compelling to the monster-smashing-enjoying genetic marker that is present somewhere in the DNA of that remainder of the public that *is* open to the complex pleasure of anti-architectural cinema that they *all* go see it and some see it more than once.

In much the same way that the president of the United States at the time *Far Gone and Out* is being filmed has to seem like *nothing other* than a string of clichés about red-state Americans in order to avoid exposing some personality quirk that might offend any part of the shrinking clique of fetishists that supports him, the monster-smashing movie must consist of little else *other* than monsters smashing things in order to avoid losing any part of its audience. Further, since the proper construction of a legible and satisfying smashing scene requires an intensity of focus in the scene such that an audience can't be reasonably expected to pay attention to anything else going on *simultaneously* with the monster smashing the city, the only story movement that can occur is that which is articulated *through* the smashing of cities (for example, "Oh, now Sony Plaza is gone"), and since the audience is self-aware enough to know the film was built and marketed around monsters smashing and therefore knows that any non-smashing scene, whether or not it is enjoyable, will inevitably end in or otherwise lead to a smashing scene, there doesn't end up being much of a story at all in any movie including monster city-smashing or any dramatic tension except for the mixture of anxious excitement and fear that is experienced by very young people during the non-smashing scenes, waiting with bated breath and possibly with their hands half covering their faces and/or halfway around a corner of a wall to see when and if the smashing will actually begin.

The broader cultural consequence of all this is that the agents of the entertainment companies, who so reliably manage to fit machine guns or Philip Seymour Hoffman into workable stories year after year, have so little experience fitting monsters smashing cities into workable stories that when they try to do it, it is damaged and unholy like that Matthew Broderick *Godzilla* (or, in the case of porn, *Brown Bunny* or *Eyes Wide Shut*), which satisfies no one, least of all those who were paying attention when all the other monsters were smashing cities in other movies. These hybrids are generally so bad that even *those* people accept that while they may enjoy movies where there are stories about things that happen to people and movies where there is Rodan and that the two things require many of the same skills and personnel to make and are recorded using the same apparatus and substance, the different kinds of films are pushed by economic necessity so far apart as to be almost two different mediums. This occurs to such a degree that people like David Thomson leave city-leveling monster films out of their otherwise maniacally all-encompassing dictionaries of film even though the man who created Rodan, Godzilla, Gavadon, Mothra, et al., was awarded the Order of the Sacred Treasures for services to Japanese culture by the Emperor himself.

A great deal of this kind of unrecognized and arguably totally misdirected creativity is evident if not in the released version then at least on the set of *Far Gone and Out*—a sense that the better minds of at least three generations are enthusiastically scrambling to figure out new ways to light and photograph Jeanna Carmine's butt. It is there in the Swedish cameraman's above shot down the inside of Natalia Dionni's red tennis shoe during the missionary on the plastic-covered mold-yellow couch; it is there in the scoring of Watch Me Burn's "Wolf That Ate the Sun" over that scene (prefiguring and perhaps inspiring the use of wolf-themed extreme metal in Leom McFreï's Sunny Carmichael scene); and it is there on the couch somewhere around the sixteenth uninterrupted hour of shooting while the camera-battery thing happens, while everyone not shooting is eating pieces of pizza, and the redheaded Cockney fetish photographer gets very excited about the idea of potentially filming two women in giant platform shoes wading through and crushing the towers of a miniature scale-model of a city and then wrestling and fucking each other and rolling and bleeding into its ruins as the spires of churches and upthrust jagged remains of buildings punch into and puncture their enormous flesh.

°°°°°°°°°°

Although several actresses later say they would have *paid* money to be one of the redheaded Cockney fetish photographer's gargantuas, I don't know if the scene ever made its way into the final shooting script of the first-and-only-hardcore-porn film he went on to direct with Max Clamm in Prague that summer. What is clear is that everyone who was there said the film he did shoot was a sci-fi/fetish-porn masterpiece and that Hustler/GSP was so repelled and disturbed by whatever it got back that it immediately canceled release and chopped it up into what it considered usable scenes and distributed these only, mixed in with scenes from unrelated movies in themed-and-plotless sex-scene-compilation DVDs they make these days, like *I Want to Cum Inside Your Mom 8.*

Likewise, GSP is suspicious of *Far Gone and Out,* and the zombie, the octopus, and the eerie blue light, and one of the girls, are cut before filming even started. When it is all finished and Osbie (who is hard not to like) asks me to design a cover for the box and I do, GSP instantly pays for it, and vetoes it, and replaces it with a photo of one of the stars standing and looking down off the porn shelf at the potential consumer exactly like all the other women standing and looking down off the porn shelf next to her—except with much much smaller breasts. No one involved understands this or takes it as a good sign.

# Plot
# Developments

**My cell rings.**

"Hello?"

"Hey . . . it's Tina."

"Uh . . . hi."

"That thing you sent about Valentine's Day was really nice—thanks for sending it. Really, I . . . "

"Ummm—sure. I mean—I don't know—I might've done the same thing in your position."

"I was all fucked up then, I mean, I was just . . . "

"Hey, *whatever*. Whatever."

"Well, I really called to ask if, um, you wanted to shoot some stuff for DiVinethings.com, because some of the girls think you're cute and we need . . . " etc.

Um, okay.

●●●●●●●●●

I get back to New York. I see my friends. We talk.

"Zak may be the only person we may ever know who has a *real* porn name, not just some porn name that . . . "

"Not like the porn-name *game*."

"Right, 'cause then my name would be Starchy Third."

"Which is *why?*"

"Revolting."

"Can you explain it, please?"

"First pet: *Starchy*—the cat, and the street you lived on."

"That's how you do the porn-name game."

"Boy, I guess then I'd be Kelly Pelican."

"I'd be Sassafras Rawson."

●●●●●●●●●

One night, Osbie texts:

"I'm riding a crowded bus to Glendale right now . . . it looks exactly like page 1 of 'GR' in here."

Meaning page one of *Gravity's Rainbow*, where a narrator escaping an explosion is surrounded by a carnival of other evacuees, tired failures. I am lying in bed at home.

Recall that Osbie's car, the Lincoln with the suicide doors, is dead. So now he rides the bus everywhere. I write:

"Glendale bus 2 the mystery meet?"

"Yep. A 70-year-old Armenian man just groped an old Filipino man's ass and ran away."

I could ask Osbie how he knows the Armenian man is Armenian and the Filipino man is Filipino, but I'm sure he knows—from some giveaway in accent or neck jewelry. Osbie knows everything, especially about Los Angeles. You can ask "What's up with *Carl's Jr*? Why isn't it *Carl Jr's*?" and he will tell you. Knowing everything, and especially eveything about Los Angeles, does not appear to have made him an especially cheerful man.

Also, his omniscience does not extend to what exactly Hustler/Gary Slynt Productions wants from Osbie on a Saturday night at the Bigfoot Lounge. Their invitation is vague and, technically, he was fired a week ago.

In New York, it is raining again.

I check my mail—there is something from my friend Clarissa, in Baghdad:

> . . . *i am concerned about the fact that my brain is so completely fried and i dont remember what it feels like to really feel normal and i am so exhausted and everyone is either dying or killing each other in this very hot and dusty, crazy place where dead bodies turn up every day with holes drilled in their kneecaps and their heads sawed off and everybody has lost somebody and people either look at you with pleading eyes or empty eyes . . .*

Which is strange because she's a reporter and her e-mails from the war are usually some sober thing about the local situation followed by something about how one of the other reporters brought an espresso machine from Israel or how she could tell the sniper posted in the skylight of the hotel the reporters have to stay in all day wanted a piece of her while she was alone in a bikini in the pool floating in an inflatable donut.

I go to the store and get peanuts. When I get home I watch *South Park* and there is a lot of stuff about porn and Baghdad, but it isn't meant to be true. On another show or movie, they get someone drunk and push him into the sea.

I write back to Clarissa but I don't expect an answer because I never know what time it is in Baghdad and it always takes her a while to get back to everybody anyway. I write to Osbie again, but there is no answer so I keep watching TV.

On another channel there's *Dune*, which is about an uprising by desert nomads who murder with their words and are on worms. On a different channel, wheelchair-bound Gary Slynt, who, of course, owns the company that owns *Far Gone and Out*, is being interviewed. And then on another channel there is part of a blackened city in the desert, blackened from fire—which is the news, about Iraq. Iraq looks like the desert planet in the movie, and one of the villains in *Dune*—a bloated, floating baron who lives in an inflating containment suit—looks like Gary Slynt, who, without the electric chair he needs to move, is likewise an immobile fatman. In his autobiography, Slynt claims to have fucked a chicken, and in Dune the baron makes someone milk a cat. I can't shake the feeling that the parallel is unfair to at least one of them.

I am half conscious and half worried about a number of things. In my daze, I keep imagining Osbie and Clarissa being caught by a hybrid of the two entrepreneurs in a spherical, white, PVC pricklesuit with radiating steel spokes that spins over the sand like a rubber tumbleweed, who forces them to do body shots off the concave remains of a trophy slave's ruptured implant in the Bigfoot Lounge (which I inaccurately imagine as full of sexy-shoe chairs) and throws them into the sea.

Something on my neck vibrates. It's my phone. It's Osbie. Blearily, in the changing TV light, I see the words:

"I received a FGAO press kit today. It is an abortion."

"O i thot they were planning 2 get u drunk and push u in 2 the c."

"I am at bigfoot right now. i told them i don't trust them, they keep running outside in secret conference. So jr high."

"Tell them u will hunt them in the nite if they refuse 2 do whatever u say." I fall asleep again.

# Pictures of Nights

**Here is something people** may have read while waiting for their baby or nose job around this time:

*With his portraits of punk strippers, indie porn stars and Internet pinup girls, Zak Smith is the Toulouse-Lautrec of the postmodern demimonde—recording long New York nights from his apartment in Brooklyn the way Lautrec recorded Paris from his corner table at the Moulin Rouge.*

Here's what *I* once read in a doctor's office:

*Newsweek* or something polled college students, giving them a long list of different activities and asking which they'd most like to do. The male students' overwhelming choice from the available options was "Drink beer and have sex" while the most popular item for the majority of female students was "Visit the Louvre with Toulouse-Lautrec."

Henri de Toulouse-Lautrec was a goggle-eyed dwarf who drove around Paris in a dog cart, fed absinthe to cormorants, and paid his friends to fuck him.

In the months before his lonely death, Lautrec, heir to a family that was excommunicated ten times over and son of a man thrown out of the army for, among other things, "playing frivolous tunes on his bugle," broke into his mother's house and demanded to cook a ham, occasionally claimed he was pursued by a headless slithering beast that hung over him in the air and pushed him into his bed, and had to be watched very carefully when he was near fire or marmalade. One night, very near the end, he was seen holding a ceramic dog and a blue umbrella, wearing red pants, and fighting the cardboard elephant outside the Moulin Rouge, who he believed was trying to destroy him.

It does make you wonder what's so bad about beer and sex.

Anyway, about the long nights, and the drawings:

I think I should probably say a thing or two about the drawings. I keep making them. I do all these things and sometimes sit and draw during them and sometimes draw them later.

My drawings are often people, and they're by and large not me. So they are social. But I am not so social, really, though I can put up a great fucking front. We can all put together a great fucking front, because we all have our reasons.

I am constantly forgetting that there are good reasons to meet new people. This amnesia strikes quickest at parties.

Do you know that party that is always going on in comedies from the 1980s? Either as a cathartic ending or as a paradisiac beginning from which the characters fall? The one where one of every kind of person is there—a rich white girl in a shiny dress, a black guy with a big Afro, a hip oldster in a jacket with elbow patches, a fat guy in a Hawaiian shirt, drunk nerds, a hippie—and they're all dancing and carried away on the happy funky wave of whatever music was owned by the same entertainment conglomerate that put out the movie? Well, Tina DiVine knows where that party is. Just after I got back from LA, she took me and Leom McFrei (visiting New York for some reason). The doormen knew her and let us all in free. When I asked for a beer, the bartender asked why I wasn't drinking at the minibus-sized bar on Second and Second instead. Okay . . .

Tina has that gene common to porn directors and Jewish mothers that makes her want certain people to have sex with certain other people. She has me all set up with someone who's going to meet us at this thing.

"I'm working in Jersey—I'm a stripper! yay. sike," the someone (Jillee Jenkins) texts.

Leom McFrei, who has been on good terms with Tina ever since they worked together on *New Wave Sluts*, tells me he also wants me in his porn. I draw a picture of him sitting in a tableless red leather booth with Tina and Jillee.

Who are these people?

I talk to Tina. The Queen of Punk Porn makes no more sense in this little drunk Model UN than anywhere else.

And Leom?

Leom McFrei invented or, at any rate, made a very big deal

of the term "alt-porn" and managed to get it to stick. He eventually got Intensity Entertainment (Pepsi to GSP's Coke) to give him a whole Intensity-Alt division, which is trying, in distinctly Lollapaloozian fashion, to consolidate all subculturey porn directors, except for ones with whom Leom has personal beef, under one roof.

He directs, and produces, and promotes, and generally plays ball. To the extent that an "alt-porn scene" exists, he wields power. He hires and fires people and gets Intensity Entertainment Group to give directors money to make their movies. Despite the fact that nearly everyone in this book has worked for him at one time or another and I have known him for years, I don't get Leom any more than I get Tina.

Like a lot of successful people who went to art school, he cultivates blankness—successfully. I can only describe him the way one might describe an animal—from his visible behaviors: Leom looks like a DJ. He also has the grassland-prey-animal-like presence common to DJs, where the eyes seem to be absolutely nonfunctional organs that merely accompany and indicate the front of the face while other, subtler senses tune and retune to signals the rest of us aren't getting. He always wears an all-black zip-up jumpsuit-type thing with two pins for bands or his company's movies near his neck. He often sleeps on the sets of his movies. He is the only person I've ever met who doesn't look more innocent in his sleep.

As for this girl I'm supposed to have sex with, Jillee Jenkins, I *do* have a second of intelligible human interaction with her. The three of us, plus a long tableful of visiting or resident porn people, are at a twenty-four-hour place on St. Mark's. Everyone is drunk or eating or making out or otherwise transported and Jillee, because of some dietary restriction or just because it is fucked, is unable to eat whatever she has in front of her. She has a bob, a lot of old-style tattoos, and is wearing a wifebeater. She is despondently staring at her plate through her eyeshadow and sending text messages to people she knows far away about how she is hungry. I slide my curry potatoes across the table, and she stops texting whomever she is texting and, beneath the general radar, smiles and says, "Thank you."

It is the first time I see any porn person in New York City doing a thing I would've done if I were them.

Mostly, though, it looks like their thing is a whole *other* thing. Tina likes Black Flag and Kurt Vonnegut—so do I. Leom likes Black Sabbath and J. G. Ballard—so do I. None of this comes up or would matter if it did. There are some people they need me to fuck, though. So okay.

And meanwhile I draw this stuff.

These days there is quite a lot of *pro*-party art—mostly photography. Like, trashy lovey-dovey glitzy fashioney magaziney itsy-bitsy-teeny-weeny-bit-obsceney-not-very-extremey-sceney photography (and the music that goes with it, blessedly metaphorless, that just goes, "Hey, let's dance, and also party, oh and also you'll probably be wanting this *beat*—oh and maybe drugs"). Like, you weren't there but it was great and everyone fucked everyone and also money.

Well it wasn't and they didn't. Their parties are just like your parties. They are excruciation and make your fellow man despicable to you.

If you go with a girl then she will usually want to leave very quickly because it is lame or smoky or there are large dogs or no cups or she just wants to fuck and why are you even here if you're with a girl anyway and so why did you go in the first place and so that's awful and you're wasting your life. If you go *without* a girl then you spend the whole time waiting to see if there'll *be* a girl, and if there isn't that's awful and you're wasting your life and if there is then you have to talk to her for a long time before you find out if she's in any sense available and if not then that's awful and you're wasting your life, and if she *is* then essentially you're on a *date* upon which situation enough scorn and ink have been spilled already except that if you're on a party date then you not only have to deal with all the date trauma but also with constant distractions and completely legal and within-bounds interdictions from other guys and possibly girls and her friend who is some mile-wide frumpfest visiting from Seattle, which is awful and could easily result in you wasting your life.

So that's parties. The second thing to understand is the subway ride home from them.

If you go home alone, you'll wait for the train forever and, much worse, while waiting, notice things. On the platforms, the scenes on the benches are like school posters about diversity, except bitter and silent. That pretty much says it. There's a clubfooted Chinese dwarf with a wire-cage laundry cart and no one on the platform talks to anyone except people carefully agreeing with a blue-eyed drunk in glasses who is saying only one thing but it is okay because it is the thing you are all thinking: "What the fuck? What the fuck is this? Who are these bastards?" And it echoes and you nod. And you notice that what you all agree on is the thing a crazy drunk person says. Across the platform there are construction workers clearly denied every perk of construction work—they have to work in *tunnels*, in *fluorescent orange vests*, and they are actually *lower down* and *within reach* of the women they would otherwise get to yell at. The air is just about exactly the way you'd expect the air to be in an underground tunnel that's been under construction on and off since you were born.

And by the time you have forgotten—in your bitter, silent diversity—that you don't actually live on a subway platform (and have noticed several people who do), the train comes. But it is not over.

Unlike the subways of Tokyo, San Francisco, etc., whose tunnels alternate noisy corridors of perspective-free black with high-tech, mall-like platforms full of expensively framed ads, the subway tunnels of New York's outer boroughs are specifically designed to mock passengers isolated and bored enough to pay any attention to them. You begin to suspect they've been contrived so that whereas people who have someone to talk to will notice only an inconspicuous rush of yellowy-gray background, the solitary passenger will see a ridiculously pitted, hollow, dim, maudlin, neglected, desolate, and forgotten maze of empty, drop-lit service tunnels, which constantly remind him or her that he or she literally has nothing better to do than look out the window during an underground trip.

Psychologically, the quiet subway ride home always lasts much longer than whatever you went out to do and gives you that special, staring depression that is so hard to let go since it seems to be trying to tell you something.

Tell you what? Nothing. Whatever it is you just did and failed to do right—that was just life on your planet. The girls all pretend you'd have to be Jesus, Johnny Depp, and Muhammad Ali all rolled into one to fuck them, and the guys all pretend they couldn't be more excited about what they saw on cable last week, and there are occasional ODs and there are occasional knives, and the dumb and the ugly keep insisting on walking and breathing to music that's just there to cover up the sound of their walking and breathing and that is never loud enough. And there are good, solid Darwinian reasons for all of this and you'd be doing the same if you were them, and so nothing can be learned from it and nothing can be gleaned and, most frustratingly for the young anarchist, *no practical action can be taken.*

This is the order of human life as ordained either spiritually or post-astrophysically. These are not technical or political problems. Nothing could ever do anything about this.

But it wears on you. It wears on you and it will make you want to be nowhere. And in the subway you think maybe you are nowhere. You're glad the subway cars are air-conditioned, so now you're breathing nowhere-air. It was awful—you think, looking at the other, shadowy you in the glass—and you wasted part of your life. And you will do it again. Here you are in the country people actually kill to live in, and the city people lie, cheat, and steal to go to, at the thing that people beg and shop and bribe to get into, and you had less fun—you did less with the hours you were given—than if you'd spent them lying facedown in a field somewhere with your head on a stump.

So where do you register your complaint, and what do you do with all that wasted experience?

The only place to put wasted experience to use is in art, and the only place to register a complaint with the very order of existence is art.

You draw it. I saw that. I'm registering my complaint— and I have made it pretty, since all things that are useless had better be pretty. Look at all this worthless not-fucking you have to drag your sorry ass across. Draw it. Send it to the gallery. They sell it. They throw a party.

Know that if I am not yet waving a menacing umbrella at the elephant from the set of *Hooked Up*, it is only because I am one stable motherfucker.

○○○○○○○○○

Iggy Pop completists will notice that all of this has been said better and quicker in the song "Social Life" from his decadent-era album *American Caesar,* in the same way the spoken introduction to Turbonegro's "Imorgen Skal Eg Daue" eerily parallels events in the first three chapters and would have obviated the need for living through them had I listened more carefully.

Anyone bent on extracting a message from things rather than experiencing them can actually save time by listening to those songs instead of reading any more of this book—along with the Bad Religion album referenced earlier, the Napalm Death song quoted near the end, and most of the cuts on the Rolling Stones' *Some Girls.* If you are in a real hurry, I hereby give you permission to just listen to the first couplet of the Distillers' "Gypsy Rose Lee" and respond to this work as if it were that one.

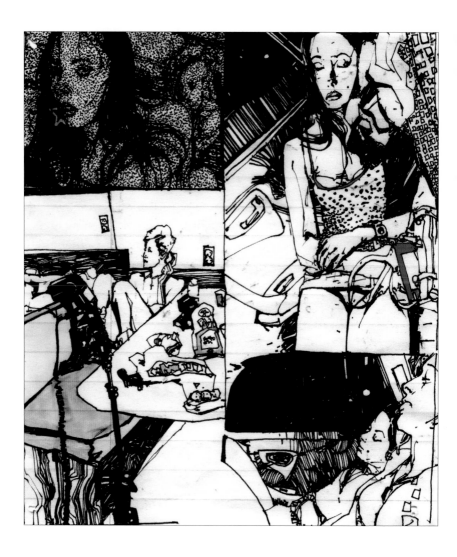

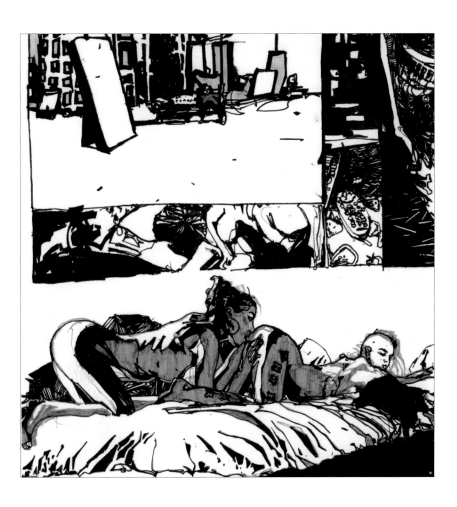

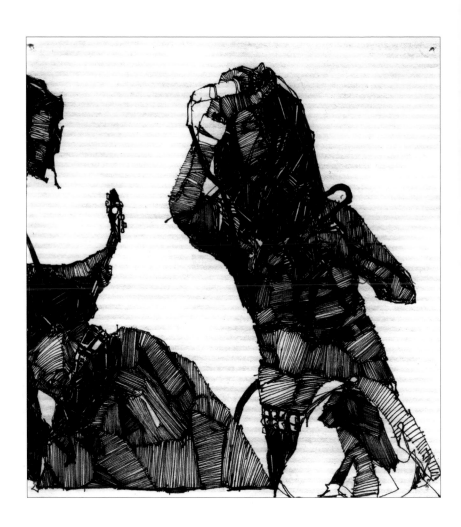

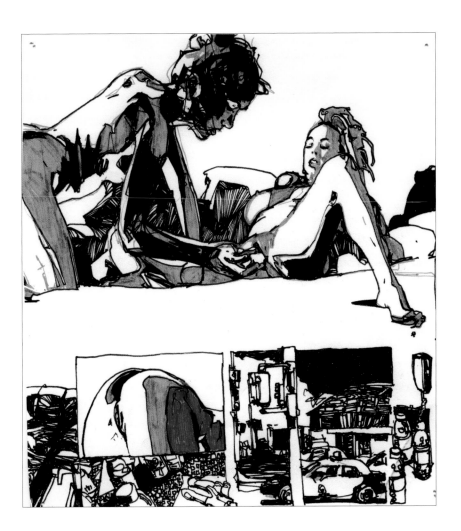

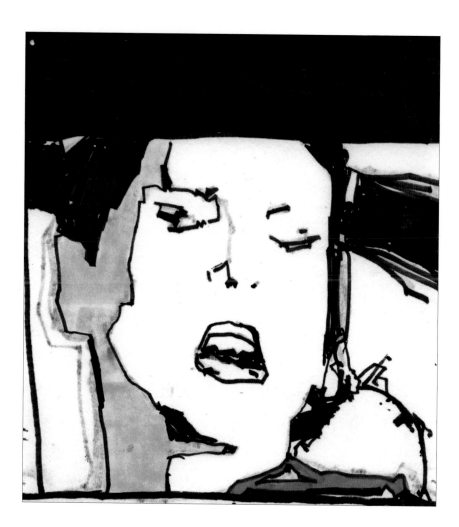

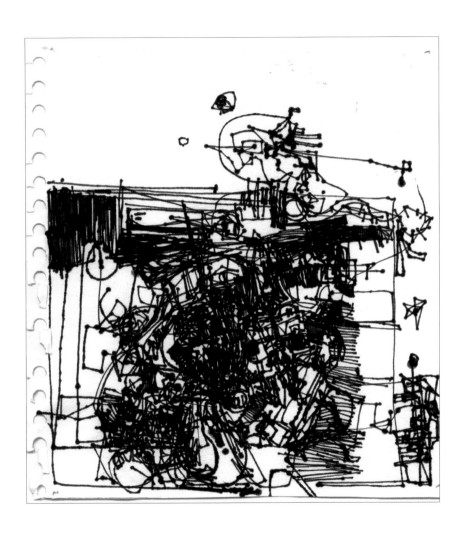

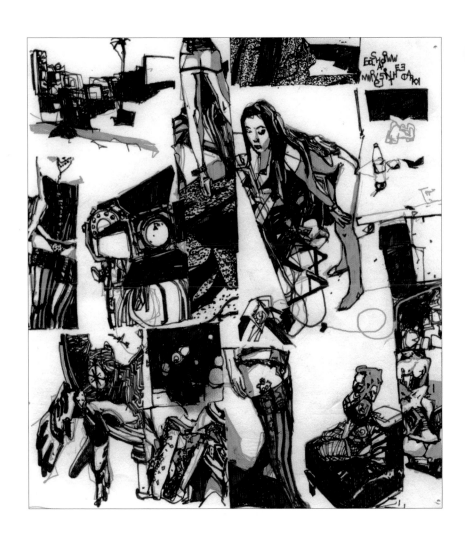

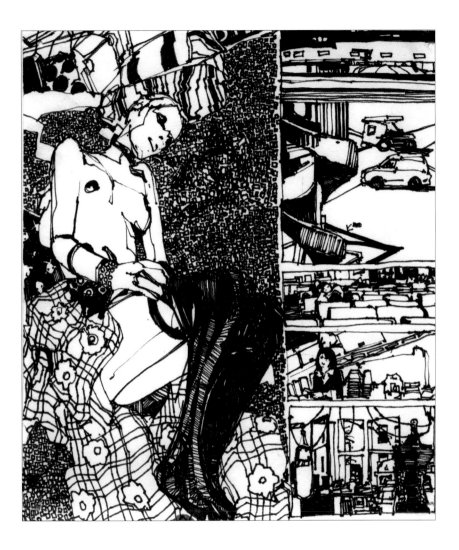

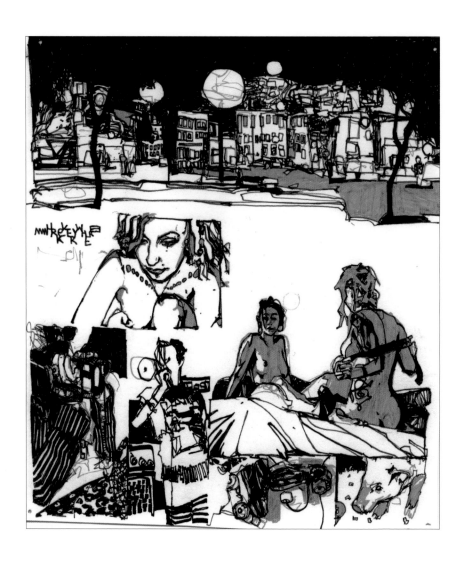

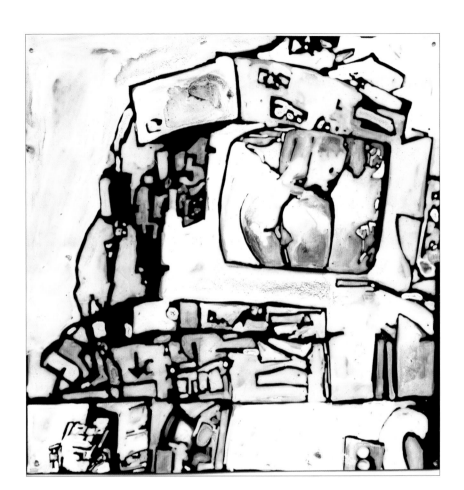

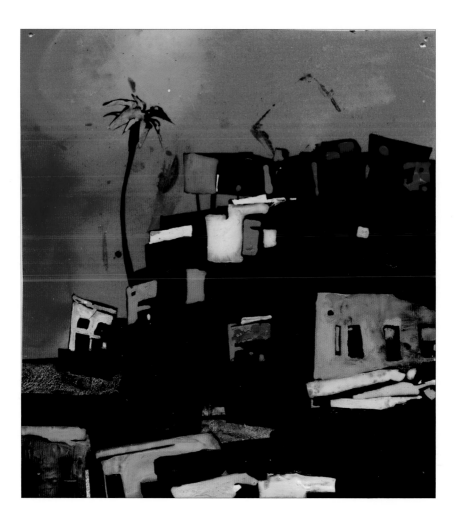

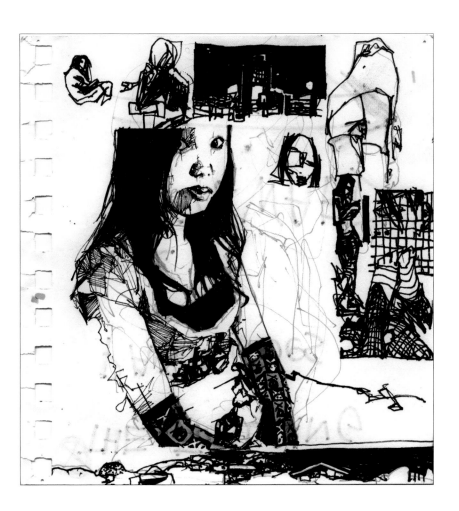

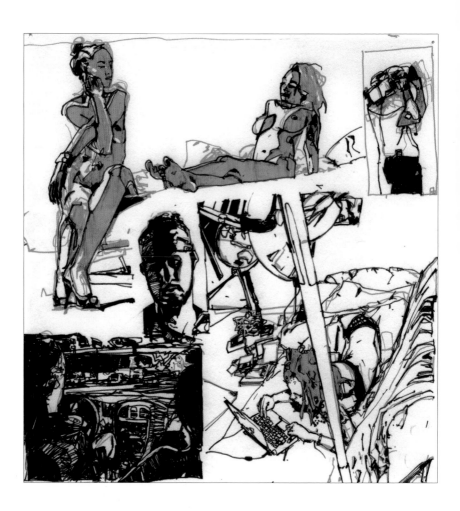

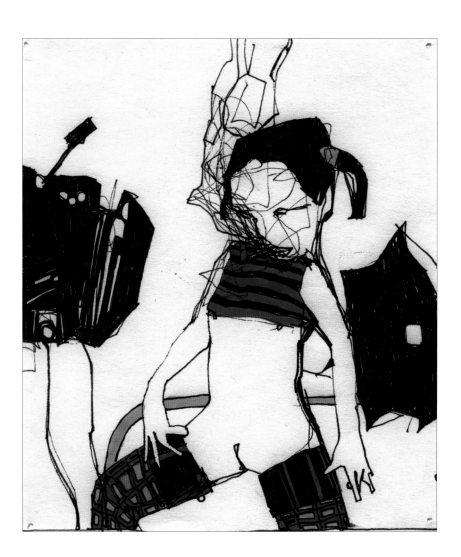

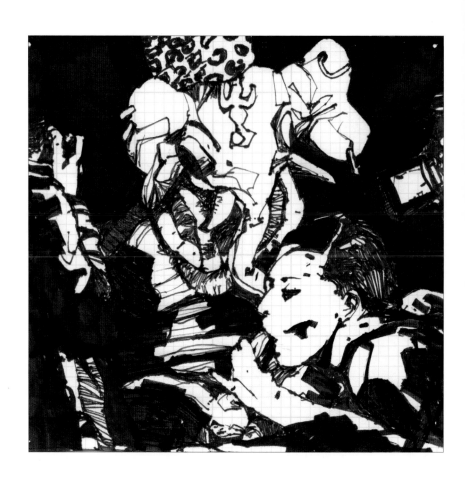

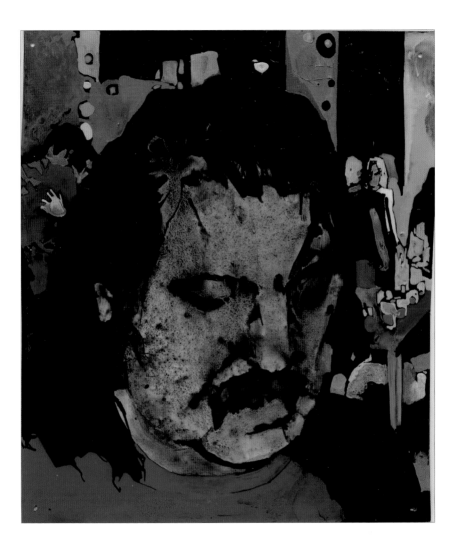

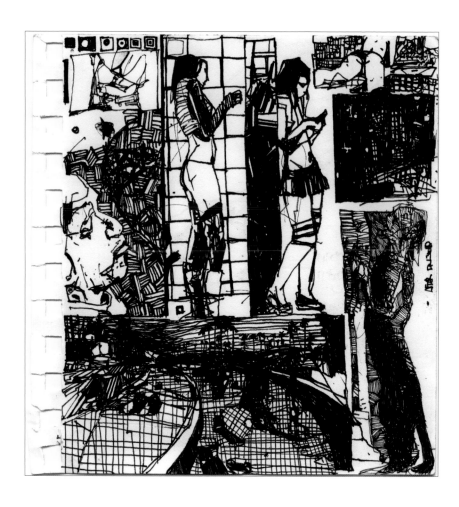

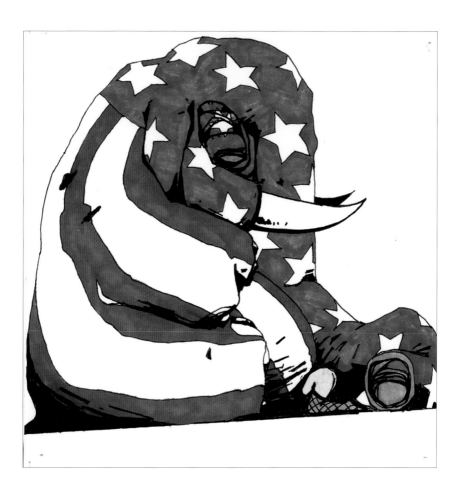

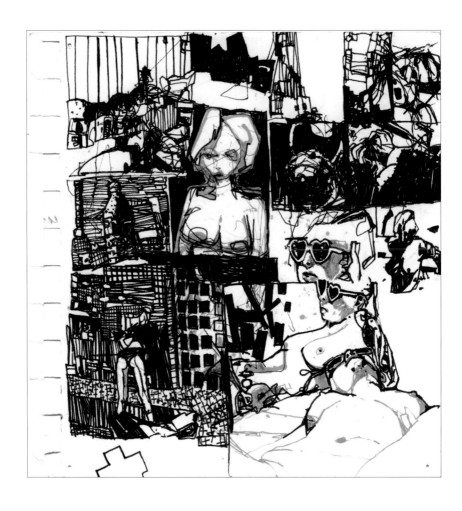

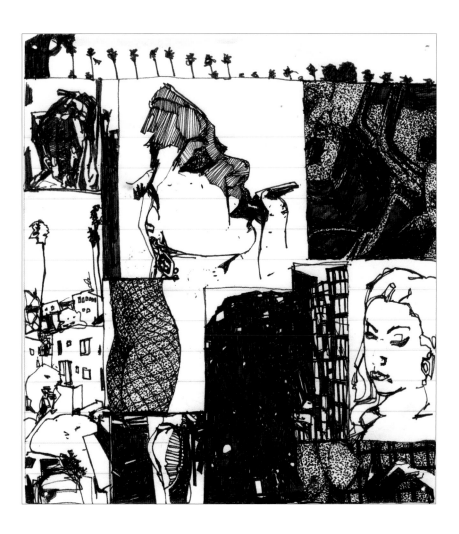

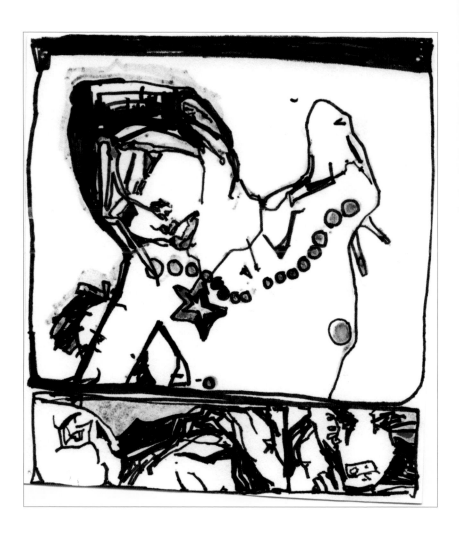

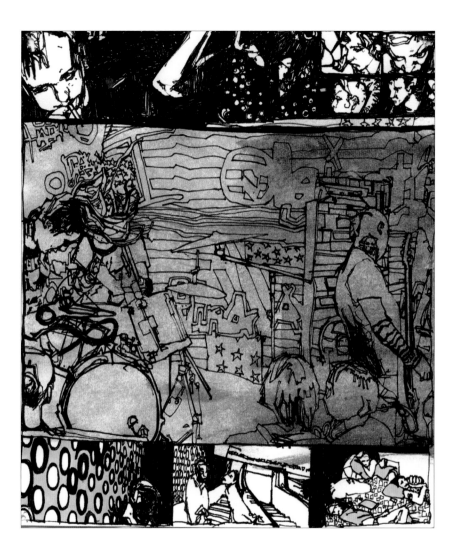

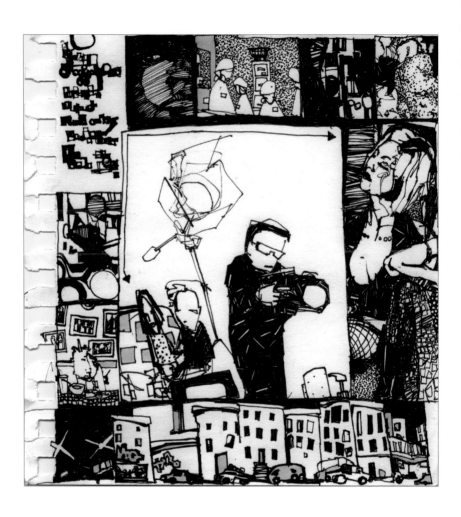

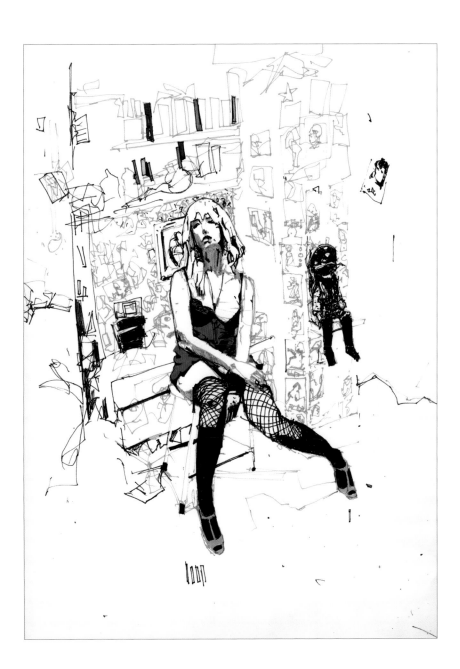

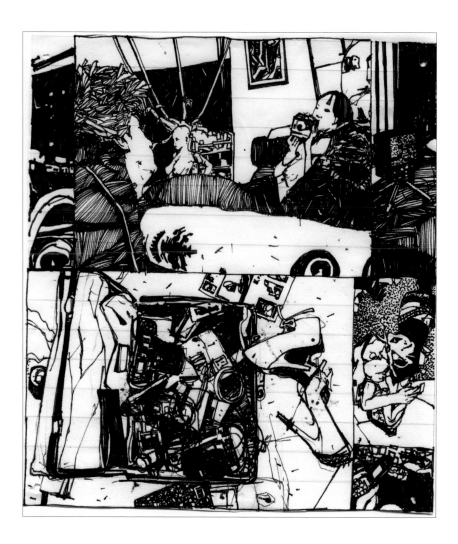

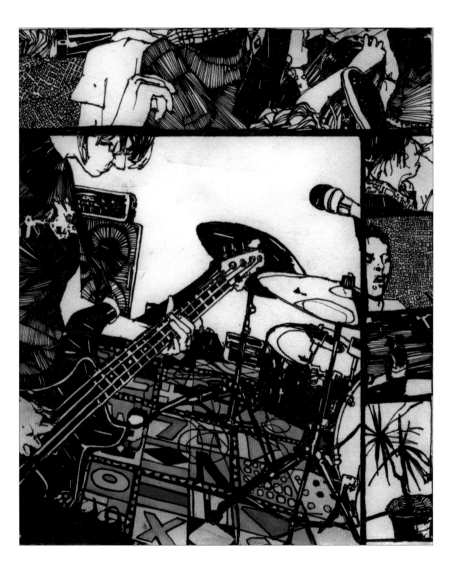

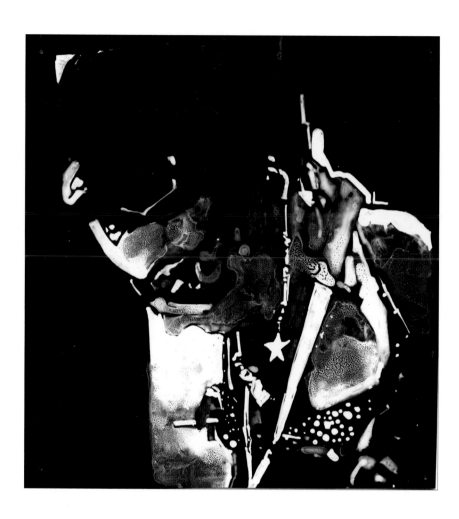

# Boba Fett, etc.

**"I feel like I was looking** at this girl, like my own age, whatever, and I'm looking at her, and I'm thinking, 'It would no more occur to her to look at me like a potential, y'know, sex-love-romantic-whatever than you would look at'—I don't know—'*that.*'"

There are three dolls on the computer screen. The first is hunched and neckless, perhaps intentionally mispainted, with black boots and gloves—maybe a neoexpressionist version of the original. The second is far more primitive, in vegetable green with no articulation and a few random details picked out on the upper body in silver paint. The third doesn't even look like the result of any industrial process at all—it seems like a helmeted idol molded by something blind, thumbless, and hateful out of blue wax with traces of earth-colored paint worn away by centuries of worship and smoke from sacrificial flame.

"What *is* that?"

"It's a bunch of bootleg Boba Fetts made from rubber molds in Poland in the '80s. Somebody sent it to me."

"She looked at you like you were a *Polish Fett*."

"She thought about fucking me about as long as you'd consider fucking that *Fett*. Just like nothing, not like '*Eeeew gross*,' but just like it would never even *occur* to you to fuck that Fett. Like that one on the far right."

"Harsh Fett."

"Yeah."

"It is the harshest of all possible Fetts."

"Indeed."

◦◦◦◦◦◦◦◦◦

Boba Fett was a laconic and doomed bounty hunter. Dented, dusty, faceless, implacable, and surprisingly ineffective, he was a villain in the second and third *Star Wars* films. These films and their predecessor are the only piece of culture that nearly everyone my age has in common, and although they have a theme and a meaning (which is: maybe you squabble among yourselves, maybe you believe in the Force or maybe you don't, maybe you worry about the odds or you kiss your sister or maybe you speak in enigmatic noises only your friends can understand, maybe you worry too much or maybe you are inarticulate and hairy, but in the end you all have a role to play in the fall of an empire, which is evil), it should be noted that Boba Fett achieved a cult celebrity status disproportionate to his role in that trilogy through good looks alone—by having the finest and most convincing costume in the history of all dented, dusty, faceless, implacable fictional characters ever. I have a picture of him on the back of one of my sweatshirts.

In the book of academic film criticism I decide to bring with me on the day I go to the disgusting free clinic in Chelsea (Tina recommended it instead of AIM since DiVinethings. com didn't pay as much as GSP) just before my first scene for her, it says,

"Fett has unexpectedly emerged as a figure Mayse nicely calls 'the polarizing neutral.' And if by mythic Mayse means a character whose utility is outpaced by portrayal, which is in turn outpaced by public reception, Boba Fett has indeed become mythic."*

I put it in my bag, with my Discman.

The day begins dreary and dripping. Jillee flaked and they'd gotten some new girl and I was a little relieved. I had checked out one of her scenes and the guy had looked really bored. With his eyes focused somewhere in a middle distance only he could see, with his tongue on her clit, and with his head on her thigh, and with only his mouthparts moving, he looked like a flesh bug listening to the ocean.

So, again, it would be some new girl—Trixie Kyle. I *had* at least gotten to see pictures this time. *Confederacy of Ruined Lives*, the Eyehategod album, plays on the Discman as I start out. I had hoped the drowning-in-tar-type effect of the record

---

* Glen Kenny, ed., *A Galaxy Not So Far Away* (New York: Tom Bissell, 2002), 27.

would bleed away all my crisscrossing thoughts and leave me empty and hungry for outside things but instead, since minds, when moving in a private bubble of music, inevitably try to make your shifting viewpoint into a movie, I keep noticing that the repeating, careening patterns of feedback and screaming don't force any order on the rain-deadened and morning-dark wet and quiet city I walk through. On a blameless day in Bushwick, rusty with lazy crime and boredom, Eyehategod is too desperate, erratic, and white.

The only other stuff I've brought—an early Rolling Stones collection—makes a passable, if dissociated, sequence out of the remains of the neighborhood and the subway ride and is always good for any situation where being cocky is a good thing, but the few photos of my costar I've seen suggest that the fickle, impressionable "you" early Stones songs were inevitably about couldn't possibly resemble the long-limbed, skulking, coiled, colorless animal with its eyes blackened by what looks like outfielders' war grease on which I am supposed to be focusing my attention. The Stones will be no help either.

The disgusting free clinic is located on the corner of a neglected, grassy lot, adjoining some dog paths and concrete ball courts in a part of the city that had once been mostly about meatpacking but is known now mostly for having art galleries and rich gay men. The clumpy thing made of docile but violently mismatched people that forms early out in front of its gates on cold mornings is less a line and more like the invisible, nervous, asymmetrical order observed in nature shows by bony packs of hilltop scavengers while they blink slowly in the wind and listen for breakfast. I am here for the second time, to get my results. At some point, through the grass, a nurse comes, opens the gate, and gives everyone numbers.

This place is everybody's common property as citizens of the city, and so we expect it to be decrepit and dulled and administered by the semi-dead and to reek with ammonia and inertia. But there is also an unsubtle element of totally gratuitous cruelty to it, akin to the kind of thing you'd expect in prison or hell, which mostly takes the form of appalling educational videos.

Somehow the testimonials of interviewed victims—all given accents, halting, naïve scripts to read ("my boyfrien' tol' me that he had never been wit' another woman but . . . "), and faces like the wet end of a grocery bag—are harder to look at than the graphically narrated stills of glistening abcesses intercut into damp but still *brittle*-looking sores or faded into pans over red infections spidering brilliantly beneath the surface of wax-museum skin, or overlapped with shots of someone's butt crisis. And everyone has to look because no matter what it is they are here for, or how minor it is, or how fast it might go away with penicillin, or how early they got here, they have to sit for a long long *long* time first and no one can read because it is on too loud and no one can wear headphones because they'll miss their number being called and no one talks to their friends because they come without friends and no one talks to strangers because every single patient has realized by this point that this floor and this waiting room are not for *all* sick or injured people entitled to free treatment but *only* for sufferers or potential sufferers of sexually transmitted diseases (the title that changes the meaning of this waiting-room picture). And they mutually respect each other's intense feelings of loathful loathesomeness and the discipline they're showing by just sitting still and just looking tired when they know that what the person in the corner of their eye or whose bald spot they're looking at really wants to do is just curl up and become as anonymous and unread as the Scotch-taped notices hanging on the suspicious-smelling walls and/or maybe just immediately die.

Even in the sober daylight, it is hard to see it as anything other than a double punishment—both for leading the kind of life that might cause you to suspect you might have contracted a sexually transmitted disease and for daring to take advantage of a public amenity.

"I'm here to pick up printed results."

"Take a number."

"No. I came in last week and the doctor specifically told me I could just pick up the printout and go *without* waiting in the waiting room."

"You see all these people here?"

Fuck you.

"Yes, but listen: the doctor I saw last time I was . . . "

In adult film, there is only one kind of nurse, but in real life, there are two, though they both come in the same range of shapes, sizes, and colors. The first remembers what it is like to be weak and frightened and tries to tell sick people the kinds of things they wish they'd been told when they were weak and frightened. They make you realize that nursing is one of those professions that maybe some people were actually, biochemically, *born* to do. The second type have the malevolent, sated languor of tropical predators and have never won an argument with a grown-up in their entire lives and feel anodyne throbs of reptilian anticipation at the thought of finally being placed in a situation where they know *slightly* more than another person.

The second kind of nurse looks on the news that they've passed the nursing exam as the first step on the path to wallowing through rich days of telling all kinds of bleeding, stump-hobbling, luckless, leprous oozers in pain not to do things and then complaining about having to do it to fellow humorless fucks over salad in the staff room.

While there are far too many people and they are far too sick for hospitals to be choosy about who they hire, if you go to a place for sick people and you can manage to get to the *little* room, you might be okay, but first you must always get through the *big* room, where nurses of the second kind bob and roam and bask and snap.

Had any patient (in the Industry, or otherwise) on that floor *ever* been together enough to walk up to the bloated administrative nurses through the degradation and obscure stains and ask, on behalf of a room full of people who could not *possibly* disagree, that they please please please please turn down the volume on the sexual-hygiene educational video? Like, what is this? Traffic school? But the nurses clearly count on shame as a sedative, and I think only the knowledge that I have

A) only come here because I am in porno movies and
B) already tested clean

gives me the strength of will to argue with them even the little that I have to.

Since my situation is too unique and intricate for "Take a number," the nurse digs deep into her medical training: "You'll have to speak to the supervisor." He is, of course, talking to someone else right now. I lean on a yellowish wall and read my book about movies. Boba Fett was played by a British actor and interior decorator named Jeremy Bulloch, his voice was done by Jason Wingreen. He had four lines of dialogue.

"You have to sit down, sir."

What is it like for the people who come here and who have to tell her they literally can't sit down?

"No, I have to stand up. She," pointing and getting a reaction from the one pointed to as if I'd just fucked all her pets and children at once, "told me to wait for this door," pointing again, "to open so I can talk to the man behind it. If I sit down I won't be able to see when the door opens."

Eyes framed in wrinkled butt-skin coast off on a wave of lard and contempt. "Think he *special*." I hear, from down the sticky hallway maze where she snarls and dwindles.

The door opens and the man in charge hands over my results immediately.

The nurses' overgrown heads ripple meatily.

Things get much worse in life than picking up your test so you can fuck a goth, but this *is* the pitiless, tinhorn, pasteboard leper place all kinds of people are in when they find out things have gotten as bad as they can ever get and this is still the last place some people see before they quit the business. It's one reason Adult Industry Medical, in LA, was invented, and why nearly everyone in the Industry uses it. Because before that the Industry was sending everybody, once a month, and more often when things got bad, down every kind of hallway in Los Angeles toward any kind of nurse. Or doctor.

Just before I walk away, with Eyehategod working nicely against the corridors and failed faces I see while retracing my steps down the stairwell ("Howling mad I greet you with my howlings whiter than death" as a famous black poet once put it), I look back at all the patients in their front-facing (TV-facing) chairs and have a sudden, vivid, irrational conviction that there is some important thing I need to let them, or maybe the brisk man in the little office, know—and that if I don't the nurses will eat them—but then one of them, maw expanding, sees me looking, and I go away.

∘∘∘∘∘∘∘∘∘∘

It isn't good to get too down on big girls, though. The one who, once I've got my test scores, meets me at the top of the same twisting stair where I first met Tina is a short-legged dollop with great fat tits barely kept in line by something yellow and very thin and is kind of gorgeous. She leads me to the apartment I last saw at the beginning of my horrible date over a year before.

Instead of mashing herself flat against the nearest filing cabinet and begging me to bounce on her ass, she gives me some forms. I fill them out. The front of Tina's place is encrusted with stickered machines and Tina bric-a-brac—sentimental and promotional. Remeeting Tina's roommate and business partner, Richie—who only ever saw me when the apartment did—I smile a difficult smile. Trixie Kyle comes in late.

She looks, in a coarse coat and with her hair in a rain-frowzed nest, a little older than her picture and than she is and taller and happier and less catlike than the twin I'd imagined. The effect is officey.

We—actors, cameraman, Richie, still photographer Brandy (and unfortunately not the office girl)—go to the location in one compact car.

Everyone's relatively quiet, except Trixie.

"Where'smyhairclip?OhmyGodIjustdroppedmyhairclip andIdidn'tknowwhereitwasanditwasrightthere.Ialways*drop*-stuff.Canyouputthisin?IjustgotthisnewTomPettyCDandI listenedtoitlikefivetimesinarowlastnight.IloveTomPetty."

"Well, I hear he won't back down," I say. "He has that going for him."

"Yeah,herocks.Mymomusedto" (okay) "listen to him in the car. I went to a Tom Petty concert once when I was like eight. I like the Traveling Wilburys too . . . "

"I like that first record—that song 'Congratulations' is, like, the saddest ever song I've ever heard. Sometimes."

"Yeah, I like them. I like whatever. My parents played all this classic rock. People make fun of me because I like classic rock but whatever, it fucking rocks, I'm like whatever, I like Pink Floyd . . . "

"Pink Floyd's great. Who could have a problem with Pink Floyd? Losers."

"You two are so cute," says Brandy. It solidifies a certain atmosphere in the car—as if we are a strange family going to see Grandma and Grandpa, and Trixie and I, stuffed in the back with poor Aunt Brandy, are kids being, for the most part, benignly ignored by adults with practical matters on their minds. It puts the two of us on the same side.

The grandparents (who immediately offer us cookies when we get to their place—some vegan DIY recipe) are played by two young, friendly, eerie men. Although one has dreadlocks and the other has a loaf of blond hair, they both give off an impression of something like hairlessness—as if there isn't quite the right amount of *matter* separating you from them. At any rate, I am glad to see that, although we take their cookies, Trixie's attention seems not to be migrating off toward them or their fantastic, rentable-for-any-occasion apartment. As I am bending over the tray for my third or fourth cookie, she says:

"Oh my God, is that a Boba Fett patch on the back of your jacket?"

"Yeah it is . . . "

"Oh my God, Boba Fett was the first guy I ever had a crush on . . . "

We talk for some time about that, and decide eventually that if you had the time and money, the thing to do really would be to make a film where, instead of being devoured by a sentient pit of sand embedded in the surface of a cruel and near-lifeless desert planet—as Fett is in the third *Star Wars* movie—the polarizing neutral is devoured by a sentient *vagina* embedded in the surface of a cruel and near-lifeless *skin* planet, which, in turn, naturally leads to the topic of sentient vaginas in general and to a discussion of the extremely regrettable French film *Pussy Talk* (or *Le Sexe qui Parle*) wherein a demure woman is repeatedly embarassed by the shrill and articulate public demands made by her horrible, speaking snatch.

The cameraman—who is very good and who never worked again so far as I know—is also a *Star Wars* man, though Richie—being a businessman and therefore perhaps having a more philosophical than visual disposition, or perhaps because he spends a lot of time telling people what to do while sitting in a chair—prefers *Star Trek*. Brandy the still photographer, being a hip young mother who likes to smile knowingly and wear bright, solid-colored skirts with light-patterned tops and sell photos to magazines about parties and beats and stripy blue streetwear and alt-porn, is agnostic. Also present and silent is another young female photographer sent by a slightly more upscale, eclectic, thicker, and worse magazine to shoot pictures for a feature provisionally titled "How 'Alt' Is Alt-Porn?"

While Brandy the still photographer takes pictures of Trixie—now in only a pink belt and posed in front of walls with hand-painted polka dots and rolling stripes—they talk about liquor and drugs and trouble and Trixie feels herself with a toy severed hand dripping rubber blood and she has pointing tits that narrow to swollen and unique nipples—and she looks tall and lean and edible. I ask, "Are we making out first?"

"Making out's fun," she says, and then we get on a couch underneath a picture of a robot and do, and then have amusing sex, which is what the porn ends up looking like. Once in a while, it again feels like we are kids—doing some job that grown-ups are supposed to do. But no—if not us, then who? At the end, from his chair and for reasons never made clear, Richie tells me to cum on her neck, and I do my best with that weird order.

∘∘∘∘∘∘∘∘∘

In a world that already has a movie about an insatiable talking twat that accosts anyone in earshot (at one point it's even interviewed) with its problems, it's difficult to be sure how much more innovation pornography really needs or wants.

Like that cunt, I am interviewed (for the thick magazine); unlike it, I am undemanding—it is good to have sex with Trixie Kyle. Alt-porn is just fine by me. The reporter also takes hours of pictures, most of which have things in them the magazine won't print. The one that makes it has my leg, a moon sliver of Trixie's back, and a lot of apartment. The article itself comes down to a two-page spread that is four or five likewise arid photos end-to-end underlined by a bumper-sticker-shaped block of text that amounts to a long verbal shrug, and the whole piece in turn amounts to another deadline met, and our work to gallons of load drained in distinct units from the balls of distantly separated clenched watchers in rooms and into tissues or old socks and into trash cans or down drains all over the world, and to another line on everyone's résumé, and money, and to someone e-mailing to tell me he is Trixie's boyfriend and that Trixie says my hair smells like crayons, and to eight more drawings for a show I have with two other artists later that month at the SFMOMA.

# Cause-and-Effect Problems

**The SFMOMA prints up**
Zak Smith T-shirts, puts me up at the W Hotel, and alleges
I *explore new visual articulations of masculine identity through
memory, narrative, and desire.* Friends fly in or are flown in
from all over. In the W, on a shelf in my room and probably
every room, there is a thick, topless, oak box with a chrome
plaque bolted to the front engraved with the words *Telephone
Book* and the telephone book is in it. I have a conversation
with a museum official explaining that my artwork consists

of a series of *pictures* that I *drew* and not some hippie "instal-lation" and therefore if an "installation element" (i.e., one of my drawings) is lost or damaged in the coming months, museum staff should *not* attempt to fabricate a crude facsim-ile or replace it with a blank piece of paper of equal size. Max Clamm tells me to check out a girl he is sending to my open-ing for possible work and I do and say she is okay. Gutter kids from Portland and Frederickschain are introduced to the heir to the Levi Strauss fortune. A bisexual Aboriginal artist on a massive Australian artists' stipend says my work represents an iteration of a typically privileged heteronormative gaze but is impressed by the technique. Someone else says the oppo-site. The other artists in the show introduce themselves and I never see them again. The yet-to-be-disproven hypothesis that every woman associated with the alternative-pinup Web site SuicideGirls that has a period has that period around the twentieth is proposed and supported eightfold by both physi-cal and volunteered anecdotal evidence from all SuicideGirls present and two not present. The hotel room is comprehen-sively Led Zeppelined. The weather is unreliable and the ven-tilation is bad. I am impressed by a photo of a fetal armadillo and everything I say is recorded for a documentary. Things end up covered in candy bars, condoms, and blood. People start to hate each other. People's steel chains and lace thongs are confiscated by airport security. I lecture at UC Berkeley. Someone secretly shoots softcore in the W's elevator. Cham-pagne glasses keep getting used as ashtrays. A curator is sent to investigate reports that a Clifford Still is hanging upside down. A two-year-old girl holds a cheese-covered Pepperidge Farm goldfish out to me, and then takes it back and eats it- and Claire LeJense slits her cynical German eyes with drawn-on eyebrows at the child and says, from a lobby chair that

seems like a carved throne on a mountain of old-world contempt, "She's *so* egocentric." We watch *Caddyshack* with the
sound off. We call down a lot for toilet paper, voltage adapters,
and liquor.

Leom McFrei phones while I'm standing alone in a room
looking at Alexander Calder's strange *Apple Monster* and asks
how soon I can fly to LA to shoot a scene with Trixie for him.
The Oakland airport is in the middle of repairs and there's
wiring and ductwork where the ceiling should be. Southwest's
flights are so backed up grown men and whole families are
sitting on the floor between the Tensabarriers eating fries
with ketchup. At Bob Hope/Burbank, the PA picks me up in
a legally totalled car. The entire passenger side is as smashed
and torqued as a dying pill bug. I do laundry at Leom's house
and sleep on the five-girl-orgy couch from *New Wave Sluts*.

On the set, a seven-foot-tall blonde—who punched Leom
last time I was in LA—to whom I have never spoken and whose
presence no one can ever explain, says, "Hey punk, make me
my drink," and so I walk away and leave the guy doing the
documentary—JJ—behind to deal with her (or him). "Young
man, can you break the ice for me?" she or he says. "Good,
now put it in my glass! NO! *Just. The. Small. Ones.*"

Trixie talks about how exhausted she is from the scene
with Jules Seizure last night and she says it so fast and so
often and in response to so many things other people say on
so many unrelated topics that it's obvious she means it, and
also is on something, and also she wants to know why we're
shooting so early in the morning, which is a good question to
ask and to which Leom says nothing but instead shakes his
head and turns to me and says:

"And Trixie here wants to be one of the pros."

And I say:

"Go easy on Trixie, man, 'cause you know there's *pros*— and then" (kindly, sleazily) "there's *poetry.*"

And then later I say:

"Keepyourhandjustlikethatgoupanddownnowsuckthe headyouwantitinyourpussyyougottasuckithardsoitgets hardsoIcanfuckyourpussycomeonthat'sgoodkeepit ontheheadmoveyourhanduptoitupanddowngetthehead inyourmouthandlookatmewhenyousuckmycockfuck yeahTrixiejustlikethatlookupatmefuckyeahputyourlips tightaroundtheheaddon'tjustshoveitintherethat's goodjustlikethatslowdownjustworkyourhandupand-downgetyourhandothetip," (Yes, I realize that these last two directions are incompatible) "stayonthetipworkyour handupanddownthat'srihtthat'srightit'sgoodwatching yousuckcocklookatmesuckmycockdon'tfuckingstop justlikethatdon'tyoufuckingdarestop . . ."

because I have to, because Trixie is actually in no state to be giving blowjobs, which threatens to leave me in no state to receive blowjobs, which threatens to upset anyone with any investment in delivering this sex scene—including her. And so I have to pretty much micromanage her through it to keep her paying attention and tripping the right nerves, and to keep up a wall of noise and interaction that shoves the fat black metal moth of Leom's big handheld camera out of the margin of my awareness. I feel immediately miserable in a lot of ways after and I want to lie down but I can't because I am staying at Alice's and she isn't home, so I just tell them to drop me somewhere on Hollywood Boulevard.

⊙⊙⊙⊙⊙⊙⊙⊙⊙

So I get dropped somewhere on Hollywood Boulevard.

While it is not true that nobody walks in LA, it is certainly true that 50 percent of all people who do are completely fucked up. They are desperate, drugged, lost, or limbless, or hold squalid, plastic-covered signs advertising *Maps to Stars' Homes* or hideous, misshapen traditional crafts. At night, they go in packs, drunk and hungry for waffles from Roscoe's.

At night on a weekday, this is as true on Hollywood Boulevard as anywhere else.

During the daytime, Hollywood Boulevard is the center of the city's attempts to ignore its own basic centerlessness, but the night empties out the Ripley's Believe It or Not Museum and the Scientology Center and the pastel Sumerian fortress/ mall on Highland and it siphons off all the ordinary tourists who, after finding their favorite star's star and taking pictures, realize there's not a lot else you can do with a sidewalk with names on it.

The "Café" in the Boulevard's Hollywood Internet Café, is, as we have all realized is pretty standard by now, a lie. It's tempting to say the "Internet" is too. It's basically an extension of the Boulevard—a hastily paneled stopping place that would seem shallow if it weren't so narrow, where the air is sour with dead snacks and twenty-four-hour neglect. There is nothing "café" about the linked spine of chairs, wires, and repeating machines—all seemingly cultured from the same family of matte-black substances—propped up against the right-hand wall and growing crookedly toward a featureless dark counter behind which an old and small and bald man bobs like an otter, but there is very much that is "phone booth." When I visit LA, I end up spending a lot of time here, waiting for whoever to get off work and pick me up or let me crash.

A young guy in bucket-sized boots and future-vampire evening wear comes in with a pair of used ninja daggers and offers to sell them to the old guy behind the counter for ten dollars. The old man—he is Indian or Pakistani—limply steps around the counter, expressionlessly takes one, looks at his own whiskered reflection in it, and then begins to cut foes unseen with solemn and spinning gestures that take him through a sequence of short-legged, but perfectly fluid, stances. He comes to a measured stop and hands it back.

"This weapon is made in a stupid way, the balance is not good—easy to disarm. Come at me!" The metalgoth attacks and the dagger is pried at speed from the pale hand. Crestfallen, the kid goes back out onto Hollywood with his weapons.

At night on a Tuesday, the only people walking up and down Hollywood Boulevard are the people who are actually *walking up and down Hollywood Boulevard*. And right now I am one of them. I feel very bad.

And I buy some homeless kids a bottle of Maker's Mark because they ask. And I sit on my suitcase next to John Lee Hooker's star leaving messages with people who don't pick up until there's no one left to call. And I go to a bar long enough to realize I don't want to talk to anyone. And I go to the Hollywood Internet Café until Alice or the guitar-playing girl or Osbie or someone else picks me up and takes me somewhere I can sleep.

And eventually someone takes me to the airport, or maybe I get a taxi. And the flight is an early flight. And we take the 405 west at dawn. And the distant palms repeat against a glazed pool of infinite and Pacific-deep pink out the right-hand window.

◦◦◦◦◦◦◦◦◦

Summer comes a month later.

Trixe and Candy Crushed and I all go get lunch.

An especially raw and treeless stretch of Bushwick separates our apartment from the only restaurant in the neighborhood that has silverware and waitresses who speak English. Years before, my roommate and I spent our first few hundred Bushwick breakfasts analyzing the puzzling Billy Ocean/Joel songs twinkling out of the easy-listening station someone thought would draw customers to Popeye's or reminiscing, over our three-piece and two-piece combos respectively, about our own days working fast food—but when women and art collectors started showing up hungry at our apartment we'd had to find somewhere else to go.

Trixie generally shows up hungry.

Trixie doesn't know a lot of people in New York, and the ones she does know aren't nice to her. She is not stupid, but the clichés of the business—drugs, unreliability, stupid arguments, classic prick boyfriends—infest her life. The problem, I think, has some cause-and/or-effect relationship to her attention deficit disorder—she has a tough time paying attention to anything long enough to see cause and effect happen as a sequence. So, once in a while, she comes down to Bushwick and it's like she's on a vacation, and even all the people yelling at us because we have tattoos are kind of funny and fun to yell back at.

Summer in Bushwick: The first or last dozen blocks of Wilson Street grow along the backbone of a low hill buried under box buildings, under cubist sidewalks cryptically chalked for utility companies or hopscotch; misspellings in two languages; stray children and balloons; dim, narrow, worn, but somehow also temporary-seeming corner stores subdivided by Plexiglas so ripped and written in it is almost opaque; threaten-

ing laughter; totally useless sections of fence; beautiful and
individual allegedly unisex beauty parlors with both their
customers and pattern-slathered furniture wrapped in plastic
and mirrored out to infinity in three directions; ruined riding
toys—tricycles; quads; ducks with pedals—scattered like the
fragments of some civic agency's just-failed attempt to build
an artificial rainbow; occupied lawn chairs; and small orange-
and-plywood zones of construction or demolition. It reminds
one curator who came to visit me of early Romare Bearden
collages, and reminds pink-mohawked Candy Crushed of one
of the cities from one of the Grand Theft Auto games—which
is itself offered by huge ads looming over a semicollapsed
building on the west end of the street, and under the windows of most passing busses, and by a girl on our front steps
with two brothers and a bulging backpack that, unfortunately,
has only GTA and racing games in it instead of the long-form
magic-world adventure games Candy craves.

Trixie Kyle talks like Bushwick looks.

At the shallow crest of Wilson, while the steel signposts,
anchored in the stressed, cooking concrete, twin with their
own shadows to imitate the hands of disagreeing clocks,
Trixie, reminded by some noticed thing, or by some cue that
has bobbed to the external and audible surface of her oceanic,
unignorable, uninterruptable, interminably broadcasting
mental monologue, moves to the always rich subject of sexual
atrocities committed by, around, and in her family.

Since these stories almost never have proper endings or
any sense of cause and effect, they are very hard for listeners
to remember (this one seems to involve a step-relative and a
faint, possibly false, impression of long dark hair and a moustache, and Native American-ness reflects off the memory),
which, given that they are full of odd and identifiable details

and are not really mine to tell and that Trixie is my friend and I don't want to cause her trouble with any of the principals, is probably just as well. Since the characters' main motivations were generally drugs, poor judgment, religion, and, occasionally, clinical mania, no pattern or unusual meaning ever emerges from them. They aren't really stories, or even prose; they are excerpts from Trixie's train of thought—a long, barely coherent, nonfiction poem made up of scenes linked by coincidence or sound—unified only by certain themes and low-frequency chords rotating under the surface.

The detail of a forced and only semisuccessful clitoridectomy attempted on a young Trixie by a shadowy, closely related or step-related male presence occupies a distinct spot in my mind—probably because she repeats it at least once and because it is unbelievably awful. It is impossible, depressing, and anyway unnecessary to follow, but, as a phenomenon, the footwork and ricochet and stray-chasing of Trixie's openly quite upbeat game of solo racquetball with the English language is definitely a thing to see, and thankfully an intact and accurate sample was recorded into the public record in the form of some filmed, improvised, precoital "di"alogue in a car in a scene she once did with Jules Seizure just before she moved—more predictably than, though just as abruptly and awkwardly as usual—from her self-sustaining and focusless chatter into the pale planet of bit-lip silence, where suddenly absorbed eyes meekly offer—from under elastic, lace, and tattooed interruptions in red, pink, and black—the long, angled hips and glacially upthrust, white, and wide ass that fate and Trixie reserve for the very patient.

Her favorite book, according to some profile she filled out somewhere on some Web site, is "The Call of Cthulhu." Though that horror classic is not a book but (even ambitiously typeset and soaking wet) a short story, it still seems far far beyond what Trixie's ADD can handle, since Lovecraft's gruesome and sublime star-monster only emerges from the sunken city after pages and pages and pages of Francis Wayland Thurston's dry, genteel, possibly monocled inquiries in universities and drawing rooms and port towns.

But then again, the opening lines—

"The most merciful thing in the world, I think, is the inability of the human mind to correlate all its contents. We live on a placid island of ignorance in the midst of black seas of infinity, and it was not meant that we should voyage far."

—may have signaled to Trixie that there might be reason to pay more than the usual Deficient and Disordered Attention to this story about a great and barely conceivable menace sleeping behind seemingly unrelated clues dropped in unconnected places and beneath a seamless ocean.

She talks about the most vile things you can imagine and we eat calamari. Trixie makes an arrow out of milk. Candy has a smoked salmon salad. The humid days crawl across the calendar.

ooooooooo

Meanwhile, I begin to suspect, whether or not *Far Gone and Out* is art, that Osbie Feel is a true artist. Not necessarily because of anything he'd made or done, but because he exhibits the classic symptom: not knowing when to be happy. When you're making it? (It still might not come out right . . . ) When it comes out right? (How good it is exists in exact proportion to how depressing it's going to be if no one realizes it . . . ) When you get paid for it? (But they'll pay for *anything*.) When it's *out there in the world*? (Because there's nothing so exciting as getting tax statements full of numbers abstractly representing an audience you'll never meet). When it gets you laid? (But people fuck *Rod Stewart* . . . )

How does *Far Gone and Out* do? It's impossible to say. No one involved is contracted to get percentage points off sales or rentals and there are no public records. Whoever had green-lit it is gone as part of a much larger internal overhaul at GSP and when it is all over there are only rumors to go on. A year later someone says he heard Slynt's niece liked it.

What is eventually clear to Osbie, in the months after his meeting at the Bigfoot Lounge, is that whoever is in charge as *Far Gone and Out* is going to release doesn't like it and doesn't want GSP to make any films like it again and therefore will do roughly fuck-all to promote it.

This leaves the potential consumer in a store trying to decide between whatever's on the next shelf over and a kimono exposing a pair of unfortunately lit ribs and the ghost of a boob.

The consensus is that it did about as well as anything else.

There is a cause-and-effect problem in the porn business. Unlike other entertainment industries (TV shows, stripping, etc. . . .), in which the quality—or at least the qualit*ies*—of the creative people involved can be at least partially blamed for the financial success or failure of the thing, porn is more like the business of very expensive art or very cheap beer.

In these industries, there is a product, and the product has sensual qualities, but what matters is not actually these qualities but *getting to the consumer first*. It doesn't matter what's *in* Milwaukee's Best or a Warhol or *Buttman's Bubble Butt Babes*

*Five*, because the people who buy these things are (and I use this term only in the strictly economic sense) hopeless addicts and decide whether to buy these things based primarily on whether or not they are in front of them. There will always be people who want the cheapest beer in the store. There will always be people who want the painting the next rich guy made. And there will always be people who have already seen all the other porn already.

As with drugs, so long as the *purity* of the product is not in doubt (no crayon scribbles on the Warhol, no ten-minute excerpts from *Brideshead Revisited* taped over the Butt Babes), the real business is not designing the product but controlling the territory from which it is sold. If it is at Sonnabend Gallery or 7-Eleven or that enormous XXX mart an hour west of Memphis on Route 40 that is the only business for miles in either direction, it will get sold.

And people like Osbie, who direct movies—who design product—are considered no unique *cause*, have no unique *effect*. They are yeast and hops.

Just as the porn business has cause-and-effect problems, and porn *movies* have cause-and-effect problems ("Oh *no*! I got it all *over* me! What'll I do *now*?"), so likewise porn *people* have cause-and-effect problems. Osbie makes a thing for some people. It may or may not do what it is supposed to do, but the people don't bother to find out before deciding they don't want him to do it again. If they *did* and *it* did, they probably wouldn't have cared anyway. He is hops. What's a good career strategy for hops?

◦◦◦◦◦◦◦◦◦

My business is simpler than Osbie's, and pays better. I get asked to do a couple movies. I meet people and I paint them.

Things happen and I draw them. I also paint some stuff that just looks like nothing because it's abstract and I put it together and that's a show. The pictures are interpreted in every fucked way by people who don't like them and in every fucked way by people who do like them. Then people buy them for a lot of money and I eat.

In obedience to ancient traditions designed to reassure the wealthy, art is, unlike porn, not evaluated solely according to whether you'd want to look at it or not. Critics judge the work according to the messages it communicates to the culture at large and the intelligence of the artist doing the communicating. This involves the critics in two hilarious fictions: that maintaining some arrangement of objects in a remote white room in an upscale neighborhood for a month is a way to communicate a message to the culture at large, and that someone who thinks it is could possibly be intelligent.

The job requires rare powers of cause-and-effect denial. Give four art people a banana and they will say: It's wonderfully yellow, it's too yellow, it's not yellow enough, I'm so glad it isn't yellow, and then say it's wonderfully squishy, it's too squishy, it's not squishy . . . and on and on until the banana gets so famous that they start getting paid to agree that the banana is yellow and good.

My work, they say, is sexy, and not sexy, and too sexy, and fringy and edgy, and neither fringy nor edgy, and too fringy and edgy to be relevant, and colorful and not colorful enough, and on and on.

So it's very hard to care or think any of it matters. Every artist's press release says the artist's work "raises issues of . . . " as if a visual artist's work in the zeros ever *raised* any *issue*. *What* people say is not as important for business as the fact that they say things and get paid to say them and the things they say them about get paid for. It is not an environment that incentivizes people to say or make things that make any sense. It is a living though, and one of the better ones.

Sometimes I think it'd be nice if things mattered.

But then again, things do, but the way they do is often a horrible way. Here's what no one said: *It is not good to be a punk, or cum on everyone you can, or make art about pornography, or make abstract paintings, because all these activities are despised by God, or, at the very least, not normal.*

But there are people who would think it, if they ever got all the way to the third floor of a museum. There is a line where what people think about things that people make actually *does* start to matter. There are a lot of people on the same side of the line as me and Osbie and Trixie and Tina and every contemporary art critic alive and anyone who has read this book this far and none of the things they say or write to *each other* about art matters much or makes any difference or changes the mind of anyone who actually has a mind. What does matter are the things being said by the gibbering horde of braindead fucks on the other side of the line.

They are stupid and there are more of them every day. During the time my story takes place, they are attempting to take over the planet, so it'll be hard to ignore them entirely . . .

# A Side Note

**You might have noticed** the small, video-game-playing presence of another alt-porn star in a recent chapter. Candy Crushed. I think I will save most of Candy for later, but some functional information should be nailed down:

First, Candy and I acquired each other shortly after my first scene with Trixie.

Second, Candy and I are *repulsive*. For example:

She had been on only a couple planes in her life, and each had been different. We sink into our seats, and at one point, over some clouds, I lean into the gap between seats toward her—"On some flights," I say in her ear, "in the aisle, they have an animal parade. It has giraffes . . . "—I imagine the dwarf giraffes into the empty aisle next to a sleeper in a cable-knit sweater—"and a funny hippopotamus . . . "—lolling past at puppy height—"and tumbling clowns . . . "

"Oh, *nice.*"

" . . . and dancing bears with funny clothes,"—spinning, they go past—"but not on all flights."

"I like dancing bears."

"You have giant ears and they're funny."

"No I don't, shhh."

Throwing up yet?

Anyway—third, Candy is not an American citizen, she's from Canada. That's all you need to know for now. Okay . . .

# Of
# Braindead
# Fucks

**Whenever** the subject comes up—usually in the context of some public blonde or breast—it is said that "Americans have a paradoxical [or "schizophrenic" or just "confused"] attitude toward pornography." This is facile and dumb. Like the question of how to treat the gay, the black, and the bug-eyed unborn, pornography is a "Hot Button Issue"—meaning an issue so *un*confusing that any lead-poisoned third grader has all the information he or she needs to have an opinion on it, and probably does.

Hot Button Issues stand in stark contrast to Complex Issues like, say, insurance industry deregulation, which, by definition, actually require the capacity to seek, retrieve, and retain information to responsibly have an opinion on. While these issues actually *are* confusing, Hot Button Issues aren't. Each American knows as much about whether and where he or she wants to see a boob as the rest of the world. What *is* confused about pornography is the Republican Party. Not individual Republicans, just the party itself. It is half made of people who like God and half made of people who like money. God hates porn; money loves it. Money love love loves it. Money fucks it this way and that way and up against a wall on Sundays.

Since this is much the same way the party feels about illegal immigrants, it is fitting that they have passed a law that fuses and confuses the two issues about which it feels so confused.

This law, passed in 2005, allows *any* foreign porn producer (with their moustaches and slippery skinny jackets) to be arrested if they visit the U.S. *unless their movies employ only U.S. talent.* "God—you happy?" "Uh . . . " "Money?" "Oh yeah, no problem!"

What? Did the porn-star unions get to them? (Can't be—there aren't any.)

The law as written is laughable—and I don't mean from any particular point of view. For example, one of the other calamities it's apparently designed to prevent is porn stars taking vacations. Consider the section of the current law, as it stands after judicious revision to reflect post-9/11 reality, concerning what constitutes a legal ID card for a performer.

So, what is a legal ID card for a performer?

The law lists the familiar forms of U.S.-issued ID cards (passport, driver's license, etc.), then says, after a semicolon:

*or, a foreign government-issued equivalent of any of the docu-*
*ments listed above*

[Okay, so a Canadian passport or a Thai driver's license,
sounds good . . . ]

*when*

[Oh, wait, there are conditions on when you can use a foreign ID . . . ]

*both*

[Not "either"—"both." So the following two conditions
must be met in order to use your foreign ID . . . ]

*the person who is the subject of the picture identification card*

[i.e., the porn star]

*and the producer maintaining the required records*

[i.e., the oily guy with the gold chain]

*are located outside the United States.*

["Are *located*"? Aren't laws supposed to say things like "are
legal residents of" or "are citizens of" or at least "reside" or
"are, during the time of the production, located"?]

According to this law, for the whole time porn producer
Shadrach Meshach and I were in Germany for the PornFilm-
Festival Berlin, putting out *Girls Are Liars* and *Far Gone and
Out* in the United States was a crime punishable by up to
five years in prison. Though if I'd had a Mexican passport,
Meshach would've been safe from prosecution.

Confused? You should be. The law is confused. The people
who wrote it are confused.

The first problem here is actually the word *or* way at the
beginning. A grown-up would've used *either/or* or some kind
of *or, if* . . . construction. Now, people on public radio are always
making fun of Republicans because of their bad grammar, but
this is because sometimes it actually matters.

I can say, "*Because the most powerful people on the planet are functionally illiterate, Candy Crushed has to brutally sodomize anyone who ever voted for Congressman Mike Pence of Indiana with a serrated bread knife; or repeatedly stand in line for hours at the DMV when the DMV has no air-conditioning and the petitioners writhe miserably through the office like blind sections of a torpid maggot."*

But this statement is imprecise. Am I saying Candy's options are

*Brutally sodomize anyone who ever voted for Congressman Mike Pence of Indiana with a serrated bread knife*

Or

*repeatedly stand in line for hours at the DMV when the DMV has no air-conditioning and the petitioners writhe miserably through the office like blind sections of a torpid maggot.*

Or am I saying that *specifically on days when the DMV has no air-conditioning and the petitioners writhe miserably through the office like blind sections of a torpid maggot,* her options are

*Brutally sodomize anyone who ever voted for Congressman Mike Pence of Indiana with a serrated bread knife*

Or

*repeatedly stand in line for hours at the DMV.*

And that, therefore, if, on a given day, *the DMV has no air-conditioning* but *the petitioners* do NOT *writhe miserably through the office like blind sections of a torpid maggot,* she doesn't have to do either thing?

Or am I saying that *specifically on days when the DMV has no air-conditioning and the petitioners writhe miserably through the office like blind sections of a torpid maggot* she MUST

*repeatedly stand in line for hours at the DMV*

INSTEAD of

*brutally sodomizing anyone who ever voted for Congressman Mike Pence of Indiana with a serrated bread knife.*

In which case, since it's hard to predict which days the DMV will have no air-conditioning while, simultaneously, the petitioners move through the office like blind sections of a torpid maggot, the safest option would be to stand in line for hours at the DMV *and* brutally sodomize anyone who ever voted for Congressman Mike Pence of Indiana with a serrated bread knife *all the time.*

The point being, it's all fucked.

What if a performer dies? Does he or she have to be buried here in the U.S.? Or do you have to move the corpse around with the producer, or make sure the corpse and the producer are never in the same country at the same time? It depends on what kind of ID they have.

But surely—there is precedent? I'm just reading this funny and splitting hairs and being a smart-ass, right? There must be some legal assumptions I'm missing or explanatory paragraph I'm . . . *No.* No one else knows what to do either—not *Hustler*, not Hefner, not any lawyer. The law is mostly untested and for the years since it went into effect everyone's been in a tornado covering their record-keeping asses and bases (especially for foreign girls, who apparently are illegal unless they have a producer who agrees to move to another country—any foreign country—forever to keep them on) over and inside out and wondering what's next and on their knees praying no one writes a law making it retroactive (where are all *those* girls buried?).

And this is just the tiny part of it that says what the word *ID* means; we haven't even got to what the whole fucked rest of the bill says.

"It's been a fucking nightmare," says Osbie. "You need current addresses for everybody, which is a pain in the ass since nearly everyone in the Darklands movies either disappeared or is homeless."

I mention to him the many difficulties faced by the children of the Lobster Boy, Grady Stiles Jr.

At first glance, the changes in the rules would appear to be like the cruising law in Los Angeles, which states that passing the same spot in my neighborhood more than once in a six-hour period is a crime (thus making lunch breaks, pizza deliveries, and part-time jobs illegal)—that is, a lite-fascist pretext to allow the police to arrest whoever they want as long as they—the cops—can sit still long enough.

But no—the consensus among lawyers is that this law wasn't even written by one. It is not written so that the DAs will have new people to arrest and parade as degenerates. It is just an awkward wad clumsily shoved through Congress to plug a hole in a platform and barely spell-checked. We are doing something about Internet pornography! View our mastery over the depraved! The usual faith-based suspects applauded it, proving that anyone stupid enough to take pornography seriously as a social threat is also too stupid to read.

I am not one of those people who will argue that the threat to our First Amendment rights is the most pressing and grave issue facing the nation. The pressing and grave issues facing the nation are almost always Complex Issues rather than Hot Button ones. It's just the people in charge use Hot Button Issues to screw you on the Complex ones.

So, Americans are not confused about pornography; the Republican Party is. Unfortunately, Americans *are* confused about the Republican Party.

ooooooooo

Oh it's heavy. Fuck it. Let's have recess. Let's drink beer and have sex and watch TV—all at once:

Trixie usually shows up having just ejected from some disaster. Trixie never seems quite alone; her arrival is like a whole carful rushing in from the snow. She comes with laptops and text messages and clips of Christopher Walken on *Saturday Night Live* and disorientation. She comes crashing in and she comes to crash. But never quite crushed, always eager to break out her baffled breakup or tossed-out story, get Candy to do something with her hair, sit and eat something she doesn't notice dripping, drink a beer or just warm tea.

It is sometime before the Fourth of July, and, between the warlike sounds of popping fireworks outside, Candy and I'd started watching profiles on all the incumbent Republican seats in the upcoming Senate races (*The senator said the rancher asked him, "Conrad, how can you live back there with all those niggers?" Senator Burns said he told the rancher it was "a hell of a challenge." —The New York Times*, Dec. 2002) (He would lose). We are not watching disinterestedly, since Candy has been having increasing trouble with Immigration and none of the porn companies in the U.S. will touch her in the current weather without U.S.-issued ID and no one at the DMV even knows whether or not she is allowed to have one. After a senator's sister is quoted as saying he'd once tossed another brother through a glass window (he would lose) I mute the TV to hear Trixie's woes.

Our room is small and has no windows. It is mostly a mattress, with a computer by a pillow and a salvaged office desk, precisely the right size, stretched entirely across the bottom of the bed—its top is like a roof over the bottom third of our low, queen-sized corner. On the desk is semiprecariously stacked nearly everything we use—music in two formats, in and out of cases, a Canon camera, a round Discman, empty Dr. Pepper and Cherry Coke bottles, slanting slabs of dozens of coffee-table books with stained spines, DVDs, a toy monkey that is all green, and paints and paintings of course, because I paint at it, and on it also is a white heavy shelf, too, with *more* stuff, and, on top, in front of a cluster of open-topped cube-shaped boxes advertising all kinds of brands and full of forgotten—maybe broken—things with wires, there is-plugged, like a postapocalyptic despot or invalid with rubberized lines into all its dark and blocky assistants, into stacks of stickered electronic submachines for games or tapes or discs (the remotes all lost)—the battered box of the now soundless and dusty black television. On it, just now, a senator whose college degree was in horseshoeing is very unsuccessfully trying to lip-synch to the Washington press corps something Trixie is saying about getting fired from a day job and how the boss said it was because he wanted a man instead. (He would lose—that senator).

It is impossible to tell when Trixie is on uppers and when she isn't. (Though usually when she is staying at our place it means she's either quit or been cut off, so after a few days it's gotta just be the ADD.) Trixie's ADD also makes any circumstance where she is the focus of attention feel like *it* has attention deficit disorder. It also makes her perhaps the only kind of person fit to properly appreciate *The Star Wars Holiday Special* ("the most excruciatingly bad piece of television ever to air on that vast wasteland," according to one critic), which she then spins laptop-wise to unveil before reaching over to *our* computer to apprise, instant message–wise, some other distant friend of her changed situation. Unwilling to focus two whole senses on the catastrophic special, Candy asks about the Boy Situation. Trixie is somewhat evasive, but it is clear she has made the boy cry (not because of porn, or at least porn *per se*).

This is what you sometimes hear from women when they've broken up and need a place to stay—the boy was crying. Betrayed or otherwise bruised, the boy often cried and/or kicked the girl out of the apartment. Personally, I feel it should be one or the other—both is appallingly bad form.

Across the third screen high above, the words *DICK LUGAR* scroll (he was running unopposed), making Trixie ask:

"What were you *watching*?"

"Just the news," I say. "I like to keep on top of things."

"Hey, Trixie," says Candy, unmoved by a pink-haired porn star seducing a wookie on the laptop, "you wanna play Super Mario World?"

"Oh my God, I *so* wanna. Okay, move over . . . "

The Christmas special, lying on the bed, plays to no audience. On the looming TV, the middle-aged face of a median-dwelling Republican senator from Maine who seems to not want to drive the nation off a cliff *just yet* goes off (she would win).

While those New Englanders are apparently unable to resist the allure of anything both slow *and* dull, Trixie is having none of it—immediately running into a deadly mushroom. While she moans about being out of practice, Candy takes over. Candy's own style is brisk and frictionless—she was born into a world that had already invented the d-pad/thumb-button interface—but Trixie narrates it.

"Oh my God, that guy sucks *so much*—those bitches—fucking turtles, fuck all those turtle-bitches in their turtle place—Did you know there was a secret there? Ooooh, what's that place? Fuck—oh that was lame."

Regrettably, when my turn comes, Mario's campaign has advanced to a Ghost House. I am a wreck about the Ghost House—I have no instinct for it at all. The massive white globular ghost that freezes and puts its ghostly white, spooky, poking, digitless hands over its eyes when you look its way but otherwise creeps inevitably Mario-ward plays havoc on my nerves. Especially in election years.

"You don't even know what you're doing, do you, you need help, Zak, listen, okay, I'm gonna do this Ghost House and I'm gonna show you how it's done because I'm the King of Super Mario World. Okay. Wait. What? Fuck! Man that thing came and—okay. Now. Alright, fuck you, *ghost*. That ghost thinks he's all gonna follow me but HA, got your ass. Alright. Awww yeah. See, nobody appreciates how my mad skills—I have mad skills."

Another thing Trixie's attention deficit disorder makes her susceptible to is Candy's very large breasts (not implants—this is alt-porn). Her eyes will periodically light up and she will surge toward them with some expression of avid disbelief and then bury herself in them for distracted seconds like a fruit bat hanging by its teeth from the drum-tight red of a suspended treat—while Candy, still both-handedly controlling her controller, giggles benevolently over her head and counsels her to remain calm. Nearly every girl in the Industry does this once they are on any kind of decent terms with Candy, but with Trixie, whose consciousness is consciously, cyclically, and forgetfully auditing all five senses for incoming data, the effect is exaggerated.

This sort of behavior is, according to what I'd seen earlier that day, what the junior senator from Pennsylvania would call "antithetical to a healthy, stable, traditional family" (along with additional statements making the clear implication that he felt that was a *bad* thing).

On occasions such as this one, it is not uncommon for Trixie to then look down, cup her own fist-sized teardrop tits, and pensively assess them. Her nipples are interesting. When erect, as they are now, it seems like each nipple is concentrically set atop another, fatter, pinker nipple. Though they were produced by an unhealthy, unstable, traditional family, it is difficult to know whether the senator would say that the nipples *themselves* are so fascinating that they are by their very essence antithetical to a healthy, stable, traditional family. However, there is no question that in their current (and as of this morning's day-job firing, *only*) profession as functional constituents of an adult performer—and since the senator, whose last name is a homonym for an unfortunate consequence of anal sex, is philosophically opposed to *all* entertainments featuring characters even approvingly *discussing* nonprocreative sex and believes that the First Amendment should be interpreted as having a three-tiered structure not unlike Trixie's nipples themselves whereby strictly titillatory speech (such as "Candy impulsively runs her callow, plump, pierced lower lip up and across the cold surface of Trixie's ice-colored breast . . . ") would be the broad, dark, and most vulnerable areolas, commercial speech (such as " . . . as they emerge, relaxed but energized as always, from their cheery game of Super Mario World and the

TV flips back to reality") would be the paler and hemispheri-
cally distended, and more ruggedly policed, central section,
and *political* speech (such as "The mere fact that any human
community of twelve million could find so much to disapprove
of in the thought of, say, Candy Crushed's mouth now finding
and tasting its way through the polar skinscape at the carved
and glitter-flecked curve at the apex of Trixie Kyle's spine, that
they ever elected someone like Senator Rick Santorum to even
a single term in any office is a fact so staggering that it should
cause any rational man, woman, or child to question whether
the responses and reactions known to them as awareness and
rational thought bear any more resemblance to the movements in the minds of the voters of that community than they
do to the mental activity behind the egglike eyes of insects
feeding on a corpse.") would be the quivering and proudly
invulnerable tip—he would have them considered, at the very
least, a controlled substance. (He would lose.)

In that case, one would normally be inclined to say that the
shirt that Trixie is now borrowing from me and putting on,
having worn the same shirt for two days, is an *ally* of healthy,
stable, traditional families, covering up, as it does, the nipples.
However, since Deuteronomy 22:5 clearly states "A woman
shall not wear anything that pertains to a man, nor shall a man
put on a woman's garment, for all who do so are an abomination to the Lord your God," and Trixie is wearing the kind of
shirt that does not merely *advertise* Batman but that has his
emblem across the chest as if she *is* Batman, and further, and
in coincidental symmetry, I happen to be wearing a shirt that
experts would recognize through very subtle indications (gray
field, *yellow* bat) implies I am Bat*girl*, and Candy, in a kind of
sidecar-coincidence parallel to the motorcycle portrayed on *her*
Batgirl shirt (which *does* actually depict the character in ques-

tion, chasing nothing down the sheer and twistless ridgeline parkway of her boobs), is now making out with Trixie, there is an undertone of transvestitism and batgirl-on-girl action about this now-entirely-clothed scene, which may be antithetical to a healthy, stable, traditional family—even without considering that both of the girls' shirts are very tight at any rate and that Batman admirably did what he had set out to do with his life despite his parents' being shot dead in Crime Alley by Joe Chill on a foggy night in Gotham City.

While one would expect both Trixie's recent firing from her day job for being female to be *opposed* and a woman's accession to a position of respect and public recognition in the male-dominated field of crime-fighting to be *applauded* by Senator Kay Bailey Hutchison (who is now waving at me over Candy's pink mohawk)—herself having risen to a position of prominence in the male-dominated field of being a dangerously shortsighted politician from Texas—her position actually has considerably more *nuance.* Her voting record actually suggests that she is a politician who would be

a*gainst* Trixie being fired because she *has* a pussy;

*for* Trixie being fired because she is, at this moment, *eating* a pussy;

*for* Bat*girl;* and

a*gainst* DC Comics' new Bat*woman* (red bat, black field, Jewish, lesbian) . . .

. . . along with late-term abortions, flag burning, and the many delightfully fur-covered animals of the Arctic National Wildlife Refuge—which ensemble of positions makes her what in Texas is called a "moderate."

(Please do note that my mention of Batwoman being Jewish and the fact that the senior senator from Texas would not support her right to work is not meant to imply it was on *those* grounds. Because that would make the future very possible presidential candidate a *Nazi*, and that would be inexcusable; not liking girls like the ones now all over each other on the bed is just *traditional*. Because homosexuals have been around longer than Jews. Or at least that must be the logic.) (She would win.)

At any rate, it is clearly fortunate that the poor woman is only on television—because things in the room have gotten distinctly Sapphic. In deference to her sensibilities, I take out my cock and try to find some place I can put it. Obliging me and Senator Hutchison, Trixie makes a soft fist around it while still insisting on fingering my girlfriend with her other hand.

So, wait, Trixie takes her shirt off, puts a new one on, *then* starts making out with Candy again? Yes. Trixie has ADD. She forgets or tapes over every other second. This gives her an excuse for anything: if you say, "Hey, let's fuck," she can always say, "I think I'm gonna get another apple out of the fridge." ADD gives people what the senior senator from Texas will need when people start asking her why she keeps voting in favor of oil and gas companies and they keep giving her money: plausible deniability. "Oh, I didn't realize."

It seems so strange that the phrase *plausible deniability* took so long to evolve—since it is the essential female pre-coital negotiation and investigation tactic—and so appropriate that it emerged from the world of espionage. Still, it's odd to think that if Kennedy hadn't tried to get Castro to smoke dynamite-loaded cigars, and a committee hadn't been formed to investigate it, we *still* would have no idea what that "Oh I thought we were just going to *study*?" business is all about. At any rate, Trixie isn't using it today.

Meanwhile, out the window, heterosexuality is out there on the streets of Brooklyn, where it sprawls and brawls and spawns and pawns and porns. And sets off illegal firecrackers. Heterosexuals keep making more of each other to hit. If they are too small to do anything but *get* hit, then they may make a new, smaller one to hit. It is pretty gay.

There is a senator on TV now who has an explanation for all the chaos being generated by all the Bushwickians out on the street—and for the degenerate behavior of the smallest girl *inside* the apartment, too—they are aliens.

Although her native land is prone to violent storms and spider infestations, that is not why Candy has come here. She has come to our country largely to be able to do what she is now doing—licking a girl's snatch while getting done from behind.

What's ironic is the anti-alien Senator Jon Kyl's own name reflects the pattern adopted in many of the comic books stacked behind the TV he watches us from, whereby aliens are given names such as J'onn J'onzz or Ron Karr, which are pronounced identically to earthling names but are as orthographically *other* as those of inhuman compatriots such as Superman nemesis and fellow illegal Kryptonian immigrant Dru-Zod and Green Lantern Corps member Leezle Pon. Although the latter is a superintelligent smallpox virus and therefore generally unwelcome in most circumstances, it *is* heroic and therefore would be welcome in this passionate and inconvenient moment because, as Jon Kyl's face fades from the screen, Candy, responding to some nimble work of Trixie's, reacts with a taut kick that, though as restrained and maliceless as the dreaming and flexing of a sleepy bunny, proves to be the last straw for my desk, which, not unlike the U.S. border patrol, has been too long burdened with a responsibility for controlling masses (in the one case, water-filled paint jars, upright oversized books, a bookcase, and a ceiling-touching tower of machinery, and in the other case, Mexicans) in the grip of essentially irresistible forces much older and stronger than it or they are. If Leezle and its species were not as fictional as one hopes they are, then that virulent friend might've been able to use some super skill to save me from having to slide, awkward and naked and at speed, between the collapsing end of the desk and the strip of wall it is eagerly on its way to meet as my life pitches like the deck of a sinking ship before my eyes and not entirely un-toward us all while I shrilly tell the girls to quit their intriguing behavior immediately and help prop the works up before something heavy maims them.

Was there ever a time when pale pairs of naked immobile gorgeous women actually held up peoples' roofs and furniture? Or was that just some Greek architect's fantasy? If it was, his dream came true fifteen hundred years later in a railroad flat in Brooklyn with no air-conditioning while a CD sang in a sort of solemn, transported reverie about earthquakes and typhoons, and the illicit, prepatriotic explosions for a democracy he would never know went off outside, at least for as long as it took me to ransack my apartment—moving as awkwardly as all racing, naked males in pointy places—for something sturdy enough to replace them—though the living buttresses were actually curled like brackets or bookends and, backs to the wall, propped up a heavy fraction of what I owned with their four feet. It seems to take for-fucking-ever, but I rig something up, and we finish our fucking.

The television, despite a drunken lurch into a new position, has miraculously stayed plugged in. I don't think much about it, though, because with a wet and talented little mouth and then a wet and talented big mouth and then both at once working their warm and moving blood-red smooth insides around your cock, you can't really think about much and you don't care and it is an immaculate mercy and it is not a lie because, really, what other thing have you really got to do that can't just fuck off and wait for as long as it takes to finish that? There is no room for the things detonating just outside or anywhere else, and there is no room for the jokes your apartment plays on you, and there is certainly no room in a two-girl-blowjob consciousness for a Utah senator to silently sing one of the songs he recorded in his other and simultaneous career as a Christian contemporary musician—"America Rocks!" "The Blood Of Christ,"or "I Am Happy." (He would win.)

# Why I Am That Fucker

**People keep making** pornography and no one serious asks anyone to explain it. This is America and it makes money, so what's to explain? When you go to Europe, though, people want *answers*. They demand *dialogue*.

Eight college guys come in to the kebab place where I'm eating a chicken filet and cheese with a side of fries. They all sit around me at my table. They are German and drunk.

One Drunk German College Guy grabs the two men on either side of him and explains about how he wants to suck their cocks.

I say, "Y'know, when I saw you walk in that's exactly what I thought. I thought: Now that guy wants to suck some cock."

DGCG: "Yah! Right *now*! Both of their cocks!"

DGCG2: "Yah! He loves *cocks*!!"

DGCG3: "His cock is also the *biggest* cock!"

ZS: "Really? I didn't know that."

DGCG: "It *is*!"

DGCG2: "Yah! You hev sen the tower of Alexanderplatz? It is bigger than this size!"

ZS: "That's a large cock."

DGCG: "*All* of the *women*, they *know* about it!"

DGCG3: "It is *legend*!"

ZS: "That's so strange—it's not in my guidebook . . . "

DGCG2: "It is underground phenomenon! Not for tourists!"

ZS: "His cock? . . . So, if it's so big, how do they know it's *his*? I mean, they must see *it* long before they see *him* . . . Umm, I'm very hungry and if you keep eating my fries I'll be very upset . . . "

DGCG: "They all know it because I am a porno star!"

ZS: "Really? I've fucked some porn stars."

All of them stop their drunk munching and look very gravely at me.

DGCG2: "Really?"

DGCG3: "The *porrrrrn* stars?"

ZS: "Yeah."

DGCG: "I am Thomas. I don't know your name!"

I'm guessing maybe probably DGCG is not a porn star but I don't ask. I am okay with not knowing, at least for now.

I am in Berlin to represent *Far Gone and Out* at the first annual PornFilmFestival. A great many important things about the world are much clearer in Berlin than they are in other places.

०००००००००

The first thing at the festival is a party. I bring three friends and we take the train from Kreuzberg.

The king of alt-porn suddenly and unexpectedly strolls toward the four of us from the rubber-lined mouth of the southbound train with his entourage and, still poking at his cell or Sidekick, asks, "Hey, are you guys a*lt*?"

We were kind of asking for it—Candy Crushed and I were looking around haplessly in leather and all black, favorably comparing the crisply painted, LED-lit Mehringdamm Station to its bunkerlike Brooklyn equivalents, and Claire LeJense and her gay boyfriend were poured in a striped and zippery heap on the platform, cooing at each other in German. Now, aside from the leather and the zippers—and the haircuts, one mohawk and three much more complicated para-mohawks— there were also the skulls. Who doesn't want to be constantly reminded that they're going to die? I notice we four collectively are marked with miles of ink and metal in the form of not just skulls but specifically skulls with accompanying crossbones: dispersed across two earrings, a battered bag, a scarf, a pullover, five tattoos in wildly divergent styles, a shirt, a belt, and a pair of externally worn fake-silk boxer shorts (all this acquired by the various parties involved, so far as I can remember, before the blossoming of skull-availability following the release of *Pirates of the Carribean*). So, yeah, okay, I get it, Leom.

There is a cloud of alt-porn directors and alt-porn stars with Leom and we are all going to the same place.

I introduce everyone.

As a genre, "alternative pornography" is obviously so open to interpretation that it could pretty much cover any image, moving or otherwise, ever made or makeable, up to and including footage of a dead pheasant bungee-corded to a pair of ice skates and being whacked with a ladle by a transvestite goatherd. As a genealogy or as a scene, particularly in the hardcore end of the porn business, however, it is basically, as of this writing, porn movies made by anyone who has ever worked in any capacity with Leom McFrei, or who wants to work with Leom McFrei, or whom Leom McFrei wants to work with and who also thinks it would get them something to market the movie as "alt-porn." Leom had been an admirer of Osbie's casting decisions long before they met, and had done something technical on *Far Gone and Out*, so *it* was alt-porn.

This is not the kind of thing you can say in interviews, so when the Europeans ask what alt-porn is, Leom doesn't know what to say. He explains his dilemma as we all get on the train. There is nowhere to sit and nobody knows what to tell him. And no one cares: Leom doesn't care as long as it keeps people asking; the same goes for Shadrach Meshach, who is with him; the porn stars don't care as long as it means they occasionally get to make movies with their friends; Claire and her gay boyfriend don't care as long as it means there are free drinks at the thing we're going to; and the other people on the train don't care because if they ever even bought porn they probably just look for the box with the juiciest shot of the body part they'd most like to shoot on. It is possible that one of the directors on the train, Diana Drago, might care—she seems like a reflective and scrupulous type.

In truth, what makes Leom's work "alt" is less interesting than what makes it Leom's. What makes it "alt" is simple: most porn movies *look* like the women were cast by trying to fill every single role with a blonde built like a mudflap girl or the nearest equivalent the agency could scrape up that day— Leom's don't. What makes Leom's movies *Leom's* is that he keeps—perhaps misguidedly—trying to make them *movies*. Not necessarily meaning giving them plots, but just trying to do, around the sex, the kinds of things that ambitious young filmmakers might try to do after graduating from art school. Stuff with color or dialogue or timing or funniness or music.

And one other thing: he tries to get in the actresses' heads— he tries very hard and he's good at it, and then he films what he finds, and it is creepy.

Example: We're talking about this girl—talent—I've met her, he hasn't. She's gonna be in something he's doing. He asks what she's like—I describe her, the way she is (I like her, she's nice), I describe the kinds of things she says and does. It takes a bit, and he goes, "Ah, so she's an attention whore." Like he'd just remembered the name of his fifth-grade English teacher and didn't much care. And you think, "O . . . K . . . I'm just gonna go look out the window now." But then you look at the movies, and you can tell that, at least once in a while, he got *in* there. He did what directors are supposed to do to actors, only with people who will tell you they can't act and with the wild card of fucking some stranger thrown in. At least he does on a good day.

Like in *Art School Whores*, there's one phenomenal moment, right after one of the sex scenes—the first Leom ever shot—where the pair are panting hard, either genuinely, euphorically exhausted or displaying more acting talent than anyone in the history of the genre—"Wow," the girl says to someone off camera, "I forgot you guys were *here*," and cracks up. He must've done something right.

If anything actually ties alt movies together *as movies,* it's style. Not any given style, so much as an attempt to have it. And what is style? Style is any part of a piece of art—or any made thing—that isn't *craft.* And what is craft? Any part of a made thing that the average person only notices when it isn't there. Craft is the part of a thing that pretends it has to be that way. The fact that this train is a series of bread-box shapes stuck together and keeps moving, the fact that *New Wave Sluts* is in focus and has audible sound and butt-fucking, the existence of a health insurance industry in America—these things come about from someone, somewhere, paying attention to *craft.* A famous architect's tower that leans like a stick of butter having a panic attack, aquatic makeup, lingering long shots in *New Wave Sluts,* saying "death tax" instead of "inheritance tax"—these things result from an attention to *style.*

Since they are much more likely to notice it, people love to complain about style—Why did that guy make that building look like some butter? Fuck him!—so mad crazy fathoms of self-righteous masturbators on, say, AdultDVDTalk.com complain about alt. *He put her in blue makeup? He is a fuck! FUCK him! He is the fuckest fuck! He should be fucked!* etc.

Meanwhile, in the large world outside the train, Intensity Entertainment (empire of which Leom's Intensity-Alt is an outpost and for which this train ride is a legitimate business expense) doesn't care what Leom or alt are about as long as Sunny Carmichael, Gina Giles, Zak Sabbath, Candy Crushed, and all the other performers in their movies qualify as "adult performers" in the pornographic economic equation that explains that two adult performers filmed having sex for fifteen minutes times six equals a film with standard sales figures (which, in dollars, are higher than the films' budgets).

It's also entirely possible of course that Intensity, which, unlike us, is a publicly traded company and therefore motivated by the laws governing its existence to pursue not merely *a* profit but *maximum* profit, might decide that the money invested in things like *Art School Whores* and *Kill Slut Kill* and *Girls Are Liars* would be better invested in projects that result in not merely *a* profit but in *more profit than any other viable project that could've been filmed at that time and for that amount of money,* in which case Leom will argue that Alt-porn = Porn (and therefore Immediate Standard Porn Profit) + Alt (and therefore small Cult Movie Status Profits *every year after the movie's made*) so that he, Meshach, Gina, Diana, and Sunny can keep riding this train for free. (The rest of us are riding the train ticketless because either we assume whatever fine-assigning clerks the Berlin train cops front for will never trace us back to our foreign addresses or we are in so deep with Berlin train cop fines already from having long ago adopted illegal U-bahn/S-bahn-riding lifestyles that it hardly matters at this point and sooner or later we're just going to have to move.)

We get off the train at Alt-Tempelhof station. In this country, "Alt" just means "old."

°°°°°°°°°

My friend Otto on alt:

"Zere is a film I get once and everyone is looking to me at the store. It is called *Scheisse Grandma*—now that, I think, I call 'Alt-porn.'"

Due to many historical factors, including a sort of been-there-over-it attitude about fascism, a convenient location in the dead center of the European tour circuit, and the fact that Iggy Pop once lived there while eating nothing but sausages for an entire year, Berlin is known throughout Europe as the punkest rockest city.* The people I know there all have a lot of skulls on them and are all, linguistic confusion aside, naturally suspicious about this *alt*.

"Zo how is the porno pahty?" says Otto.

"Lame."

"Yeah, zis is what I think it will be."

"We saw Fuck for Forest people there. The guy looked like a caveboy; he's—just naked with a loincloth and, like, crystals in his hair or something and Claire's like 'Get the fuck away from me, you are scaring me, hippie.' I was trying to be like, 'Oh hey, I know you guys, you make pornos and give all the money to Save the Rainforest; I do the same thing, only with Food Not Bombs,' but Claire's just fucking *unloading* on this hippie and then he was like, 'If you don't care about the rainforest you should kill yourself, just take a pill or shoot yourself!' or whatever and . . . yeah . . . guh."

"Yeah, I look to their site from a flyer I get and I see, but who wants to see this hairy fucking with trees and so? Gross."

"Yeah, it was . . . yeah . . . the party was . . . I don't know, the thing was at this sex club, y'know, and there was like this guy with underwear that said '100% meat' and like this pink stump with arms on the wall, I think it was supposed to be a pussy, and all these sad-sack Berlin S&M people with like no hair and leather armbands."

"Yeah, I know, sounds like I expect. And was there this men with the . . . you have this word *lay-teks*? . . . yah . . . this suit they wear and fat spilling around?"

---

* If you've never heard punk rock this is what it will sound like to you: the earliest stuff will sound like people yelling about unspeakable things happening (for example, Fear, or Crime), the second wave will sound like people yelling *while* unspeakable things are happening (like Nausea, or Conflict), and the most recent achievements will just sound like unspeakable things happening (Terror, Tragedy).

"Yeah, pretty much. Well, y'know, I figured it's the party for this festival so I should go and talk to whoever, but really it was just they let us into the club for free and that was basically the party. I brought people with me and it's all dark and like nobody's gonna go, 'Hey, one of those punks sulking on the giant rubber ottoman is Zak Sabbath.' I kind of knew but I had to check it out. The bathroom mirror made you all weird colors though."

"Yeah, I know zis people. In Augsburg I have this kind of job to be the guard of this place and there is cocaine and all of this that they do and they are saying it is okay you have piercings to your face and whatever and your hair but you must wear this and have such a *tie* to wear. Do I have a *tie*?"

"Right, yeah, no . . . "

"Yes, but the point is I *wish* I have a tie because they are saying if you do not have it we give it to you and they give me zis *leather* tie and zo . . . "

"Jesus . . . "

"Yeah, can you see me in such a leazher tie? It is fucked. The sex people are kind of weird cocaine fuckers, I think."

∞∞∞∞∞∞∞∞

Claire LeJense on alt:

"Hold on, I need a cigarette."

"Hey, I called 'cause we were eating Indian food over near your place but you didn't answer."

"Yeah, I slept at the hotel."

"Hotel?"

"*Their* hotel."

"You mean . . . "

"Yeah, it turned out totally unexpected. It was . . . *yeah*."

"Okay, so now there's a story so tell me the story."

"There's not much of a story, just that porn girl ended up eating my pussy while Frederick watched and jerked off."

"'Porn girl'—*Sunny?* . . . I saw that coming."

"How? I didn't!"

"Because I've gotten used to the fact that when girls say, 'I want to fuck you, Zak,' it's some kind of code for 'Although I have no idea who your friend Claire is, as soon as I meet her I'll eat her pussy.'"

"Well you guys left and then Frederick started hooking up with this guy and . . . "

"At the sex-club thing?"

"Yeah, and so I was kind of standing guard and these stupid S&M morons kept coming over like, 'Oooh, watch this guy fuck the gutterpunk,' so I was calling them things to keep them from masturbating all over him and the people in charge wanted to throw me out but some of the porn people were saying, 'We have beer back at the hotel,' so, y'know . . . "

"You *always* do this to me. I mean, who was the last girl you did?"

"I don't know . . . Sylvia?"

"See! You hang out in Berlin and only fuck guys, and then I show up and *bam*!"

"Well maybe she was scared off by your girlfriend . . . "

"She didn't seem to mind that your boyfriend was right there."

"Frederick was fucking some *guy*. Besides, I'm always stealing boys from Frederick, too."

"Honestly, I can't take you *anywhere*."

"And that guy *with* the porn girl—he kept talking about how 'dominant' he was and how he was a sadist and I made him suck my tampon."

"I always miss *everything* . . . "

"Oh boo hoo, porn star. It was actually really bizarre, before she got between my legs she was totally talking like it was porn, like she was really submissive, and talking to me like I was a *guy*, in this voice like, 'Oh, do you like these titties, do you want to touch my little titties?' the whole time."

"Weird, weird—that's totally how she is in her movies, too, like she just keeps talking all cute and it sounds really fake but you can tell she's kind of into doing it, so it's also real, and then you know that it's kinda the way she is in real life and it's—and like she's all like some blonde stoner-cheerleader and imagining her with *you*—and y'know you always wonder about the full-time girls, which ones just like the money and which ones are really into it."

"She was into it, but she was like a machine. Like a little porno machine."

"Weird."

"Weird."

⊙⊙⊙⊙⊙⊙⊙⊙⊙

Dear Osbie,

I'm sending you this from an Internet café on Wiener Strasse. All around me Turkish schoolkids are jabbering in German and first-person shooting each other.

On the other hand, these lemon yogurt/white chocolate things taste much better than you'd think.

Doing research, I find my original plan for this afternoon, to write something brief here making fun of the guy who organized the festival—for being hard to find, for not having watched your movie, for throwing lousy parties, for his brimless hat, and for being (ha ha!) German—is somewhat undercut by the sheer volume of stuff he's been presiding over and presumably worrying about all month long. There are performances, lectures, exhibits, contests, workshops, mad screenings, stuff from Paul Verhoeven and Lars Von Trier, and people from Belgium and Bologna on panels discussing gayness and queerness and blackness and transgenderality and net-neutrality and glamour and class warfare and dildos and rubbers and cybernetic lovers and "the other" and fucking your mother and objectifying your brother and hate and images and facials and lesbians and everything Japanese. Everything that lives underground and has semen on it is in this city, now.

In addition to all this business, the mainstream porn world is simultaneously hosting a trade conference called Venus. There are billboards everywhere. Their tempting, awkward site says: "Enjoy a gala and parties which cannot be more glamorous and spectacular. With stars and starlets who you will find only in the erotic market."

So Berlin is unimaginably pornographic at the moment. Girls who've taken more on every surface in a year than I'll ever lay out are out there trying to kill the daylight hours. But where? Where are the starlets I can find only in the erotic market?

There are allegedly a lot of art/porn types here too, like Annie Sprinkle, but I haven't run into her either.

Meanwhile, Vaginal Davis (whose "personas reject the internal counter-cultural mandate to refuse self-criticism, instead problematising [sic] the functions and assumptions of normative trends within the margins," according to the magazine she quotes in her write-up) bafflingly conducts a lecture "designed specifically for cosmopolitan whites looking to explore and bring out their inner dinge. And for assimilationist blacks ready to re-connect with their Mandingo/Mandinga jungle realness." Which, y'know, sounds like a thing.

And I'm here writing to you—the only human noise I can understand out of all the action in here is some kid saying, "Taliban boy." Maybe these Turkish kids are playing some cooperative game where they are in Spec Ops and shoot at the Taliban and not at each other. It's so hard to tell.

So anyway the idea is that people who are doing the stuff above—or want to see people do it—are the audience during your screening. I will try to make you look as good as I can. I'm not sure I can charm German couples whose idea of fun is to show up for the pornographic movie they probably know nothing about in the smaller, secondary theater rather than the pornographic movie they probably know nothing about in the big primary theater. Should I tell them jokes? Will they pass the displays and say, "Oh, that's the pornographic film by the guys who tell the dumb jokes, let's give it to Gerty for her birthday, it was hot, I'm sure it will make her want to masturbate"? Please advise.

A porn actress just died and no one seems to know why. She was found in her hotel room. According to *Berliner Zeitung*: "Die Berliner Poilizei ermittelt, der Arzt schliesst einen Allergie-schock nicht aus." Autopsy on Monday. The consensus among the American alt-porn people here is it's nobody we know.

What else is going on here . . . stuff, but maybe nothing worth telling. A couple years ago, pretty much any sequence of events that ended in sexual intercourse would've been a story, but, you know, once you cross over to dealing with all this managed nymphomania, sex kinda loses its weight as a narrative punch line, which really only leaves you with injury, death, or unexpected animals, as far as the classics go.

My perspective on what's worth remembering is further distorted by the fact that the only nonpornographic people I talk to much in Berlin are Otto, who is only interested in porn inasmuch as it gives him the opportunity to grill me with the kind of lefty political questions concerning exploitation and the representation of women that you'd expect from a vegetarian anarcho-punk even when he is letting you stay in his apartment, and Claire, this chain-smoking she-wolf who . . . well, okay, sample Claire dialogue:

"Boys are so *exhausting*."

"What do you mean?"

"Well I just fucked those two guys at once a couple hours ago, and now I should probably fuck you, and then I've got to go fuck my ex tonight to keep him happy."

"You need to get some sleep—I release you from your obligation. I'm gonna check my mail. I'll wake you up before I leave."

Anyway, like I said, I'll try to make you look good. I hope your uncle is alright and you are too. Let me know, if you get a minute.

—Zak

⊙⊙⊙⊙⊙⊙⊙⊙⊙

I'd assumed for months that the *Girls Are Liars* blowjob was just one of those regrettable projects in life that just hadn't made anybody happy. I was wrong, though, because Leom liked it so much he left all that audio in. And judging from my mail since *Girls Are Liars* came out, it has female fans, too. The woman who grabs me in the otherwise empty lobby of Kant Kino during the premiere while I'm trying to see if they've got Milk Duds in this country is not at all one of them.

"Zo you are ze fucker who tell zee girl how to zuck you cock?"

This is not said in a chummy way, either.

I explain that I am that fucker.

I can't blame her—I didn't want to sit through it either. Kant Kino is a real movie theater, and the screen is not small.

Imagine being in the front row of a theater full of turtlenecks and glasses while your screen twin bosses someone around his cock in cruel, massive Dolby. For a long time.

Also, whenever I hear the sound of my own voice—in any context—I am amazed that anyone ever has sex with me.

Also, I am, incidentally, reminded about how I look when I have sex. I know now, but it took a long time to find out. I look angry. From the movies, I now know that whenever I'm on a porn set and not having sex I look stupid and pleased. But when I'm fucking—cold rage. My eyes are evil little marbles. Why? This is how I look when I'm concentrating on something. I know because whenever I am working intently, or looking at a picture or ass I like, or trying to think, someone always interrupts and goes, "What's the matter?"

An ex once said to me, "Why don't you ever smile when you're drawing?" I said, "Okay, there, how's that?" She said, "That's not a smile." "Yes it is." "Go look—hold that face and look in the mirror." I held exactly the face and got up and went to a mirror. There I was, not at all smiling. It felt like a smile but it wasn't one.

I realized then that every single time I had ever smiled at myself in the mirror I'd asked my eyes whether I was smiling and every time I smiled anywhere else I'd asked my muscles. And the muscles were liars. Even leaving aside the idea that, as a painter of portraits, it brought into question the traditional excuse for my profession—that is, that the face reflects the inner reality—it was disturbing. For, like, twenty-five years, for at least a quarter of what would be my life, I thought I was smiling and I wasn't.

But if you want to see your eyes and muscles *violently* disagree—have someone film you while you fuck. This leathered six-footer in the lobby in front of the candy with the dying blonde hair and unlit cigarette had very likely had sex. Had she ever filmed it? This was not the thing to ask now.

I try to explain about the blowjob. I try to explain about the morning and Trixie and I say, *Pretend to be me*: You're shaved and naked on a strange floor and everybody's job is to wait for you, so you have to keep hard. Or, if it's easier, pretend you have to stay wet—I say this to this six-foot person (Are these two things rough equivalents? Nobody will ever know). So what will you do? Just about anything. You will say *whatever* to blot out Leom and the bored people in the room down the hall who you barely know who kept giving you food and rides and paper towels, the kind people whose workday is inversely proportional to the length (timewise) of your erections and who will have nothing much new to talk about that night at the bar besides with what, if any, panache and dispatch this relatively new guy with the voice like pushpins in Kool-Aid shot a wad on Trixie's face.

So you'd keep on, and you'd say some stuff in a pornography voice and hope it keeps Trixie on the tip and hope the audio gets cut (since *your* mouth isn't in the shot) or else that it all just sounds like pornography.

The woman is a weary Berliner and so has irony on her side—no matter what she says, I have no idea how convincing any of this really sounds. I *am*, however, completely sure I do a very bad job introducing *Far Gone and Out* the next day. I miss the slot for opening remarks entirely and arrive—sweating from running and squeaking into my seat—in the middle of the first scene's Fake Internal Pop.

There is not yet a school where you can major in porn acting and do a unit on FIPs, and so no one tells you beforehand that they shoot certain angles and moments for the softcore version and that for this version you will be required to loudly pretend to have an unseen orgasm, even if in real life you have roommates and are the sort of dead-eyed silent finisher who maybe at most emits a barely aspirated rasp or slowly pushes his teeth into the girl's shoulder at the heavy instant, and that when you are performing your unconvincing FIP nobody will tell you when to stop FIP-ing and you will try to think of some noise or otherwise terminal-seeming action you can perform to make it clear that the fake-moaning cable version of the scene is now over and someone should say "cut," and that if the best you'll be able to come up with is a sort of consumptive cough, which is so totally asexual that you have to do the whole FIP over again and have exactly the same dilemma again and you will sort of try to end it by convulsively grabbing the back of Rebecca Black's head from behind and she'll say, "Ow!?" more amused and surprised than anything else then everyone on the set will laugh audibly into the mikes and this will strike the director as so funny that the whole FIP sequence will actually be rescued from cable-only obscurity and left in the final cut of the hardcore version in two separate places and that this is what will greet you if you agree to perform in a film that turns out to be creatively ambitious and gets into an international film festival and you forget that some streets in Berlin have addresses that go down in one direction and up in the other.

It looks like the room is still full, at least. Audience attrition is a serious problem during these flicks, though people leaving does not necessarily mean the movie is sucking.

While it works alright for the arty European stuff where the odd existential rim job might crop up in *any* kind of movie, the film festival is really not the ideal format for American hard-core. The general lack of avant-garde movie infrastructure in the U.S. means that American alt-porn has to use the same advertising-and-distribution channels as mainstream porn and also means that, in many essential ways, it has to be *like* mainstream porn—mostly made up of long sex scenes that, beyond the minute or two it takes to register and appreciate the music, camera angles, and wardrobe choices, have absolutely no entertainment value to anyone not simultaneously engaged in the pursuit of an orgasm of their own.

With all these couples watching and no option to pause or rewind, porn is, at best, all the chemical damage of three high-school years' worth of unresolvable turn-ons jammed into a couple hours and, at worst, a sort of long smothering under a blanket made of slathered parts and moans of varying degrees of plausibility that makes you never want to do anything resembling what the gleamy, hairless giants up there are doing ever again.

So a lot of people leave during the movies—and more leave during the credits (so, directors, *cut the credits out of the film-festival version of your movie*). Because of this, it's clear, before they even open their mouths, that whoever the pairs and clumps of university-ish men and women left are, they are *serious* about pornography.

⊙⊙⊙⊙⊙⊙⊙⊙⊙

A lot of the questions are about politics and porn. Politics and porn make people nervous in the same way.

While a frog might show up on your TV, or a comedian, or a teacup, these all appear as supplicants—*Please be enter-*

*tained by us, please stay here with us! Look, I ate a fly! I told a joke! I want you to buy a certain kind of cheese!*—but neither the president's head nor a twat would be on your television if they hadn't already won (they had your vote—or someone's—or your $14.95). And yet, while they don't actually want anything from you that you haven't already given up, they both, more than any other thing on TV, try to make you believe that the machinations on the screen are the result of, and response to, your will. Consequently, when it's most clear that they aren't, the curved glass that stops your flying bottle or wad of jizz from hitting the face on the screen feels much more like a prison wall than when it's separating you from a basketball game or a family of four having zany misadventures.

No other thing on TV can make the difference between you and its target audience so clear and so insulting. The political and the pornographic are *not* akin to the honest entertainment familiar from the beginning of time to any king or juggler— with the screen just there to collapse the distance between you and people trying to amuse you—as in, *Hey, watch me juggle! Wow, nice job, I like watching you juggle!* This—the cock and the Congress—is watching something that, in a healthier world, you'd be participating in instead. It is isolating and worrisome. People get touchy.

So a woman in the audience complains, on essentially political grounds, about cum shots. She complains that this is something only for men.

While there are many things in porn that are only for men, this is not one of them. If you don't know this it may be because you've never read it—"Happiness writes white," as Montherlant said. "It doesn't show up on the page."

(Which, incidentally, is why the British Secret Intelligence Service, during the reign of Director George Mansfield Smith-Cumming, started using semen as an invisible ink.)

Sunny Carmichael fields a lot of the questions during the *Girls Are Liars* screening, which is helpful, because she is the kind of woman *this* kind of woman thinks doesn't exist.

Before we got to Berlin, I showed Candy a picture of Sunny Carmichael.

Candy thought, then said, "She looks kind of like the 'hot' girl next door."

I said there were no girls like that next door to me.

"Like one of those girls in eighth grade," she said, "that would talk about getting drunk and guys shoving bottles up her ass."

I asked Candy where exactly she went to eighth grade.

Even before I was in porn, it was obvious that either some-one had been making *new* kinds of women or we'd been sys-tematically lied to about the old ones.

The evidence for the latter theory is good. Ever wonder why God creates "male and female" but then he's only got Adam by himself and then Eve doesn't show up until twenty-two verses later? Certain writings suggest Eve was Adam's *second* wife, after his first wife, Lilith, demanded to be on top. So she got edited out of the Bible. In later years, she shows up as a sort of patron anti-saint of masturbation—every time you jerk off, she collects your cum and has an evil baby. She was also alleged to be a killer of normal babies, and also an owl.

Things like that are not easy to prove, but it does suggest that tradition—which is a conspiracy of unimaginative par-ents and unloved old men in funny hats, that is, people with a vested interest in slut-suppression—has retained a remark-ably consistent attitude toward sexually aggressive women for the last few thousand years: They don't exist. And if they do, then they kill babies and make you masturbate. They do seem to have dropped the owl thing.

This is all to say that the please-cum-on-my-face girl *is* known to empirical science. I know one guy—promiscuous, but not in porn, and older than me—who *only* creams on faces. He, like everyone, has been thrown out of bedrooms for different reasons, but never *that* one. There will no doubt be, sometime soon, a sort of anti-daytime-talk-show where each afternoon a powder-blue-sweatshirted housewife is paraded like a grotesque so an audience of twenty-five-ish women in halter tops with lower-back tattoos can cluck and jeer together at her for not wanting cum on her face on the first date and tell her she needs to get herself a *job*.

Another notion the cum-face-question woman wants to discuss—that men form unrealistic expectations about the desires of women from looking at porn—is transparently not at all so. In fact, a man generally won't be looking at porn at *all* unless his immediate estimate about what women want from him is relatively bleak. One might say the heterosexual male masturbator, who expects *no woman at all,* has the lowest *possible* expectations. He expects to be *ignored*—which in anyone's book is not expecting much. The cum-face-question woman seems to be indulging in the popular myth that male sexual requirements are *relative.* This is likewise transparently not at all so. If you're pretty, there will always be men who want to ejaculate on your face. It's not porn's fault any more than it's KISS's fault that some people want to rock and roll all night and party every day.

The popularity of porn is not the cause of sexual dissatisfaction in men, it is an effect. Which is a much more frightening fact, if you think about it.

Expectations, in this case—as in the case of all expectations formed by fiction—are only an issue when dealing with the pathologically stupid—and the pathologically stupid are a perennial problem no matter what they're watching. They will ruin lives because of some shit they saw on the Weather Channel.

In general, most of the questions the Germans ask are predictable and easy to answer because they are the same ones Americans ask, including that hot chestnut: "What made you decide to do porn?"—although this particular version of the question is thoughtfully appended with some Sensitive Intellectual multiple-choice options: "Was it just something you were always *intrigued* by? Or . . . was it an *impulse*? Or . . . for your *personal development*? Or . . . "

(People never ask why I decided to be a painter—I guess wanting to stretch colored pools of liquid plastic until they look like a pretty girl who likes sex is easier to understand than wanting to put parts of your body in her.)

Thinking up new smart-ass answers to The World's Stupidest Question is one of my hobbies, but, to be honest, very few things make me feel as profoundly and self-righteously sealed off from any real sympathetic understanding of my fellow human beings than the fact that people all over the world keep asking this fucking question. Nothing else puts me in so much danger of reading the population as twelve billion red eyes in the night, all day just breeding and winning bread to no good end. People are so strange with the strange things they want more than sex, the things they will willingly have less of the most intense participation in the visceral world to get at, things like God or babies or heroin or quiet or large televisions or attention or pride or autographs or a bigger place or a feeling of accomplishment or a sense of identity or pricey shoes.

*And*—they are often lying. If you could see what they were thinking, if you could see what you can't see, you'd see pornography. Are you in the city? Have you seen the cars? The pornography industry is bigger than the car industry—in money—that is, people want porn more than cars and they have it more than cars.

So how much porn is there? To make the real-but-invisible visible, we have to imagine that, instead of a yellow Chevy Impala parked across the narrow side street covered in graying fall leaves, there's a little blonde cheerleader in soaking moist white cotton panties parked across the narrow side street covered in graying fall leaves and instead of crawling each morning into a bone-white Corolla, you crawl each morning into barely legal brats just dying to suck you off; that there are desperate, wet MILFs upon MILFs where once there were fleets of cop cars and cabs; that the freeway traffic jam that interrupts any attempt to feel a day in Los Angeles is vivid and continuous and urban is not a drab steel sea with passengers under glass but sixteen lanes of hand jobs, tit fucks, cream-guzzling teens, and oiled-up bubble butts glistening under a rush-hour sun and going off in both directions, quivering past all the exits and dust-caked, arrowed names of subcities and streets; that, indeed, all the rest of the city and planet is constantly crisscrossed by fantastic snatch moving at every speed, so much that we can barely breathe without inhaling a wet, pale tide of nocturnal emissions so vast it threatens to eat away the shell of stratospheric molecules that keeps us from being fried alive by our world's own nourishing sun. Then we can grasp the extent of what people refuse to discuss.

"Did you fax it over?" "When was the last time you heard from them?" "Are you an unreconstructed fiend for tight, dripping twat?" "Oh yeah, a few times every day!" Unsaid. Written in white.

And then you don't think about it anymore, because if you did then it would be impossible to impersonate a professor, or pilot, or parent, or any of the men in collared shirts you see looking bored in public places and in private places. The point is, if you were going to build a psychological city to parallel the physical one (of which it is the engine), you'd need an ungodly delirious amount of pussy.

In this frame of mind, the girls who do all the porn seem like a division of field nurses, racing with their kit bags full of shoes to obscure warehouses to administer purely symptomatic relief to the secret pain of a secret empire.

Or, short answer—no, it's not the people staring at me naked, it's not the free doughuts, it's the *having sex with the attractive women*. Next question . . .

# Oh, Also, about Porn Girls:

"I wish Vin Diesel was a porn star."

"Why? If you wanna fuck Vin Diesel you can just . . . "

"Yeah, but I would wanna get *paid*."

"I don't get it, I mean . . . Oh wait, okay—I get it—*insurance*."

"Exactly."

"Like, if it's not good, then you can go, 'Well, I'm getting paid whatever' and you don't have to be all, 'Why the fuck am I doing this?'"

"Exactly."

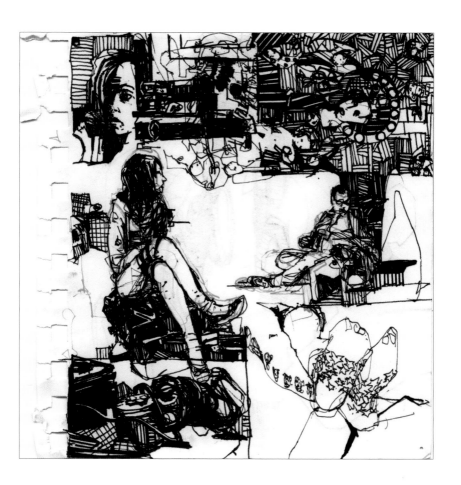

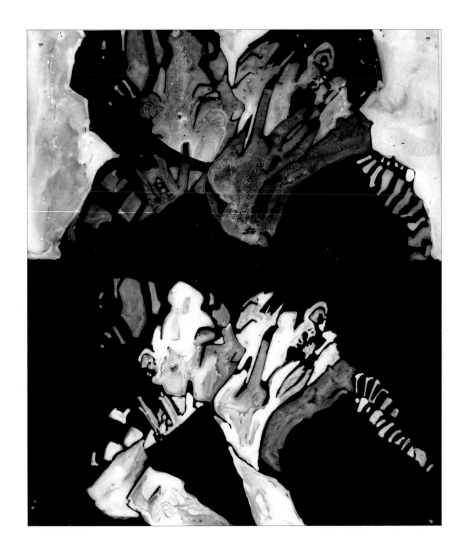

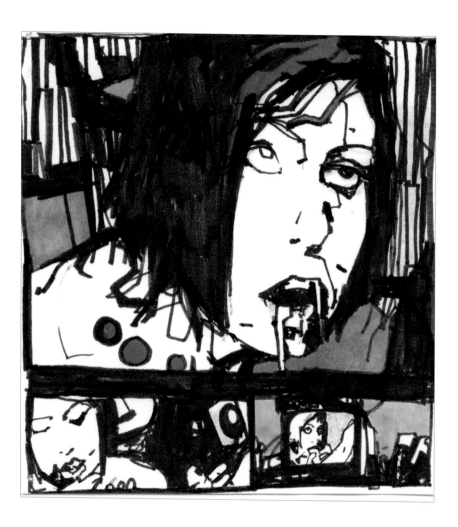

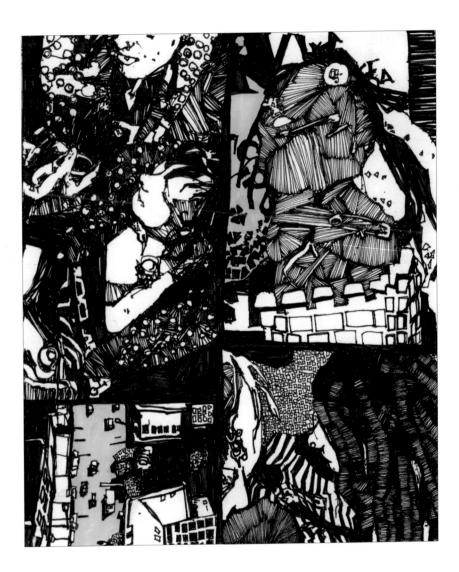

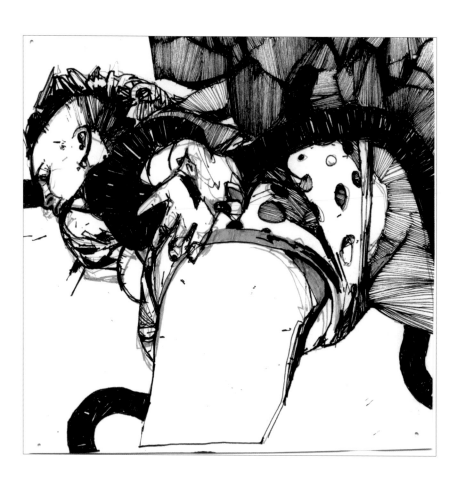

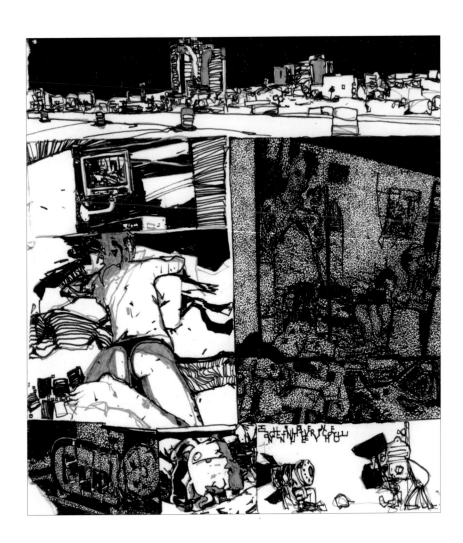

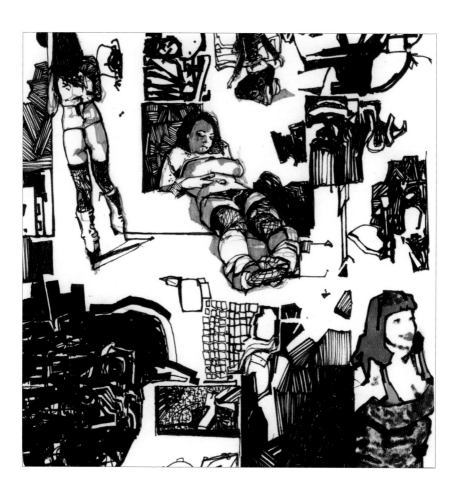

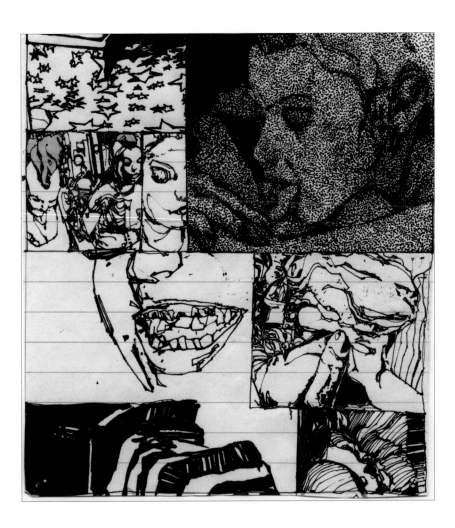

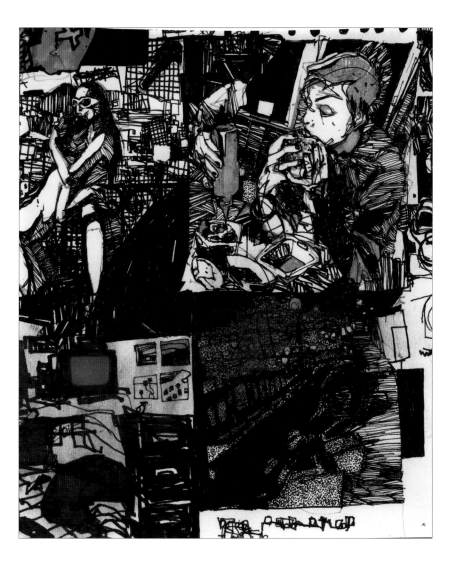

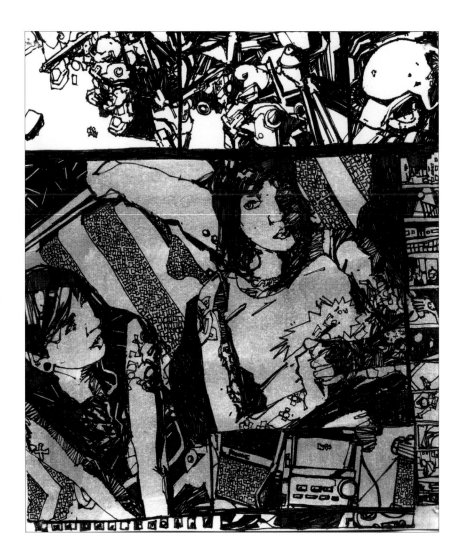

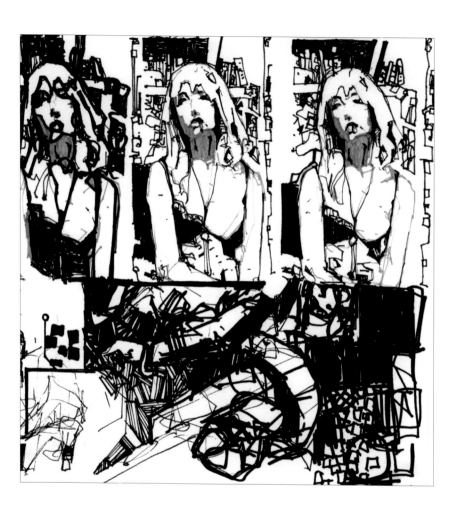

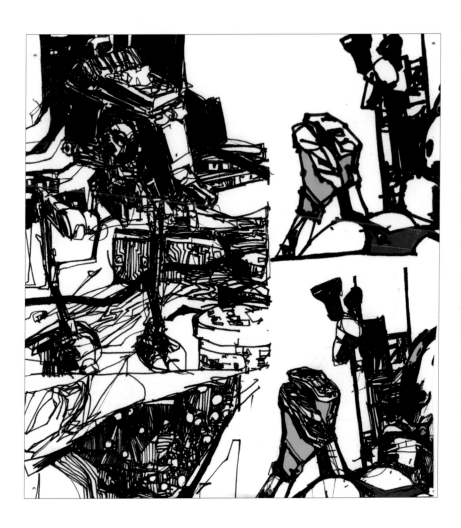

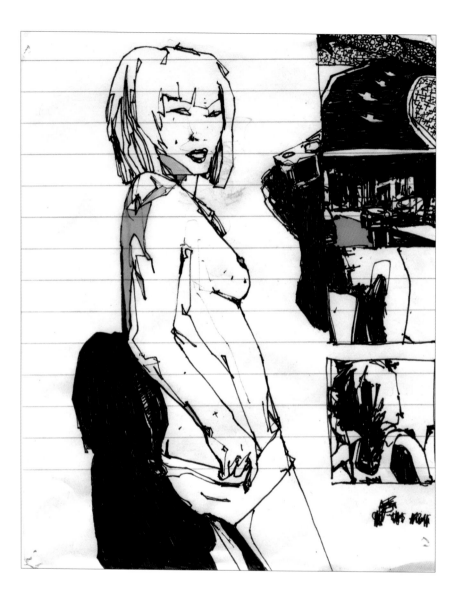

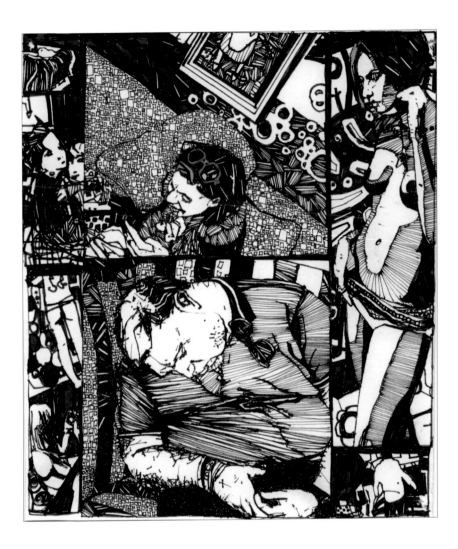

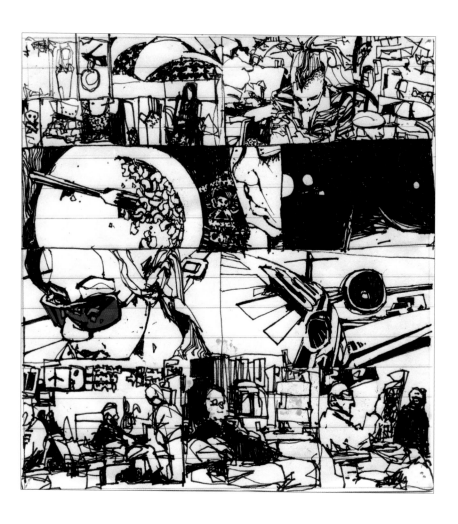

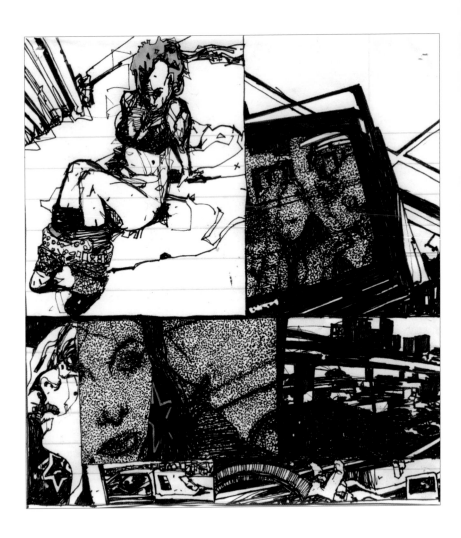

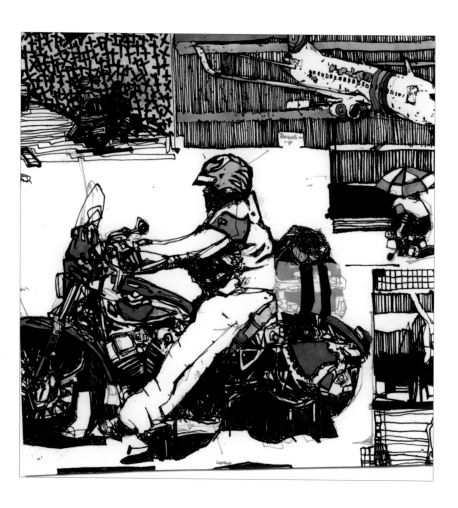

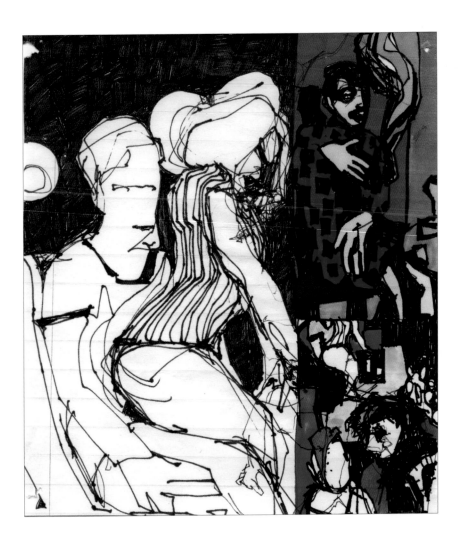

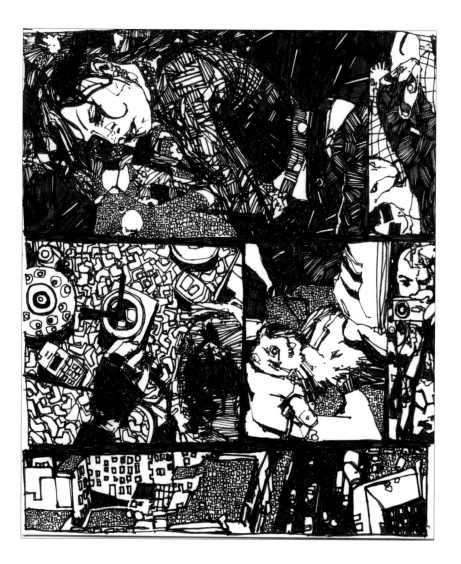

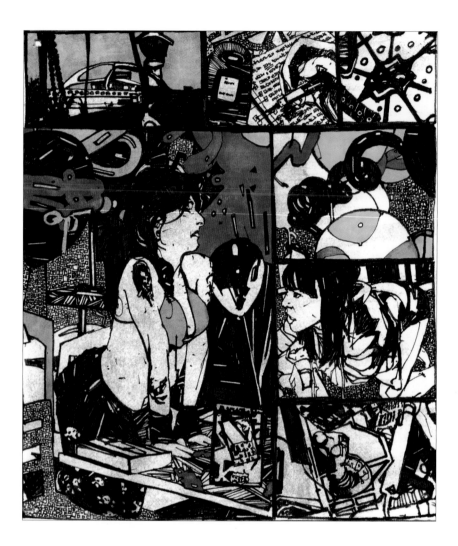

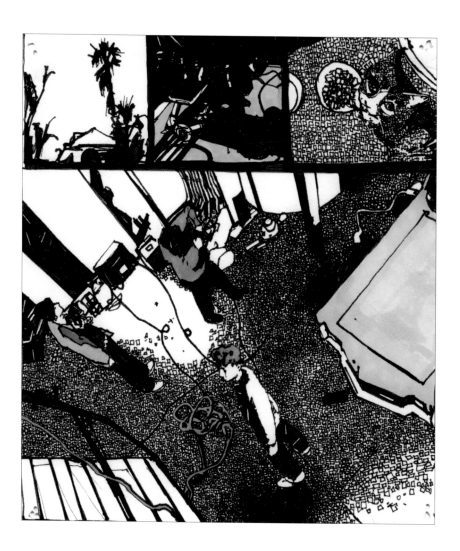

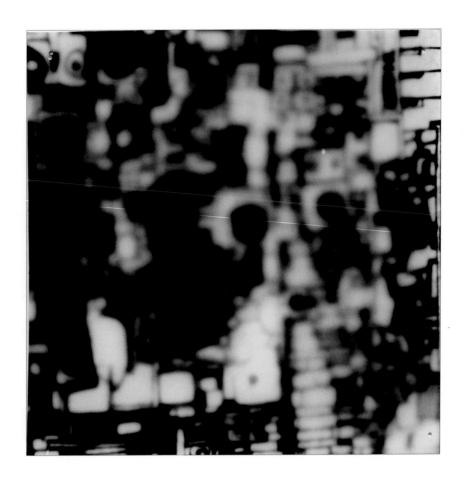

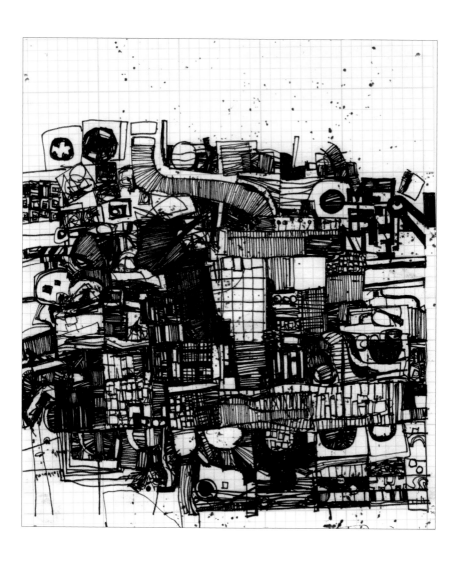

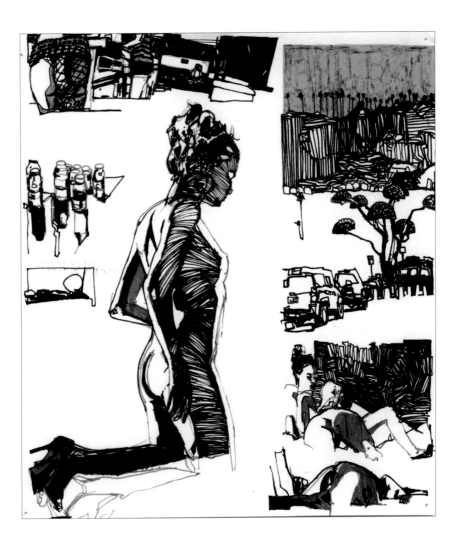

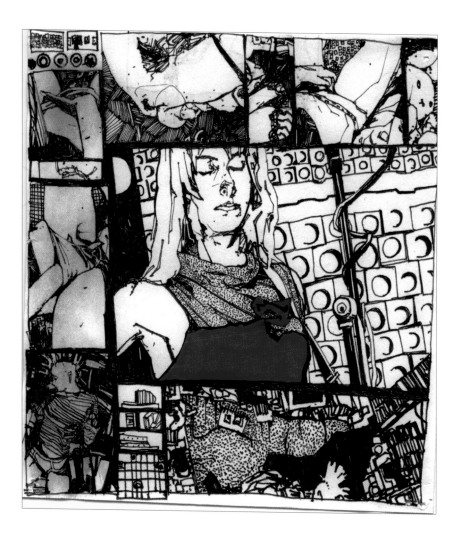

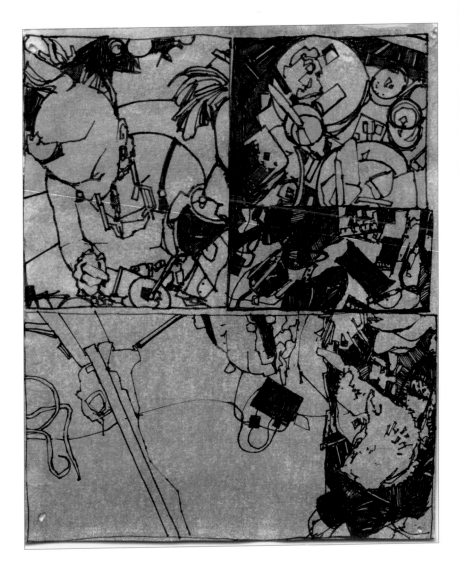

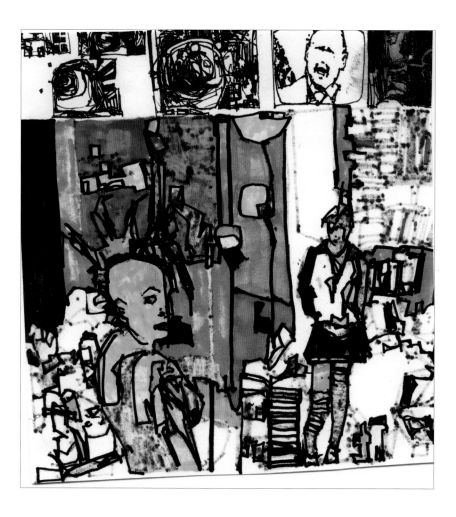

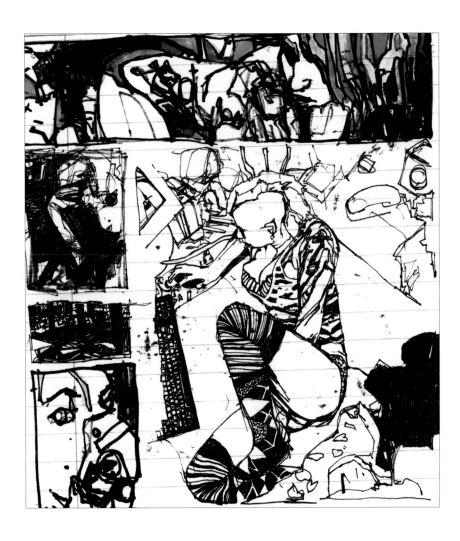

# How Do Your Friends Talk to You after You Start Making Porn?

**Home again.** On the phone.

"What's up, Craig?"

"Hey."

"So, what's the score, are you . . . uh . . . comin' to samurai night?"

"Am I coming? I don't know, what are we doing?"

"We're gonna . . . uh . . . go to BBQ's and then go watch, like, *Goyokin*."

"'Guy Oakin'? What the fuck is 'Guy Oakin'? Is it, like, gay Finnish porn?"

"Yes, Craig, it is gay Finnish porno, that's what I really want to watch. I want to go to BBQ's and then see mad Finnish loads. All over. Creamy."

"Is there, like, reacharounds where they're, like, *Finnish*ing each other off?"

"That was so stupid."

"Well, what the fuck is it? I don't want to watch Finn fucking."

"Oh, y'know, it's like it's a fucking samurai movie! You know, there's like vengeance and honor and . . . stuff."

"Is it gonna be like that last one with, like, people rolling around in barrels?"

"*I don't fucking know.* I haven't seen it. It's a fucking samurai classic or some shit, there's like some fighting in the snow or some shit and a kabuki face."

"A 'kabuki face'?"

"I don't know, I saw a still somewhere . . . okay, I got the box. 'A young samurai returns to his home and discovers a higher calling . . . revenge.' Okay? 'Directed by . . .' Okay? 'Tells the story of a haunted samurai . . . past massacre, revenge . . . . soul' . . . .another massacre . . . there's a woman and 'Mangobei absorbs a truly phenomenal amount of punishment as a way for atoning for the sins of his clan.' See, good, right?"

"And what's it called?"

"*Goyokin.*"

"Why is it called *Goyokin*?"

"I have no idea."

"And where are we eating?"

"BBQ's."

"Do I have to wear one of those greasy bibs?"

"I don't know, you wear whatever you want."

"No, but I mean, I'm just saying . . . "

"What the fuck is wrong with you?"

"No, I'm just *saying*, if I wear something *nice,* then are you gonna, like, drool *barbecue* sauce all over me?"

"I don't know. I have not yet come to a decision about that. Are you coming?"

"I guess. What time is it at?"

"6:30."

"Okay, but if it's fucking Finn porn I'm not watching you jerk off."

"Get off my phone, you freak."

# Like Porn
# Only a Place

**After the Berlin festival** **in** the fall, the next big porn thing is the Adult Video News Awards in Las Vegas in January.

It is of an altogether different character.

At the terminal we pass the slot machines for people who have to gamble as soon as they land and the cube-shaped glass-walled stores to buy chocolates and McCarron International's shockingly competent and stylishly executed stone-carved statues of oversized desert animals, which are the most, and possibly only, intentionally beautiful inanimate objects inside the city limits. Our hotel is next to a charred ruin. We go to Max Clamm's party at a place he's rented for the weekend called (like, on the actual documents) "The Pimp House." I start playing pool in a purple room with Clamm but he trundles off halfway through and lets his Vietnamese assistant finish for him. This is the way Clamm—with his shop-teacher glasses and rickety jokes—does everything.

Scholar, author, activist, intermittent dominatrix, and ex-whore Auspicia Clay and I sit in a giant chair shaped like a man's hand instead of doing what everyone else is doing, which is standing in the kitchen watching a girl shoot darts at balloons using pussy air squeezed through a blowgun she holds to her twat with her feet. She usually misses, and then Nasty Carl puts on a film he directed where I have sex. I ask why there aren't any dwarves and someone explains that the dwarf or little person who had been at the Pimp House had been a nuisance and had left or been made to leave. I eat lasagna and nachos and Wheat Thins while the man with the world's largest genital piercing asks me to choke him. People who are sex clowns or have sex with clowns watch themselves in movies where people have sex with clowns or are themselves sex clowns. One of them explains that he supports our troops and sends them his clown porn (and this has been independently confirmed by servicemen). I don't think anyone has sex at the party and people are mad at the man with the world's largest genital piercing (which you could put your hand through, but I don't—and I also don't choke him) because he pushes someone into the swimming pool.

The next morning I go to a corner store that has the alert, dangerously unreadable personality of someone on a lot of something and afraid of running out of it, to buy something for pimples or razor burn. One of the three clerks behind the counter at the corner store says, "$11.95? Damn, I go to Wal-Mart!" and they all laugh a lot and keep saying more things and I go away because the corner store scares me.

I walk across the parking lot, passing the burnt ruin, which someone at the hotel had explained had been a pizza parlor but last week a man came and set it on fire and stood and watched it burn until the police came to take him away. I pass two drunks, who heave themselves across the morning. It is pretty cold for a desert, and the street is quiet, and so are they, but one has a comb and combs his wet head while stumbling into his fellow and I, likewise preparing, smear myself with the corner-store stuff Candy said would work on me.

Osbie, Auspicia Clay, and I are interviewed by a lesbian for television and then we drive down the strip and I ask the cameraman what is the most fucked-up place he ever went to shoot and he says maybe a jail he went to to film transsexuals, or maybe Chernobyl.

Then we go to a tall-ceilinged hollow place with a broad black stage for Max Clamm's Porn Star Karaoke. There are not a lot of good songs in the book to sing. The tall porn journalist Monte Pentagram sings "Girl, You'll Be a Woman Soon," and one of the men who is a sex clown dresses in women's clothes and sings a song from *The Rocky Horror Picture Show,* and also a country song in his normal clothes, but also a cowboy hat, about being a "big dog"—which is distressing. Candy says she's bored and I start to say, "Hey, if you're bored it's because . . . " but before I finish she has taken off her shirt. So then I put my hand on her boob and then also another hand on Auspicia's boob—because she'd immediately taken off her shirt, too, when Candy did—and I lean back into the candy-flake red cushions of the booth, well satisfied with this state of affairs, but it doesn't last because a bouncer tells them not to show boobs. And then Osbie sings:

> *There is nothin' fair in this world*
> *There is nothin' safe in this world*
> *And there's nothin' sure in this world*
> *And there's nothin' pure in this world*

and the rest of a Billy Idol song and is good at it because you believe him.

Then, secretly and mushy-faced, Max Clamm takes Osbie aside to tell him two things:

1. It comes down to you and the sex clown man for Clamm's $500 singing prize
2. It is important that you sing another song and win because he doesn't have the money for the $500 singing prize

and then Clamm goes in the corner with a pack of likewise large, grave-looking, dark-suited men bent over some things and looking like a dissident cell in a cold place. Then Daisy Wallace from clown porn—the only female porn star to sing that night—sings:

> *I'm sailing away, set an open course for the virgin sea*
> *I've got to be free, free to face the life that's ahead of me*

and the rest of "Come Sail Away" by Styx, and then bites Osbie in the stomach.

No one knows if the low turnout is because of the twenty-dollar door price or because of some other and more fundamental conceptual flaw in Porn Star Karaoke, but the men who own the karaoke house are angry with Clamm and hold him. He will pay them back, he says, but not soon, and they, shrewdly demanding collateral, confiscate a set of custom hula hoops from the pussy-darts girl.

Meanwhile, hungrily, we ride out looking for food downtown in the night, but there is none. The dizzy optical rugs and mirroring walls of unusually empty casinos lead around curves and past brass-handled glass to closed places, so finally, our numbers dwindling, we settle for a floorside place on the strip with a parched, butter-resistant, tomato-garlic bread and Osbie throws up.

There is a lesson in vomiting—when the mind finally forgets, the body remembers.

In Las Vegas—on any day—on the strip and its tributaries, you will see every freak, cheesy men, ads for things on stages no one sane would sit through, ordinary citizens with balloon animals on their heads, the worst version of every idea, guilelessly ugly human faces that have lost long before the wheel even spins.

"I got a . . . onamgolubla . . . gnuasbahuh . . . its . . . is *black!* . . . I give . . . umblesnuh to you for . . . two hundred—one hundred dollars?" says one on a corner.

"No, but thanks." The light changes, and with our first step away from him, like it pulled his plug, like selling or pimping off that onamgolubla was really his last chance, he falls smack over—the way a telephone pole would, with straight legs right past forty-five degrees—facewise into a curb.

"*Damn!* Maybe we should get a . . . "

But no, there's already an ambulance there. It was picking up a different unconscious bleeding drunk ten feet ahead.

You would not want to be a Las Vegas cop because this is

normal. This is the constant landscape of the place; chips in boxes broken in alleys; ads for twat wrapped round poles; an exhibit of the mutilated corpses of Chinese men in formaldehyde; the thawed-out leather face of an ancient, gaunt quadriplegic steering his retrofitted tin chair over uneven pavement and past scrims in safety orange with a black joystick; always a choice between several equally cornball options; the Luxor pyramid—nothing but a colossal, leaking roof—and rows of absolutely implausible deceptions all down the Strip. This is not the Taj Mahal. This is not Versailles. This is not a Gold Mine. There is a wild disconnect between the spangled, exotic night-show dream that the city dreams out loud and the staid convention fumblers at the felted tables, who are no more able to grab that dream than they can grab colored light.

And there is always a lot of vomiting. This isn't easy on the talent on the floor of the AVN convention because many of the ones most likely to have to go throw up also want and possibly need escorts (a director or a makeup girl) any time they leave their booths to shove, chunky-shoed and bustily, through fans cut loose from the autograph lines that organize them.

Anyone on their way to vomit will first pass the complex and muscular Chuck Devil—The Man Who Has a Pussy—because the AVN, which will make him Transsexual Performer of the Year, put him next to the restrooms. He is, about this, as he is about many things, as *you*'d pretty much have to be if *you* were a man with a pussy, both philosophical and practical—"Hey, this way everybody sees me, right?" Not only is he a male transsexual (words' meanings become more subtle around Chuck) sex performer with a vagina, he is also quite possibly the only human to have ever been very attractive as both a man and a woman without looking in any way androgynous, having gone from a completely doable oh-

my-God-why-would-you-wanna-be-a-guy model-type chick to
an economically significant chunk of leather-daddy fans' idea
of a very good time despite never having bothered to get a
cock. He is a man of wide and varied experience who also has
a lot of female fans, including one of the in-no-way-unhouse-
wifely waitresses at the Mirage buffet (whether a waitress is a
waitress if she works at a buffet seems like one of the easier
category questions here), where Chuck downs the mad carbs
that, along with doses of hormones, fuel his black-tattooed
biceps and triceps and where, near the table's other end, the
cable cameraman is saying how he knows my paintings, and
likes them.

What do you say to your fans? With his, Chuck jokes easily,
waving his cigar, because if you like Chuck you probably have
a sense of humor, because you find yourself stirred by the
sight of something that might seem, by quite a few measures
that like to think of themselves as normal, totally batshit crazy.
I am, as usual, at a loss—behind my mounded tray of olives,
quesadillas, and manicotti—not because I don't like compli-
ments, but because I feel like there's something I should be
able to learn from or share with a nice-seeming cameraguy
named Kasimir, who likes things I make, but I don't know
what that is yet. Especially considering that the only other
thing in Las Vegas that he likes is Cirque du Soleil (which
I've never seen but which Patton Oswalt described as a show
where everything "is wet and French and gay and on fire").
What do you do with fans?

When I ask Courtney Tables (who doesn't vomit, so far as
I know, during the convention, but does it in her movies a lot)
if she noticed a small zone of sweat and deodorant residue
that some girls notice on their shoulders from being repeatedly arm in arm with a weekendful of fans for photographs,

she says no, but then explains how, one day, after the convention, she noticed cum jizzed up on the side of her clothes and, though at first repelled, decided she was impressed with herself for inspiring this discreet wad and it was hot that, when just touching her, some lonely soul had quietly shot and smothered a humble load on her dress, and she went out wearing it, without cleaning it, all night.

Unlike a comic book convention or a trade show, the fans don't talk to each other, because, although it is seen by as many people and generates far more money than the other movie business, porn is not a mass medium. A president's hand-picked man almost got thrown off the Supreme Court for discussing what happened in a porn movie in mixed company.

So even though there are crowds and crowds, the autograph hounds look, in this context, even more alone than they probably usually are. They lean heavily toward a wobbling kind of man wearing a blatant black T-shirt telling people about loving porn, that maybe they only get to wear there or, maybe, they wear inside during dreary all-male days. The porn stars' days with them, with both fans and stars now in outfits that make obvious what is usually not noticed or assumed when a five-foot blonde hottie in a frumpcoat and wool hat passes a closely-grocery-holding engineer in an LA shoe shop or car lot, are strange.

ooooooooo

There's this thing Lana Lespalier said while I was in LA to shoot *Girls Are Liars*. We were at the 101 Diner and I was trying to decide between corned beef on rye and huevos rancheros.

"It's strange," I said, seeing a huge lightbulb-shaped blonde with half her tanned rack peeking at the frank moustache of the man across the table, "in New York, in like Williamsburg, you go to a diner like this and you see all these people there trying to look like porn stars. But you come to LA, and you look around and most of the people look just exactly the same, but some of them actually *are*."

"Most people," said Lana simply, "are weird losers."

That may be true, but most people are also normal losers.

The average man, or, at least, the average American man, the average consumer of American pornography, who might've been recognizing Lana at that moment, over a tuna melt, from, say, *Ass Theatre Volume 3*, is white, thirty-six or thirty-seven, married, has two or three kids, lives in a house, either voted for George W. Bush in 2004 or didn't vote, watches football, and believes that *as Elisha was on the road to Bethel some youths came out of the town and jeered at him, saying, "Go on up, you baldhead!" Then Elisha turned around, looked at them and called down a curse on them in the name of the Lord. Then two she-bears came out of the woods and mauled forty-two of the youths*, and everything else it says in the Bible—or at least thinks he does.

I'm not sure I know anyone like that. So where are they?

Airports, mostly. Airports are where Industry people usually see normal Americans and airports correspond roughly to the mental image Industry people have of Normal America. That is, a huge, occasionally carpeted puzzle palace of metal, glass, Cinnabons, and magazines where you follow the instructions of uniformed people—sit down, stand, wait, give or take things, show things, take things off, answer personal questions—and follow signs through corridors full of listless women and men where nothing ever seems to happen past the logos of corporations and on to other labeled rooms that you have to go through to get from New York or Miami to Los Angeles or San Francisco.

And what do all the jerseyed men, and girls in sweatshirts saying the names of colleges, and all the other weird losers, want? And where are they going? It's hard to be sure, but in airports you'll notice that every television is tuned *always* to CNN, and on it Lou Dobbs is *always* complaining about immigrants, and also *always* there are a disproportionate number of flights and announcements of flights going to Las Vegas, Nevada. In the zeros, Vegas is very big, and growing fast.

Among Republicans I know, half are alcoholics and half are wealthy gambling addicts. These halves both like to go to Las Vegas and are its fauna.

Alcoholics have earned, through centuries of articulate literary achievement and amusing behavior, a certain amount of tolerance in the public imagination for themselves and for their illness. The wealthy gambling addict, however, is at the moment impossible to grasp without recourse to some theory of devolution deduced from studies of Risk-Reward-Reaction behavior in primate research labs. The ones I know already have everything they want that money could possibly be traded *for*.

The third thing of Las Vegas is sex, which is easy. As a Digital Playground contract girl pins Candy between a brass slot machine and its dedicated chair and mutters, "I'm *so* oversexed" while creeping over and into her like a taut albino spiderperson, it is obvious that sex is the brightest and cleverest of the three siblings—the one with a future. You take its side and are glad it has its city and pity it that it has to share.

The talent that gathers around the Circle Bar in Vegas's Venetian Hotel during the annual Adult Video News Awards is full of such pussy talk. *Le Sexe qui Parle*—"The Sex That Talks." If sex could talk it would ask everyone to stop staring at it and to stop talking about it when it wasn't around. And ask why it couldn't sit in the front and why it wasn't allowed in bars. If sex could talk it would say it was hungry and tired and ask why everyone couldn't just let it be by itself instead of going on this endless trip stuck in the backseat between Money and Confusion. But then again, if sex could talk, it would also say it wanted to be in movies.

At the convention, the two rules of the 101 would appear to be in full effect—everyone who looks like a porn star is one, and most people are weird losers.

∘∘∘∘∘∘∘∘∘∘

Let's drop a few sentences about porn *guys*. I know—*ew*. But know that whatever it is about porn guys, it also is about *guys*, because porn guys mirror precisely the male population, at least before they go to the gym. Any demographic skew is more down to opportunity than anything else. Personality-wise, the range of men you see in porn is exactly like the range of other men, only nakeder and lucky. And the physical requirements of the job, despite a lot of lore to the contrary on both sides of the aisle, do not display themselves in any observable off-the-job behavior.

If a baby is born, it is more likely to grow up to become a U.S. congressman than a porn guy, but whatever. People don't line up to gawk at luck. There are no waddling lines of women waiting to have things signed by porn guys (except *very* rare celebrity-status-getting-interviewed-on-non-adult-channels-because-they-actually-tried-for-a-long-time-to-get-mainstream-publicity ones like Ron Jeremy).

So then, since we're in Las Vegas, let's turn our attention to their brothers, the *other* porn guys. The guys who like porn.

Consider: There was once a (mainstream) movie called

*Groundhog Day* about a guy cursed to live the exact same day in the same shit town millions of times until he convinces Andie McDowell to like him. Because, despite being one of the finest films ever made, it was executed as a light 1980s comedy, he gets the girl in the end. However, it becomes clear to anyone paying attention that it takes more time and more attempts than he would have otherwise had in his whole life.

One of his schemes involves taking advantage of finding out that she majored in nineteenth-century French poetry. "I've got some French poetry here. Baudelaire. I will read to you . . . " But of course he never does read Baudelaire out loud—he says something else in French at one point and then reads some other thing later about a tree. He doesn't because, the very first time anyone (a whore) agreed to have sex with Baudelaire, Baudelaire got syphilis—totally untreatable in that luxurious, velvety, magical French century—and he spent the rest of his social, medical, psychological, and creative life dealing with its consequences. Reading out loud to Andie McDowell the majestically dire things Baudelaire wrote in that thirty-year grip would have not only introduced the sound of *real* pain into *Groundhog Day* (which had to keep its light-'80s-comedy clothes on) but also stretched the credibility of peppy Andie ("I want what *everyone* wants—home, family, career . . . ") who probably also would have liked to go to the Louvre with Toulouse-Lautrec rather than drink beer and have sex.

And the *only* way to deal with guys—porn guys, groundhog guys—these hounding, mobile bags of pain, is light comedy. These bumblers in lines, programmers, two-handed clutchers, these bloggers with their pictures near breasts, these meat-stacks, sad-sacks, these weezing mouth-breathers, nodding Cro-Magnons, ghost-costume-sized hip-hop shirt roamers, these collectors, these enthusiasts, pederasts, Ozzytees, these waist-touchers, wasted brokers, jokers, grinners, tit-seekers, watchers, these bulky humans and beanpoles processed in bulk, these barn-door-sized target audiences, these red bosses and red employees and simultaneous electronics-convention attendees, these *men*, these fat-ass motherfuckers in their bloatiness and massy fat pants. Whatever, *civilians*. Because the other option is *thinking* about them in their caterpillaring lines around booths as they shuffle.

A girl once took me to see some special-needs kids she worked with, all adopted. There was one kid there, fourteen, brains and senses totally normal—*totally aware*—but he could only really smile or not smile, or shift a bit in his wheelchair, and, of course, drool.

I looked at him from the quiet edge of the visit (I was just some boyfriend) and I thought, *I've got two choices here.*

The first choice is to just think of him as a fourteen-year-old boy—like a little me—sitting there in his chair with his also-adopted-and-damaged sister in the next room hopping up and down and masturbating herself in front of some cable kids show and groaning, and his damaged little foster brother off in his crib staring at a ceiling and looking like Jabba the Hut, and this foster mom and dad massaging his fourteen-year-old shoulders and all in his face going, "Oh, Stevie likes it when there's pretty girls on TV! Don't you, Stevie—see? Look at you *smiling*!"

In his position, what would *I* do? He has a normal brain, remember, it is just his body that has got him here. If it were me—if I were him—I would be trying to learn Morse code. Then I could bang out, "Fuck *off* all you people, let go of my head and stop joking with me about all the tits on TV I can't ever touch and just park me somewhere and let me die" on the wall until someone did or until I knocked myself forever unconscious. That is what I would do.

And this is a horrible thing to say, of course, but it's what I thought when I extended my sympathy over to this paralytic. And it was so horrible I could barely look at him.

Imagine the life of a kid who on handing-out-lives day opened up the little envelope and found out he got assigned *unremitting misery forever*—and everybody is just like, What's with your boyfriend over there, he doesn't like Stevie? No, I just can't *handle* Stevie. My heart goes out to him. And then it comes right back, sweating, and it jams the door shut behind it and tells me never to let it go out there ever again. And I just stare and deal.

Because the only other option is much worse, and I can't take it. The other option is just *not* thinking of him as a person, pretending he's some little subhuman. And I can't go there, even if it would help me make it through the hour without wanting to just stab shit.

Every time you see an abject life about which you can do nothing, you make some version of this choice.

The girls look at these fans, and they *have* to just go: "Retards," and then ask exactly how much they're getting paid to let the retards hop all around them today. But every once in a while one retard looks up while you're going through doing your little boyfriend/bodyguard escort-the-babe-through-the-throng routine and you see his eye and you think, "Yeah, buddy, I know. You know who I am? I'm just the schmuck who got there first. That's all."

It's just a tiny gap but it would take the world to close that gap. Hey, most of them are already even walking around with paper cups drinking *beer*! Hey, *halfway* to heaven already. One thing the anecdotal evidence would appear to suggest about drinking beer and having sex with girls is: it's a *real* thing—people do it. No one is ever going to the Louvre with Toulouse-Lautrec ever again.

And if you look at our split species—the men with their male pornographies of *Girls Next Door* and *Drunk Sorority Babes*—and then knock with your pizza box on the door of the actual girls-next-door who are deep in *their* pornographies—their romances of Toulouse-Lautrecs and Baudelaires and Boba Fetts and pirates and chivalries and musical gypsy river-rats and good-hearted land-owning duelists and a million other things that could never, ever be, and never were—it is difficult to figure whose dilemma is more heartbreaking. The one pining for a phantom thing, or the one pining for what could so easily be arranged if only the world were not so poorly organized.

When you consider the thirty-six pornographic videos that are being made today, and were made yesterday, and the day before and the day before that, and are made every single day, and if you add in all the romance novels and soap operas and socially acceptable sentimental movies and all the other brands of entertainment that exist not because their inventors hoped their audiences would find them, y'know, interesting as things, but because they allow their audiences to pretend to be wanted in the way they want to be wanted by ones that they want to want them—instead of being wanted by people they don't want or by no one at all—and then remember each represents an entire *audience*, then you will immediately see how arid and failed the human project is and how, when you ask people to give up their addictions, they are bound to ask you just what then they are going to get in return.

∘∘∘∘∘∘∘∘∘

*My Hot Wife Is Fucking Blackzilla* beats out *My Daughter's Fucking Blackzilla* for Best Interracial Series, *Cheating Housewives 3* wins Best Specialty Release—MILF, and *Big Wet Asses* wins Best Anal-Themed Series (quite deservedly, from what I've seen), but none of this means much to anyone at the last party on AVN weekend. The big news is that DiVinethings.com's Jimmy Gun won Best Male Newcomer and Lana LaValier's house burned down.

At the by-invite-only alt-porn party, held, with symbolism lost on nobody, around the balconied rim of a larger and louder normal porn event charging all its guests and thick with smoke and jerks, there are wandering men who wind easily over the porn/alt-porn border. One gropes everyone like a crustacean and wears a turban, and another sidles in to say, "You're making music with your thighs," to Polly Morning, while in a curtained booth a crone sits offering to tell people what the future is. Candy and Sunday Dark sit off in a corner looking like bleak mohawked twins of hate and another Las Vegas bouncer tells another girl to put on her clothes. They don't let in Leom, who arrives late and confused from the awards, Intensity having arranged for *New Wave Sluts* to win something in the wrong category.

The rest of the weekend is full of unexpected reversals and creeps.

At the Venetian, I spit on a giant in an electrical hat because he suggests to me out loud that I like My Chemical Romance while a carpetful of photographers watches. No one knows who he is, or why anyone would do a thing like that.

In the depths of the hotel, between immobile women posed like guarding columns, there are lizard-men at fetish parties, obliging and ill-proportioned, of unclear age, sober and eager, whose facial hair is incongruous with the shining lizard-dark man-suits they aren't pulling off and that you sincerely pray they won't pull off. A stubbly faced and stub-legged one in bicycle-like pants that stop short of the knobs of his knees, whose badged shirt in blue rubber and moistly energetic manner mark him as some chief of theirs, warns, "Keep quiet in these halls, there are some serious high rollers in these suites who will have us tossed out," before he hobbles hunchingly back into the sheathed, saurian rituals inhabiting the underlit block of linked rooms.

We do keep quiet—and we look for a different party. Candy, Osbie, Auspicia, and I leave an elevator and land in a spoked room, precisely identical, from its bone-white fixtures to the marble table at its hub, to the room we'd just entered the elevator from. We are uncertain if we are where we intend to be and uncertain if we wanted to go there anyway.

A hotel full of guests, with seventy restaurants and canals inside, and it is making no sound at all. The patterned carpets absorb all sound. When we manage to get people on the phone they give us room numbers that might not exist. Immobile guards in deep blue with unsympathetic eyes direct us to floors we've already seen, make impossible demands, or simply tell us we should go away from the Venetian Hotel. We wander lost through identical levels, occasionally switching back, but are never certain that each place is not exactly the last place, with the elevator button simply serving as a trick trigger, spinning all the room numbers up or down.

I imagine that if we don't leave we'll be found dead in a week or two by room service at the end of a long corridor, taken out by a poisoned fountain or cursed statue or just starvation, so we get back in the elevator. There we find the boss monster: a dreary sodomizer—five feet tall and carved from a brick of skin the red of dog food—Jack Fuchsmore, the endpoint of every dwindling, humdrum discussion of porn's horrible potential. With his misogyny, true actual depravity, and deep wrongness, with his egotistical and yellow cowboy hat balanced like a Pringle on his crude, moist head, he, like all nightmares, is, in every sense, What You Expect.

He makes movies that look exactly like the movies people who think you shouldn't watch porn imagine when they imagine porn.

The girl strangely accompanying him is both making eye contact with me and grinning, despite the fact it is 11:00 P.M. and the convention is long over. She must be insane or a whore, since none of the talent smile at people they don't know after convention hours. Fuchsmore, who has a record of harvesting unsuspecting talent from Osbie's movies and therefore has probably seen most of us having sex, says a measured, howdylike "Hello," with a generosity that seems to welcome us not only to his elevator but to all the elevators, hotels, sprawl, and desert for miles around.

"Hey," I say back on behalf of our half of the little moving room, and, before leaving, as we tensely count the fisheye views of ourselves in the numbered brass buttons, the degrader mutters a dirty little song secretly to Candy, that only she can hear, the only one of us not yet in Osbie's movies and so, as yet, not anointed by his defiling and seeking looking.

We get spit out somewhere. As we head away, Osbie's girlfriend or ex-girlfriend, drunk and high, via cell from New York, moans demented lies at him until he cries.

⊛⊛⊛⊛⊛⊛⊛⊛⊛

"Coco's is so alt," says Auspicia, as the Coco's sign—blue on an indecisive cream—blossoms out of the dark edge of Tropicana Ave. We all think this is funny. It is that late and we are that drunk.

To anyone not wild to shop, to gamble, or to pay to fondle unavailable snatch through dry fabric (or, for a further fee, to plunge in), that is to anyone not caught in the grip of capitalism's most familiar fevers, the Strip collapses into a network of stage flats behind which a real city, with actual inhabitants and unplanned events other than vomiting, may or may not be hiding. In bad weather it's no fun to roam around, and everything is farther apart that season because half the lots are just half-constructed or half-demolished hotels. When the errands are done, we spend days making semimotivated choices, like crawlers in a mediocre zoo—Do you want to see the vulture? Yeah, sure, let's go see the vulture—before fetching up during every night's last phase at Coco's.

A short trip off the Strip, it is, if not exactly safe, then at least defensible, with clear views of the only entrance from all tables and a sparse and sluggish clientele of senior citizens and the unconscious homeless.

We talk for hours and complain—Candy, Auspicia, Osbie, and I—and say all the things we would do if we were in charge of alternative pornography or Las Vegas or America and also talk about things that are far away or happened a long time before and eat pies and eggs. And we are grateful for the warmth of the cheap chain restaurant and to be an entire city block from the sound of slots.

People often say: "Why is porn so *boring?*—and it's not even *hot*, it's just the *same thing* over and over." This is a distressing attitude to those of us who see widespread promiscuity as a desirable social goal. People who hold it would do well to visit our corner at Coco's on Tropicana and breathe its late-night atmosphere of frustration and old ketchup, next door to the dead remains of an incinerated pizza parlor.

Here, drinking lemonade, is Osbie Feel: half-Irish, half-Mexican, one of those shipwrecks of wasted talent you see sloping, overdressed, darkly sideways out of bars all over Los Angeles—whose dream is a retelling of the entirely nonfictional connections between Hitler and the Bush family during World War II overlaid with an apocalypse of fat-assed Nazi sluts in crisp leather getting violated in appalling ceremonies—who can't even convince GSP to properly distribute an aimlessly modish movie about cute, pale women in stripy socks fucking half a Jew, one-point-five Mexicans, and a black guy.

Here, bent over a salad, is Auspicia Clay, who looks like an assistant veterinarian and for whom the words *adult industry* are not just a euphemism for *porno* but rather a useful term to describe a long and irrational résumé tied together only by the fact that nothing on it should be done to children. She *might* try to persuade another self-described female-friendly production company to fund a movie where girls fuck boys who fuck other boys in places all over New York City, or she *might* try to find a fetish-friendly production company to help Ella Revenge shoot a movie where she's fucked with a loaded gun—or she might just relax into steadier and better paychecks, writing reviews of dildos and kicking businessmen in small hotel rooms.

Here's Candy Crushed, barely five feet and eating toast, who people want for all kinds of movies but who only likes to watch ones where big-titted girls get done from behind by monsters with tentacles.

Auspicia and Osbie talk about which people's movies they've seen and whether or not they're idiots, Auspicia and I talk about trying to explain porn to people who aren't in porn, Osbie and Candy talk about *Star Wars*, Candy and I talk about how hard we should try to get anything done in Las Vegas, Osbie and I talk about class warfare, Auspicia and Candy talk about the orthopedic benefits of breast-reduction surgery, but mostly we bat the convention and all its tired porn clichés around until the corner booth is a sauna of listless hate.

And all over the margins of the Strip, there are other parapornographic people in other diners who would like to think they are trying to do something better and different and find it exhausting.

It is a lot like what happens after art openings.

In addition to the ways already mentioned, the porn business is like the art business in that there's not a lot of percentage in trying to expand into new markets.

You can make a record for people who hate all the music that's out there and get rich and famous doing it. You can make a movie (a regular movie) for people who hate all the movies out there and get rich and famous doing it. This is because everyone listens to music and watches movies.

However, people who hate all the art out there aren't even in the museum to begin with. In fact, they think everybody who *is* in the museum is a total asshole, and so if you make art for people who don't like art they'll never know it's there. So then what? So the people who make good and innovative art for people who don't like art stop making art and go back to their day jobs like they never existed. The art world has so successfully eliminated so many people from its audience that it's created not only the illusion that what people most want to see is some quote from Alexander Haig written in Hunt's Ketchup across a photo of Mary Kate Olsen but also the illusion that the only kind of art any art person would ever want to make anymore would be something roughly equivalent to some quote from Alexander Haig written in Hunt's Ketchup across a photo of Mary Kate Olsen.

Would-be good and innovative pornographers have this same dilemma. If you don't see how, reread the paragraph above with the word *porn* where it says *art, adult video store* where it says *museum,* and *Ass-Whores from Planet Squirt* where it says *some quote from Alexander Haig written in Hunt's Ketchup across a photo of Mary Kate Olsen.*

And as easy as it is to see all these would-be-difference-making pornographers as cells of grumpy dissidents, it is equally easy for them to see themselves as not that at all, because it's hard to think how different porn might happen or matter, and because it's hard, period, and because none of them agree, and because everyone's half inclined to get the fuck out of this business next year anyway, and because money, and because the awful awful rest of porn is way bigger than they'll ever be, and because, most of all, it's just *porn.*

There's always that way out. Better porn might matter and it might make things better, but nobody's proved it yet, and so you can always just say, "Fuck it, it's just porn," and get off your high horse and go do whatever else and make some money.

°°°°°°°°°

And then the last morning—cold again, and deadly dull, and with hours to kill before the plane out of Vegas.

We watch *Mythbusters* on TV—the show where they try to figure out if things in movies could really happen. They test whether you could chop a sword in half or bounce down a series of awnings. They do not test out what really happens when barely legal sluts have a sleepover. Osbie tells The Story about the Man Who Shattered His Arm Because It Got Nitrogen on It, The Story about the People Who Sold Their Babies, and The Story about Being Disgusted by the Ocean.

We check out and wait for a cab on the corner, sitting on our bags in the unfairly seasonable weather, next to the frozen pond at the foot of the icicled fountain in front of the Tropicana. The tourists end up throwing their dimes at, rather than into, the pond and the coins skid and ping off the sealed-in green glass of half-sunk beer bottles and leave the year's first wishes faceup on the ice. A cab shows up and we go home.

After a couple months, a lot of dicking around, and a lot of frantic phone calls from Max Clamm where he jabbers to anyone who'll listen about a TV idea he's trying to sell to Disney built around a girl he knows who thinks she's from space, Clamm manages to convince Bill and Hillary Productions to let Osbie do another movie. Candy and I head back to LA to help out.

# Fish, Pig, Bug, etc.

**Alice had moved** to North Carolina, so Candy and I start each morning at the Aura Hotel with the cameraman, Rob Chuckler, a balding pinup photographer whose remaining hair sticks out in a caricature of slow confusion, and a production assistant named Fish. From a parking lot that slopes and laps unevenly around the stilts holding up the balconies as if the asphalt had set in midslosh, we drive over the 101 and take a wide road down to South

Central. Heading south, the signs change colors, and grow and get less regular and farther apart. As the buildings flatten, Rob tells stories about hotel rooms or recording studios or we try to figure out Fish, who, even early in the morning, is absolutely inscrutable.

A native of some town or village between Kyoto and Tokyo, he is eerily enthusiastic about passing the big Staples outlet, which shines out from downtown LA like a mouthful of great glass teeth at everyone on the freeway. When asked whether he likes working on porn, Fish says, "I like doing the jobs no one else wants to do." Since, on this production, "the jobs no one else wants to do" include ridding a warehouse set of not just human shit but the waste products of up to a quarter of the Chinese Zodiac, while the jobs everyone else *did* want to do included having sex with porn stars two at a time—you wonder. He might be a virgin. He throws up after watching his first scene.

The project is plagued by the predictable sorts of problems: the lights from Clamm's last production, somewhere in Eastern Europe, are being held as hostage or collateral by its director, pending fulfillment of some pact no one else properly understands; the police accuse the property manager of giving marijuana to a developmentally disabled child; a man is found who is willing to rent out a pig, but when the time comes to pick it up the man says he's going out and will be too drunk to receive visitors when he comes back. "Also, it will be very dark," he says "and the pig is black."

The first morning of actual shooting, Candy has a strange dream where I continuously ejaculate against an uninterrupted field of multiracial flesh. It is a pretty fair, if abstract, summary of my character's part in the movie. I can't remember my own dreams, but somehow in the night I remembered the name of the guy helping with the lights—Spurgeon—and it is comforting. This is in addition to Fish—and these are the people using their *real* names.

No one knows the pig's name; I name it Puggsley. Someone else names it Apple. It's his first movie, too. They tell Clamm to feed him dog food, but there isn't any. Marisa Hart and Candy visit him, bringing cornflakes, but he doesn't want to see anyone. He is in a bathroom, unhappy, not squealing, just turning the dark, oily bulbs of his animal eyes on everyone over him and squeezing the pull cords of the bending muscle under the stubby rubber-leather length of his seeking pig nose. He paces through the dry, bent flakes, scattered on square tiles sinking and darkening and distorting toward a storm drain blacker than him, on tapering hooves as light as a set of corks, like he is something on the wrong chessboard, too big to be a piece, too small to play. The girls want to hold and comfort him, but when Marisa reaches out a long, polished stripper arm, he scrambles into an impossible corner behind a toilet, and they leave to let him eat in peace. When it's time for his scene, he's violently ill all over the AVN's 2008 Performer of the Year.

The script is based on Osbie Feel's loose, and radically politicized, interpretation of the famous death of white dock worker William Lyons at the hands of the black pimp "Stagger" Lee Shelton during or after a card game at a saloon on the corner of Eleventh and Morgan, Saint Louis, Missouri, over a hundred years ago.

Everyone knew it would only be a matter of time before Feel ran afoul of the studio—and he does. Although it is a staple of the many songs written about the murder since 1895—by everyone from Mississippi John Hurt to Huey Lewis and the News to Nick Cave, the Clash, and Modern Life Is

War—Bill and Hillary Productions feel that Stagger's job, that is, his status as an entity primarily concerned with arranging for women to have sex for money, makes the murderer an inappropriate subject for a pornographic film.

So Stagger Lee (played by martial artist, World of Warcraft enthusiast, and ex-Wall-Street-type Skyler Wright) becomes the owner and operator of a burlesque house, and all his whores, dancers. Other liberties are taken—largely the result of Osbie's attempts, in the tradition of musicians before him, to give a plot and/or a meaning to an incident that has neither. There would be a gruesome surgery scene, anachronistic steam-powered machinery, an illegitimate child played by a pig (actual children being, like fictional pimps, banned from porn), and the much-celebrated porn veteran Ron Jeremy would appear in a tasteless barrister's wig.

The thing is shot in a massive warehouse, in a district of truck lots and snack-cake factories, where the sun bakes wary factory workers on smoke breaks leaning on corrugated steel fences and the air smells like exhaust and the spongy hides of Little Debbies.

On the chain of film-set complexity, Osbie Feel's studio productions rank below most TV commercials, but distinctly above most studio porn films. They drag across the weekdays—sometimes three or even four, leaking money.

From any kind of distance, it is like watching your friend turned into a fly on a window, crawling in rain specks.

# Like Porn
# Only Good

**Someone gets arrested,** someone gets fired, someone gets nauseous, Clamm's life is plausibly threatened by the costume designer, and the pig gets explosive diarrhea, but no one is injured or goes insane, and people keep making out in the makeup room, so really, so far, so good for *Stagger Lee*.

Rob, the pinup photographer, is also shooting a movie, his first, and wants me in it, so we get in a black car and head to a ranch in the desert where some guy makes furniture and rents out his property to people making commercials.

Gina Giles, who's driving, stars in it and helped write the script.

She is warm-eyed and long-limbed and blonde. She's in movies and she directs movies.

In the backseat with us is her costar, Natasha Crash, who's talking about someone or something she's going to go see at the Hollywood Bowl while she's in LA for this movie.

" . . . do you know him? He's a DJ."

"I don't really like electronic music. But I like *girls* who like electronic music, because they're usually sluts."

"I'm a slut. I fuckin' . . . *yeah.*"

"That's good, that's good to hear."

"Yeah, I really need to get fucked today."

"See, it's good to have this two-hour car ride out to the set because then you can have a conversation and find out these important things."

"Yeah, like a lotta times on movies you say something and guys don't even wanna talk to you—it's *stu*pid."

Then she talks about how her pussy is real tight today. Then everybody else in the car talks about how tight their pussies feel or whether they can tell—except me and Rob, who don't have pussies.

So it's a good day to be me.

ooooooooo

What if I weren't me?

I sometimes think:

What would you do if you were Natasha Crash?

You would drive around Miami, with your deep tan and

long nose, and thick lips, with your long black hair pinned and clipped up, in the cockpit of your Escalade.

You would smoke barefoot, twelve floors up, on your balcony, and say, " . . . and I caught her, this fat whore, this fat cookie-eating whore, and I bought all these cookies and didn't get to eat *any* of them" into your cell phone.

You would make drawings and your boyfriend wouldn't even look twice at them.

You would tell Candy that you want to take her to the doctor with you on Monday so you can show your doctor what you want your tits to look like.

You would go with your friend to fuck Dwight Eisenhower after a show, and he'd have his babymama there on the bus and you'd fuck him after he sends the babymama and the baby into another room on the bus to watch *Harry Potter*, and then you'd want to go then and fuck the guitar player afterward but Dwight Eisenhower would tell you that the guitar player was on a different bus and once you were on Dwight's bus you'd have to stay on Dwight's bus and so you and your girlfriend would be stuck with him for a whole leg of the tour because the other guys in the band are afraid to take girls off Dwight's bus and you'd keep wanting to leave and then you'd hatefuck Dwight and then when you got home he would e-mail you for years after and ask for naked pictures and you'd know he was an asshole.

You'd wear ski-goggle-sized frosted Gucci sunglasses the color of your Mediterranean skin and earrings with intermeshed, inch-and-a-half gold stars on circle-linked chains and a rhinestoned black shirt saying "Rebel" in an Old English font and a gold necklace saying "Vodka."

You'd sit at a convention next to a science-fair-style display in folded foamcore that you made with "Natasha Crash" written on it in pointy purple, green, red, blue, red again, purple again, yellow, green again, red again, and blue again Magic Marker and also "Videos" and "Autographed 8 x 10" in black cursive and "Polaroids" in magenta and also stickers on it: smiley faces in two colors, peace sign centered in flower blossom, rainbow-patterned star, green flower, orange flower, blue star, blue star with yellow center, multicolored polka-dotted white heart, rainbow-patterned heart, straight rainbow, smiley face with hair bow (but no hair), as well as other round stickers in aqua and pink and a photo of yourself—tanned, tits up and panties half down, in a kitchen in front of steak knives in a wood steak-knife-holding block—glued to it. And not ironic.

(And you'd be across from a—professionally printed—display for another exhibitor's product: "Blowguard: Takes the *job* out of blowjob.")

You would have a closet, with very many shoes, including a pair of PVC platform ankle boots in toxic green and a silver pair of those kind of stripper shoes that have, like, a porthole running through the heel, and a bag in purplish candy-flake shaped like a giant radio.

You'd see a printed list, pinned to the wall of the club where you're feature dancing, of various local strippers along with, down the center column, the reason they're banned from the club: *stole customer's wallet, drugs, drugs, scams/pimp, walked out, lost her mind, crack.*

You'd think about how Miami's all fucked up because the guy who works in the parking lot of the club you usually work at just got hit with a brick and they took his money.

You'd count out your night's pay—four hundred dollars in mostly ones.

You'd lie beachside, with tanning oil, and say how all the guys on SugarDaddies.com and RichMen.com are just fucking lame-ass guys pretending to be rich and it's retarded.

So, yeah, Natasha:

If someone were trying to put together a reality show about a porn star, where someone goes through all the things porn stars go through while acting just exactly like a porn star, but where the producers also wanted to make the audience root for that porn star and admire her tenacity and antihypocrisy and will-to-trashy-power and really really *want* her to find that roxy she dropped on the floor or the guy who spilled beer on her Dolce and Gabbana handbag, then the producers would cast Natasha Crash. And even if they didn't, Natasha Crash would watch it, on her forty-five-inch flat-screen TV in her almost-empty penthouse in Miami, or in her other house full of cats in a gated community in Tampa where the lawn's totally haywire because she hasn't paid the landscape guy but the homeowner's association can't do shit to her because the house is in foreclosure anyway, or with her boyfriend in his mom's basement.

And Gina Giles? What's going on in her head?

Here is the kind of conversation I often have, to this day, with Gina Giles:

Gina: "Oh, that'll be good—we should shoot there—because we haven't moved in there yet and it's totally empty still—how about that?"

"If you're asking me," I say, "then no way. If it's real life and it's like I have to fuck this girl on the floor or maybe not ever, then fucking on the floor is what I'm doing—but we have a *choice*. There's the fucking floor and bits of glass and kneeling and scrabbling around and so, like, why bother? Let's just do it here."

"But you've already *done* a scene here, won't that be boring?"

"Again, if you're asking me, then *no*, having sex with two girls at once—this is not boring, this is as exciting as life gets.

If this is boring, then I am done and cooked. Who gives a fuck about the bed?"

Gina Giles gives a fuck about the bed. Male talent, largely, does not give a fuck about the bed. If you look at movies directed by guys who used to be performers, you will notice a distinct lack of giving a fuck about the bed.

Gina Giles, though, gives a fuck about the bed. Gina Giles does not, however—and this is crucial—care how or why you ended up on the bed. This is probably why Gina Giles movies usually go off without a hitch, and she usually gets exactly what she wants.

As opposed to most porn, which happens because the director wants to fuck sluts, *ambitious* porn emerges out of the following aesthetic conflict: the director wants to make the next *Blade Runner*—and fuck sluts—or *Texas Chainsaw Massacre*—and fuck sluts—or *Clockwork Orange*—and fuck sluts—or whatever. The film ends up a cross between a low-rent approximation of what they want to do with a camera and a low-rent approximation of what they want to do with sluts.

Gina Giles is not this way. The artist in her wants to look at *this* slut doing *that* slut in *this* way in an atmosphere choked with *that* and *this*. And the pervert in her *wants to masturbate* to it. The ambitions of the artist and the ambitions of the pervert are identical. They are not at war.

Gina has a lot of fetishes. I am not going to call her up right now and ask what they all are, but it's enough to say I'm having a hard time thinking of one she doesn't have. Of interest today is the fact that Gina has a fetish for anything white-trashy—diners, trailers, tweakers, scorched desolation.

And so all these Ginas are pleased about the ranch in the desert, and the dust, and the cast, and the fact that the exact week of shooting there is, by coincidence, a picture of her on the cover of *LA X Press*, which is a cheap paper you can find in glass boxes on every corner in LA, full of ads for phone sex and jack shacks, and which is a totally perfect prop for the movie since it's a movie where she plays a dumb trash cracker who hitchhikes to Hollywood to get famous.

And who is Rob?

Readers who are stupid are probably waiting for me to say that my movies are Art. I won't. Whether or not any given thing can be considered art is about as interesting and complicated a question as whether or not any given thing can be used as a paperweight. Both a Bible and a needle can be used as a paperweight, but all you want to know in an office when the fans are blowing full speed is which one of them makes a *good* paperweight.

Rob Chuckler is the only person on earth who even comes close to making things that work well as art and as porn. While there is no shortage of great art that uses sex as a subject or pornography that, by design or necessity, requires creativity to produce, Chuckler is the only one who consistently creates images that make every gland in your body shriek at you to cream all over the girl in the picture so that you can go back to looking at it without the distraction of every gland in your body shrieking at you to cream all over the girl in the picture.

It is somewhat ironic that Rob was brought into hardcore originally as the cameraman on *Stagger Lee*—which was sold to Bill and Hillary as a "burlesque" movie. Chuckler's pictures are—on the scale of erotic aesthetics—the opposite of burlesque. The girls in his pictures seem to be straining across time and distance and the glass to show you what they've got. There's no classy teasing. Chuckler's wide-angle pictures scoop up their subjects and throw them in your face. They are aggressively unmysterious and completely vulgar in the best sense of the word. They are like what porn would be if it were any good.

So these are the people in the car. Natasha, Gina, Rob. They are people with exactly the right temperament to make porn that looks a lot like porn and still like doing it.

ooooooooo

Shooting goes well.

The ranch is an amazing ranch and mostly just sky. Rob's lens will distort this sky and pull it down at the corners, but this is okay—when you see Natasha and Gina Giles wandering around under this sky between scenes, it really feels like they're under it.

No one can get over not being surrounded by cars or buildings, or in Los Angeles or Miami or New York City, respectively.

"I like those things in your hair, they're so cute," Natasha says to Candy.

"Thanks!"

"Everybody says that," I say. "Everybody likes those things in her hair."

"Well," says Candy, "of course. They're all pretty and sparkly—girls like stuff like that."

"Girls love sparkly shit," says Natasha.

Natasha says she wants to be in more movies like the ones Candy and I are in. I tell her the alt-porn directors won't hire her because she has a tan. She says that's stupid.

It's hard to say porn should be any kind of way—it's hard to say porn should *be*. But if porn should be any way—and still be more or less what we expect porn to be—Rob's movie is exactly the way porn should be. People get along and then have sex and then someone who is paying attention films it and puts funny dialogue bits in between featuring girls who convincingly act like girls who fuck everyone. It doesn't have zombie cocks or five-hundred-foot women fucking on a city. It isn't that different from regular porn—it is just like it but good. It is obviously doomed.

# Things Are This Way

**Then a plane home** and back to New York. Night. Rain again. And a friend's art opening.

Strangers and art for a while. Coming in wet off the street like you're a tiny thing walking into a hollow piece of ice. The room is tall and the facade is glass and the art feels like some ideas about movement and life being kept in storage until the weather clears. Then here's the person who made the art.

"Oh hi, hey, how's it going?"

So first it's like, "Oh hey—how are things, did you . . . "
—but then almost right away you remember you're standing
right in the center of all the overlapping sight lines of all the
people all around.

They are trying to figure out why she made all this stuff,
and they now have a new piece of information that may or
may not explain that—she knows me. Cameras pop at us.

Certain powerful people give you a look—not really a look,
more of a stylized, herbivorous head movement—that con-
veys the message "I know who you are and I realize you are in
front of me and I have nothing to say to you right now—but
I've also got plausible deniability about that."

Then you are like a wedding guest—you say, basically,
"I realize you have to deal with a lot of people right now and
I am gonna let you stop worrying about me—I'm good, I see
some of my people over there, you can go back to work, congratulations."

(People say "Congratulations" when you have your first
show, but then, strangely, keep saying it at every show after
that—mostly because "I'm glad to see you haven't failed yet"
sounds impolite.)

Friends of the artist hang generally in the third tier, near
the walls, beyond the layers of family and VIPs.

This is work, and the friends greet each other with the flattened words you use when you just get to the office. Hey. Hey.
See that? Yeah, fucked. Totally.

This is the watercooler talk, and artists are artists because
they don't like watercooler talk.

Nothing has ever happened at an art opening ever.

Sometimes they are three hours long and sometimes they
are two. No one knows why. For the artists, it's dodgeball and
they're always on the dodging team.

People always ask, "How did the opening go?" Which is like asking, "How did brushing your teeth go?" They got brushed.

Here comes Marty Place . . . although I know very little about him and what I do know suggests we have nothing in common, I always feel warm and well-disposed toward Marty because whenever I see him he says "Hi" and then says his name.

He tells a story about how he wanted to bring the limo but his kid said he shouldn't because the kid would be embarrassed, which is unexpected because mostly what you see in this room is people walking around trying to show each other how rich they are. Anyway, Hey, Marty, nice to see you again, okay, good-bye.

At least two people come up after Marty who are talking to me *professionally*. That is, these are people who read somewhere that the way to be a famous artist is to go hang out at art openings.

One of them, Chuggsy Whimplerumor, is spectacularly bad at it. Chuggsy Whimplerumor is, of course, not his real name, but maybe it is, because Chuggsy's first mistake is he just says "Hi" and doesn't say his name.

So whatever small thing I'm saying now to Chuggsy is just a way of keeping him at bay until I remember where I met him before and why and—this is key—whether during any of the previous meetings he ever said or did anything to suggest he wasn't the megachoad he now appears to be. He makes other mistakes, like his "Hey, I'm a quirky nerd" outfit with a happy tie, and also he is not interesting.

"Hey," he says. "Look at her, she's a piece of ass, you should go talk to her."

She isn't and I shouldn't. "Hey," I say, "maybe you should go talk to her!"

"Well I'm not gonna do that, I . . . "

I realize maybe the most fun I am going to have at this opening is trying to convince Chuggsy that he should go talk to this girl. It's more appealing the farther she walks away from me. I encourage him to seize the day. Be bold, Whimple-rumor! Dig that bitch! She is wild for you! Her passions rage, clearly! Touch her with yourself!

He goes away. He bothers some of my friends, which I like, because maybe it means they know who he is. But they don't. I decide that wherever I recognized him from must've sucked.

Things are tough. My friend Jeronimo is forced to talk to Bosley Harndleson for fifteen minutes and just now realizes it wasn't even Bosley Harndleson. The second Professional shows up, remembers to introduce himself, but then has an unforgivable haircut. Everyone is getting restless and scared. We are not dodging the ball.

Oh, but now it's ending and it's time for our friend's art dealer to buy us all dinner. The lights go away and people leave.

There are place cards—which is not usual. I don't sit where I'm supposed to, which turns out to be a mistake.

Someone I don't know is begging me to sit next to her. Some high school friend of our friend.

Why me? I don't know. She's drunk. She has a dim-eyed sidekick who allegedly runs a gallery specializing in Renaissance art. They discuss astrology and leave the room together at intervals for no clear reason. I eat a lot of bread. I think they are both trying to sleep with me, but they are throwing signals that would be confuse even someone who cared. I make up birthdays and listen to the wrong horoscopes.

The woman on the other side of me is a whole other story. She looks alert and sober. This is also bad.

After two hours fending off a pair of useless drunks I then have to deal with an art person who spends the *next* two hours defending the way things are in the art world by constantly contradicting herself. I argue loudly and hotly, like you never should.

Then there's a necropolitan afterparty where all the guys wear scarves. Like, "Hey look, I'm sophisticated, I'm rich, I have a *scarf* even though I'm *inside!*"

And this is all normal. Ten years of this.

It is obviously time to leave New York.

∞∞∞∞∞∞∞∞∞

For her part, Candy says, "I like LA. There are girls to make friends with. In New York, girls are mean and unfriendly."

We move in with Suzanne Lin, a friend of Trixie's who used to do movies for DiVinethings.com.

Suzanne looks like one of those heavy-headed flowers Japanese gardeners tie at right angles to sticks. She lives in Silver Lake, has a slight deformation that they call, in the Far East, "snake thumbs," and drives a dented car. She is a hot Asian coed. At night, she fears the Ghost Lady with matted black hair, who comes from the television and sits on your chest and takes your soul. She buys a tall shelf and puts her TV on it, so that the Ghost Lady will fall down if she creeps into the room while Suzanne sleeps. She's from Orange County and wants to be a food writer. She is twenty-three years old.

When Candy and I move to LA, Suzanne takes us to an all-night diner where they're playing Social Distortion and have pork chops on the "diet" part of the menu. Because of this, I decide—perhaps hastily—that Los Angeles is a much better place than New York City. Candy says, to Suzanne:

"So what are we doing tomorrow?"

"Yeah, Juan was really vague."

"He wasn't vague," I say. "He wants you two to just do whatever you want. That's what he said, over and over like he was really high."

"I don't know what I want," says Suzanne. "I'm a sub, people tell me what to do."

"I don't know either."

"What do I want to eat? What are you guys getting?"

"What is this? Sub lunch? You want eggs."

"I don't want eggs."

"I'm having smoked salmon and avocado and spinach salad with raisins and capers and goat cheese."

"I want that."

"So you're wearing ears and a leash, right? What else? Are you doing a strap-on?"

"I *could*—that'd at least be, like, interesting, like *action*."

"Yeah, *action*."

"We could do that."

"So you're saying you need to get a strap-on?"

"Yeah, I guess, I mean, I'd have to cancel my pole-dancing class. Is there a sex shop around here?"

"I don't know."

"Do you know anybody who'd know?"

"You know lots of people who'd know."

Cell phones.

"Hey, Gina, we're at a diner in Echo Park. Do you know if there's a sex shop around here? Candy needs a strap-on to fuck Suzanne tomorrow."

"They should just borrow mine."

"I guess they should, like, boil it first?"

"Yeah, can you come over now?"

"Sure—Okay, you're borrowing Gina's."

"So I'm fucking Suzi with Gina Giles's strap-on? That's kinda hot."

Driving to Gina's, then, "Oh hey, this is Liza, she does *Barely Legal.*" "Hey, didn't I shoot you," "Hey, are those real," etc. Gina Giles asks me to masturbate for her new site where boys masturbate.

°°°°°°°°°

On Gina's set the next day, at a studio in the valley, the guy before me has some trouble, and has to use a *Playboy* to get going, so it's a wait and I read a book. Around me, porn guys waiting to do different things to different parts of different girls in different parts of the building talk to each other. The book I'm reading is *The War Against Cliché*.

"Yeah, my therapist, he says it's a totally codependent/coenabling relationship, y'know?"

"Yeah, *totally*, that's how mine is—codependent, co-enabling."

"He got me on Selox and Xanax."

"Hey, what's up dog!"

"Hey!"

"Hey man, how's the novel?"

"Good. It's gonna be a best seller. The ghostwriter I got from Chicago—he checked it out, he's like, 'You wrote this in one night?'"

"You're writing a novel? What is it?"

"It's fiction—it's prophetic—it's a realistic version of what it would take for the Antichrist to rise to power."

"Whoa."

"Yeah—I don't believe in any of that shit—God, the devil—
I got it all figured out, it's gonna be a best seller. What's up
with uhh . . . "

"Oh man, I was just—what did you say?"—he points, he
thinks—"It's codependent coenabling! Totally, I'm . . . "

I jerk off for one of Gina's sites, Str8boyzjerkoff.com. After
twenty minutes I tell her—this is true—I'm really bad at jerking off and there's no way I'm going to cum unless I get some
help. She bends over a counter and I do her for thirty seconds,
then we scramble back into position and I shoot on the lens.
Gina drives me home. Then there's a party for a fetish-porn
girl at a sushi place.

Everyone there is wearing a black T-shirt. Two people spend
the whole time talking about how to buy a used car. I discover
that certain porn stars are capable of looking guarded, bored,
and self-satisfied all at once. Someone says:

"He's a guru, he's really in tune. He had this one woman—
she called and he's like, alright, come out to the Center. And
so she drives out there, for fifteen hours—in Nevada—and
then she gets there, and as soon as she pulls up he says, '*Ok,
now turn around and drive back*' and that's it. He's a *genius*."

There's someone named "Ancient" and someone named
"Sorcerer." Someone introduces himself to one of them. They
talk:

"Are you initiated into the ancient mysteries?"

"What?"

"Well, I just thought, because your name is Sorcerer,
maybe you were."

"Ancient mysteries?"

"Yes, do you know who Aleister Crowley is?"

"No."

(A short, inaccurate history of the intellectual lineage of early twentieth-century occultism, with pronunciation errors.)

" . . . and he was on the cover of a Beatles record, too."

"Really? Why?"

"Well, they were into, like, alternative spiritualities and exploring . . . "

After that both of them nod dutifully and say, "Yeah, interesting stuff, for sure."

I might've cut in then and mentioned that, at the beginning of the Russian Revolution, Crowley wrote a letter to the Communists offering to head a task force dedicated to the extermination of Christianity from the planet.

But it wasn't that kind of party.

◦◦◦◦◦◦◦◦◦

"All movies sold by Bill & Hillary undergo one of the strictest approval processes in the adult industry—a process so exacting that we have helped create a much more positive image for the adult industry. Each title is scrutinized by a qualified internal reviewer and an outside expert, a qualified therapist or psychologist, to ensure every item depicts a positive and healthy portrait of human sexuality. Rejected videos are trashed. Click here [dead link] to learn more about our sexual review policy."

—Bill and Hillary Productions official Web site

When they get Rob and Osbie's movies, Bill and Hillary throw a general fit, Max Clamm finds some excuse not to pay half the girls, and both directors struggle to keep their footage out of his meaty hands.

While GSP's impediments on *Far Gone and Out* came generally only from the aesthetic Right, Bill and Hillary's come just as often from the parental Left.

Their beef with Rob's movie, it emerges, is a scene where Gina and Natasha stumble onto a house in the middle of nowhere. A couple takes them in, then—because they're secret perverts—they tie Gina and Natasha to chairs and have butt sex on top of them.

The tying up is done with no realism at all and the rope is slack and hangs off the edge of the chair, but apparently this does not strike the company as making Rob's portrait of human sexuality any less unpositive or unhealthy. He will spend a year trying to buy back all the footage from them so he can put it out with someone else.

The consensus from the female cast members on the set of *Stagger Lee* is, if, after giving you the usual list of things they don't want you to do to them, they gave you another list that had all the things they *do* want you to do to them, this second list would be identical to Bill and Hillary's list of things *they* don't want you to do to them. If such a list existed. The first thing they want taken out of *Stagger Lee* is the sound of me slapping Tasha Rey's and Grace Domaine's asses during a threesome. This is apparently also antithetical to a positive and healthy portrait of human sexuality.

Now, Grace is one of those girls who, in private life, cheerfully has a "master" instead of a boyfriend; Tasha first came to prominence at age eighteen by *asking* to be punched in the stomach on a set; and you'll just have to take my word about me. We are all okay with that. Presumably, we are not the only ones extant who are okay with that, and presumably some of the people okay with that occasionally have nothing better to do than watch porn that reminds them that other people are okay with that, thus making the "portrait" desirable to that party and therefore definitely "positive." "Positive" being covered, the problem must be with "healthy."

So, either Bill and Hillary's alleged psychiatric professionals' insight into human nature falls somewhat short of what's available in the average AC/DC song or we are all—ass slapper, ass slapped, observers of ass slappery, AC/DC—unhealthy, fearful maniacs of sex and so, by definition, have some condition in our minds that, if left untreated, will eventually result in something bad. Perhaps more ass slapping.

But anyway, assuming they're right, we are therefore freelance employees who are clearly exhibiting—on a tape that is the property of Bill and Hillary Productions and that was reviewed by someone in their employ with the necessary credentials to make a clinical diagnoses—symptoms of mental *illness*. Shouldn't any company that makes such a big deal about being employee-friendly and giving money to charity and that argues that their "success rests on a history of hard-work [sic], dedication, and a willingness to fight for what's right—regardless of the cost" get us some *help*? Or at least *recommend* we get some help? Or at least stop hiring us over and over?

After all this, the ass-slapping sounds are eventually and mysteriously put back in, but only after the editing of the entire film has been turned over to a Clamm pawn.

When *Stagger Lee* is released, a year after it was shot, no one agrees with Osbie that it is entirely an abomination. On the other hand, the released version of *Stagger Lee* does seem like a movie going out of its way to prove how totally pointless everything in porn except the sex is.

Half the script is removed and the between-scene sound is mixed so muddily that

A) you can't really tell what's going on anyway, and

B) the general high-school-drama-department fuzz over the dialogue combines with the sort of wink-wink stage-set po-mo-via-vaudeville aesthetic of the whole thing (one of the only funny—or audible—lines is Tasha Rey saying, "Stag, I love your gangster ways—fuck my pussy night and day," in a comatose monotone) to imply that all the plot stuff is just self-knowingly ironic "hey-listen-to-this-con-trived-way-we've-found-to-set-up-another-blowjob" bullshit anyway—which every other day is what Osbie will tell you it is (only not on the days when he's actually typing the script) (or shooting the dialogue)(or shooting the dialogue again because he feels like we didn't quite nail it the first time).

# MSA-0011 [ext.] EX-S GU et al.

**"We were shooting in here** with her—and I'm like, okay, cute girl, tattoos, whatever— and the cameraman knocks against the wall and the girl goes, 'Umm, Osbie, it looks like your RX-78 GP02A fell off this shelf and got broken and I don't think you'll be able to fix it!' And I thought—'Yeah, I'm gonna remember her.'"

I've knocked over the RX-78 GP02A myself, I'm sure, despite having developed a sincere affection for it.

It watches over my grateful sleep—from a post against a wall painted mandarin-whorehouse red whenever, after a long night in LA, I crash at Osbie's while he stays at his girlfriend or ex-girlfriend's place—along with an RGM-79 (G) GM, two RX-75s, an RX-77, an MS-06J (or C?), an MS-07-B3, an MS-09, an MSM-03C, and, Osbie being hopelessly sentimental, an RX-78-2. In the mornings, after a shower overseen by a framed photo of an MSA-0011 [ext.] EX-S GU, I generally go downstairs and check my e-mail on Osbie's computer, whose massive hard drives, when not fully occupied with rendering, capturing, or editing video footage, contain almost nothing besides endless photos of porn girls and pictures of toy robots.

Nearly all of Osbie's own toy robots are modified in some basically invisible way, and a few are scratch-built. Osbie used to work in special effects and sci-fi production design, and all his spare talent goes into these robots and it's impossible for anyone else to tell. They look just exactly right, as if the factory built them that way, just like as if some guy who has a bunch of toy robots on his shelf.

"Osbie," I say, "here's what we should do: we should build a big robot together. We'll sketch it out and work on it together and make it really detailed and cool and beautiful and so much not like anything else anyone's ever seen that it's not just a robot it's a sculpture and I'll show it at my next show and it'll be a collaboration between Zak Smith and Osbie Feel and we'll split the money."

And Osbie thinks this is a real good idea. So we start doing sketches. In the meantime, I have a movie to do in Barcelona, and then a show in London.

# Other People's Cities in the Dark

**Flying into London—**
on a nearly empty red-eye flight—I'm drinking a Coke in
the little corrugated cup they give you, and all of a sudden
there's this pain. Severe and dental. I zigzag down the aisle
to the bathroom to see how much my gums are bleeding. But
no. It doesn't look fucked. It just feels fucked. (Max Clamm
joke: "Doc, I feel great but everyone says I look awful." Doctor
looks up the symptoms—"Ahh, you're a *vagina*.") But *I* look

fucked—some new message written red all over my face in a squalid cluster like a sore-colored moustache wandering up around my nose. Like a completely talentless tattoo, red and on me.

It's not a disease; it's just an unbelievably militant eczema bent on overthrowing my face. I am vain, but you don't have to be vain to see a problem here. Like What the Fuck Did I Ever Do to You, Face Distributor?

When we land I go into a store at King's Cross—past a cornerful of British people shrieking at one of their coworkers or co-fans to drink some kind of lava-chili in a glass—barber shop in back, cosmetics up front.

"Hey, hi—what should a person do if their face is doing this?"

"Ah," he makes his face like one of the great and serious African king faces that decorate the halls of high schools in Baltimore, DC, and Prince George's County and nods—this is some Old Testament shit here. "Tear no a creme for dat. Is a *reaction*. What you got to do is to be right in yourself, man. In *here*. You relax, it go away. Be good in your way."

Good in my way? I *was*. I *used* to be good in my way—in an *American* way. I was healthy and obnoxious. Looking around I think I'm now good in the local way—teeth fucked, skin fucked—that's doing pretty good for King's Cross. I'm not sure they *have* a cure for this on this island.

I have a public thing in two days, an opening. Relax relax. I take a bubble bath in the hotel room with every pillow in the room behind me so I can sit comfortably and read a book. A hot drink and a cold drink balanced on the rim of the tub.

Afterward, sweating through soap bubbles, I pull these pillows from the tub and they are *unbelievably* heavy—heavier than a dog. Like a body. Try it sometime. Try getting a fluffy hotel pillow soaking wet. It's not easy to haul around something as heavy as a body.

Wiping steam off the mirror, I notice I am still fucked in my face. My body is doing this to me. Stress, you'd have to say.

But I don't *do* that stuff. Anger, depression, and bitterness, sure—but *stress*? Never have done it. And all those things that are supposed to do it *to* you—deadlines, screwy family, ex-girlfriends, friends on heroin, money, no money, Ivy League, fistfights in bars, running from police, public speaking, DC, New York, LA, painting—never did it. Neurosis is just that band from East Bay. I do not do stress.

This is obviously because of the porno I just did in Barcelona. And what did it add up to? In the scheme? Nothing. Nothing I can think of. But my face is thinking and so are my teeth.

Your body has its own revulsions and repulsions that it knows and you don't know—and its own morality. It is not easy to haul around something as heavy as a body.

And I don't know anyone here.

I've been arguing with the art dealer about music for the afterparty since he first starting planning the show.

"Yeah, *sure* we'll do wha'*ever* you want. What kind of music do you want?"

I tell him.

"Oh, there's no DJ in London who can play *that* kind of music."

What I wanted was punk rock from the zeros. And now I *need* punk rock from the zeros. Clinically speaking. A good dermatologist would've said, *Lie down, take some Leftover Crack, and call me in the morning.*

I go to the all-night Internet place across the street from the hotel. What I do is this: write to Candy, copyedit a paper Suzanne sent me (more on that later), and then put on the big black rubber headphones and listen to music on the archives of a radio show I used to do. And hear my friends' voices.

Then-roommate Sean says that the singer from Graves at Sea reminds him of the voices of the giant spiders in the old *Hobbit* cartoon. He then goes on to say that his favorite part of that cartoon, and of Tolkien's entire *Lord of the Rings* saga, across all media and iterations, is the part where Bilbo says, "*Cakes.*"

Bilbo is climbing a mountain in the rain—Sean explains—with the wizard and the dwarves. In order to keep his morale up, the wizard says to Bilbo, "Think of pleasant things." Bilbo says these things out loud: "A warm fire," says Sean into the microphone, " . . . my library at twilight," then a long, poetic pause, and then, with an isolating simplicity, and, in a humble rapture: "*Cakes.*"

Every time I open my mouth to drink out of this Coke bottle I have here, it rips apart the skin on my face to the left of my mouth. I am wretched.

In the headphones, this notion of thinking of pleasant things then prompts another co-host, Jeronimo, to talk, and to tell the listening audience that we'll soon sign off and all together visit Chelsea galleries, to look at art, and we may then have to *think of pleasant things*—wandering Twenty-fourth Street thinking, "*Cakes*" . . . "*Pussy.*"

Which reminds Sean of a time he did just that. We had taken Sean to Coney Island for his birthday. Sean is afraid of roller coasters and once said that the only way he would ever go on one is if he could eat a pussy the whole time, but, thinking it looked the least intimidating, he agreed to ride the swinging Pirate Ship.

But this was unwise; as Sean explains, the swinging ship " . . . is the part of the roller coaster that is *most* terrifying *over* and *over* and *over* again . . . I was completely freaking out." He was.

So sitting next to my friend, who was white-cheeked and hyperventilating in mortal panic, I said, at Coney Island, on that Pirate Ship, "Okay, Sean, just imagine you are eating a *pussy*. There's a big pussy in your face—one leg over one ear, one leg over the other."

On the radio, Jeronimo cuts in (in his Spanish accent) to note that I was *screaming* these things (which is, of course, true because I had to be louder than the ride, and louder than all the loud children all around). "And you were just, 'AND A WARM WET POOSIES AND . . . ' and we are all, 'What the *fuck*?'"

And meanwhile, Sean began shaking and sweating and repeating "It'sokaythere'sapussyonapussyonmyface okay thighs, thighsonmyface . . . okay" and did survive the ride.

There's a mirror on the wall behind me—oh, I still look fucked. I am unsuccessful at relaxing. I seem to have lost the instinct for it—maybe that's why all the Italians in Barcelona hated me—I am an insult to their culture. Fuck. Fuck.

*Cakes.*

Fucking Barcelona.

°°°°°°°°°

The initial query letter was long and polite and had links to their other movies and said Cassandra Maniace would be there and promised to soon deliver an English translation of the script. All I wanted to know was who they wanted me to fuck. It was my intention to follow up by asking if the people they'd cast wanted to fuck *me*—but they never answered and so I was again going off to fuck some random people. But hey—Spain, adventure, whatever. And I was supposed to be in Europe anyway.

At the passport office, there is a war-on-terror-length line. I am told I can't bring that in here. I say, I know, and, That's why I'm holding it up in front of your face and asking what to do with it, etc., for far too long, then they let me upstairs. Upstairs, I explain why I am there, fill out the appropriate form, and give it to a guy at a window who immediately throws it away. He asks me what he can do for me today and I repeat myself until he is made to understand that I filled out the appropriate form, and gave it to him, and he then immediately threw it away. When I do get my passport I go to an airport, and then another, and then maybe another, and then maybe another. It will suprise no one familiar with air travel in the early twenty-first century to hear that this takes somewhat longer than it was supposed to. I'm fairly sure I'm in either Dallas or Philadelphia at one point. All the bars look Irish. Every time I wash my hands the sensor is in a different place. In DC/Reagan I think they have a button. I also take some buses. I get to Barcelona around midnight.

Now, is it a city where you come inside off a street and that's the first floor? Or is it a zero floor? It's an important thing to know if it's the middle of the night and there's no one to ask and you've been told to go to the *third* floor.

On the third, or second, floor I look at a door that might be the door I'm supposed to go through. It doesn't do anything.

I stare at it.

After forty hours of not sleeping in all kinds of seats, and of waiting to be digested through lines, and of terminals and terminal food, and of unmarked streets and unfortunate, unexpected, unavoidable delays, and of casual threats from governments at the bottoms of forms and on posted signs, of other languages, of taking shoes off and putting shoes back on, of time zones eating hours, of eating peanuts, of the guy sitting next to you, and all other travel riddles, this last test, in its frank laziness, seems especially cruel and drab and unusually petty.

And also, impossible to solve without possibly waking and scaring sleeping people who speak no English. Fuck you, door. There should be numbers on the floors and there aren't. Then I notice that the repeating brass niches on the margin of every hallway would make much more sense if they turned out to be elevator doors with heavy glass and not a series of pitch-black telephone booths. They are. I press 3.

The real third floor is identical to the fake third floor—a ring of wooden doors around a dark red carpet—except now one is open.

Inside there is a lean, silent hallway leading to a dim, slantlit room. There is going to be talent in here from several different countries and I am going to have sex with some of them (they still haven't said which ones), so I look for a shower. I find it without making noise and go in.

The bathroom is a low-ceilinged, irregular, five-sided, pale-tiled architectural incident off the long hall. It looks like nothing in the Western Hemisphere. Although it's stuffed with nozzles and dials and appliances and white tubing, experiments make it clear that the light is not just broken but actually just not installed at all.

So I take a long shower in the dark, and sink against the porcelain wall with my eyes closed, and inhale steam.

This is very good.

I dry off using a spare shirt in the light from a window-slit cut through the wall behind what I think is a water heater.

The apartment seems to have been designed, like certain castles in the Orient, with the intention that no one be able to sleep so long as anyone else in it is awake. In place of what they called, in feudal Japan, "nightingale floors," the place has a sheet of fake hardwood that rucks like a low and squeaky wave extending nearly halfway down the main corridor. There is no way to avoid it. When I reach the edge of the far room, I see a moaning shape with long hair, half made of blankets.

"Hi," I say, in a low voice.

It is on a twin bed, which has an unoccupied twin to its right. After a murky exchange in some language, possibly English, and some pointing in the dark, it seems that the safest place to sleep is neither twin, but a square of futon on the floor in the opposite corner. I nod at the shape, wondering if I'll have to fuck it, and drop heavily into my corner on my stuff. Checking the time (which requires silently sliding someone's nearby recharging cell from a teal velvet case—the cell I'd picked up in Berlin was either useless here or totally useless), I'm pleased to see I'll have seven hours to sleep. I crawl under my coat. The girl—it sounds like a girl now—speaks clearly and suddenly and impatiently in an accent I don't know: "Are you going to sleep?"

"Yeah."

Proving, through a tracery of uneven dark, that she is young and is a woman and is naked and is very probably talent, she moves toward the hallway light, turns it off and silently gets back into the bed. The room is full of quiet for some time, and the darkness is broken only by the Christmas stars of scattered LEDs burning colors into the surrounding surfaces.

Then something huge comes in, a man, and soon he too is naked, and moving heavily. His face is impossible to make out but his muscles are everywhere, which makes his great

smooth-skinned seamless gut seem like an unnatural preg-
nancy or hog-sized symbiote. The whole shadow-universe
of the apartment suddenly rearranges itself around him and
creaks under him. Bright, narrow light-shapes from doors he
opens shoot across the room from unexpected angles where
he discovers new spigots. The voices in my head debate about
whether to try to sleep through this. When he passes again
I have my eyes totally open—sedately, I wave strangely, with
fingers spread wide (anthropologists say waving originated as
a way of saying to strangers, "I have no weapon in my hand").
He returns it, slower, as if learning by mimicry. Eventually he
gets in a bed.

He is Ghazi Purcigliotti, a bald ex-mercenary. The next day,
sitting on the clean sheets of the spare twin bed, he has the
bright and moist look of a chick in an incubator, his knobby,
shaved face gleaming with morning light and weight-gain
powder as he bats a distracted paw at his distended cock.

Mikki Fabb, who sits smoking, dead-smiled, on the edge of
Ghazi's bed, cried when she finished letting Ghazi Purcigliotti
do his fantastically violent version of the thing producers pay
him to do, and then her car had been totaled in some city far
away and then her luggage had been stolen. Now she is supposed to fuck me, they tell her.

She has one of those rare faces where it's possible to pin-
point exactly what it is that makes it unattractive: a handful
of otherwise decently molded features set into a surface posi-
tioned an inch too far back in the head and flattened in the
middle, as if the whole face were sinking into a hole some vital
structure underneath the nose had left when it collapsed, or as
if her eyes were trying to recoil back into her brain.

Across from Fabb, Lisa Donna stretches lazily in rhinestoned jeans, wearing for me the look friendly bakers wear

when they're giving new customers a good deal on a new muffin they're sure they'll like (I was supposed to do her, too), while Ilse Break (the girl from last night) asks stupid questions in her accent:

"So . . . why are you staying here?" (Squinting.)

"I'm on the movie."

"He's an *actor*." (This is Lisa.) (Thank you, Lisa.)

"You are an *actor*?" Incredulous (she may never have seen a punk before). "*Ghazi* is an actor." She points.

"That's what they tell me."

"Ghazi is a real serious fucker. So are you a real fucker?"

I explain that I am a real fucker. Appreciative but also witchlike laughter all around.

"Do you do *drugs*?"

∘∘∘∘∘∘∘∘∘

No, but I haven't eaten anything but Gummi Worms in eighteen hours.

Where the fuck did these people come from?

To briefly explain—not long ago, Barcelona sat about a thousand miles from the border of a great empire as large and apathetic as all the deserts of the earth put together. The cloistered, pale, aging, anxious murderers who ruled it had seized power in the name of the people, but instead they behaved like kings—though with a thoroughness rarely seen before or since, and on an unbelievable scale. It was a world of rust, famine, and poison rivers, and of systematized theft and neglect constantly justified with naked unreason by smiling liars. It went on for only a handful of generations, but each was schooled in desperation, poverty, and pragmatism. Therefore, when the Bloc, as it was called, began to fall apart, these clever millions were loosed on a barely guarded Western European Candyland of privately held cash—many sold their daughters immediately into prostitution and many of the daughters took to it fearlessly and with something approaching bitter pride.

Porn producers on the continent started hiring these women, realizing that it was cheaper than what they usually paid to pry Western European girls away from Catholic families or subsidized educations. The typical result of this geoeconomic train wreck is a sort of vain, dishonest, jewel-encrusted animal with lots of hair that feeds on shoes.

Ilse Break is a good example. Mikki Fabb is not quite. I do not yet know about Lisa Donna. I'd like it if she were prettier, though.

The day drags itself together; tanned people in T-shirts lug gear and converge on a loft overlooking a Mediterranean plaza, drink espresso, plug things in, talk in every way, and I am glad when I see Cassandra Maniace.

"Hey! It's you!"

"What's going on?"

"Who fucking knows?" she rattles. Her voice is like rusty warm water and twice as old as she is.

She does her best to explain things—which isn't very good. Italians lived with the Latin Mass for a thousand years after they couldn't understand it anymore and had riots when someone tried to change it. Explaining things is not part of their culture.

If you stay with Cassandra, for lunch she'll bring you a dripping, goldfish-colored ball wrapped in butcher paper and if you ask what it is she'll say, "Eat it, it's Italian."

If you take a bite, steam pours into your face and the cheese goes spiderwebby and it starts to fall apart and you have no choice but to eat the whole thing because it is on you.

But it *is* Italian, so it's usually good.

In the circles I run in (do I run in circles?), you get to a certain age and it's not babies and weddings—it's everybody takes their hobbies *pro*. The guitarists become sound engineers, the drunks become sommeliers, the tattoo guys get tattoo shops, and I'm even having sex for money now.

Cassandra, who got me this job, is a photographer and essentially a multinational concern: shooting runway models in London, transvestite orgies in the Czech Republic, vanilla sex in or on the Coliseum, pinup girls in New York, Los Angeles, and abandoned mountaintop ex-Eastern Bloc border hotels no one else knows about.

The lazy, generous, and reassuringly cynical look of all great porn photographers—which seems so natural when they're middle-aged men—wears weird on a girl in her twenties spaghetti-strapped between an unwashed bra, an undershirt, an army knapsack, and the black, chrome-buckled leash of a very expensive digital camera. Her exhausted eyes keep peeling back and going all avid and sly, as if basically life is a guilty pleasure.

Her job is, mostly, convincing insecure young girls to take off their clothes and do whatever she tells them to because if they do she will make them look like crystalline goddesses who crush civilizations under their stripper shoes. Trust her. So the basic "Just eat it, it's Italian" philosophy dominates here. You are presented with some unknowable thing, you try it, trying it gets you in too deep to escape, and you have no choice but to finish it. In the end, you're lucky if there's anyone around who speaks your language well enough to tell you what you just did.

What I can understand of the conversations—in six languages—around the set seems to go like Italian traffic:

obscene, loud, circular, and with everyone on cell phones: "No we donnawant Chinese *food*!" "They are all fucked up! They want *Chinese!*" "Well tell them we don't want Chinese!" "Our friends want Chinese food, they are all fucked up." "I know, you said that in English."

oooooooooo

Cassandra and I sit on a couch in the increasingly wired-up living room while the loft takes on a busy, kitcheny feeling, with bodies being basted and dressed and moved through short corridors and up narrow stairs and lamps unfolding over us. The director is one of Cassandra's exes, a fuzzy bald chunk on a lot of crank. Ominously wide-eyed, he comes over with a notebook to explain that what the production company has hired him to do is to imitate the kind of movies I make in California. Then I am interviewed by someone from Italian *Rolling Stone*.

They excuse Mikki Fabb from having to fuck me and put her in an albino-leopard cardigan and wool socks and a topknot—which flattens her head even more—and begin to shoot.

As you know, whenever shooting starts on any movie, they say, "Quiet on the set," but what you get isn't a normal quiet—it's an uneasy, electrical quiet that is waiting for sound. It's room-tone.

Mikki goes through the girl-girl part of the scene, mirroring whatever look Lisa puts on. If they could be isolated and abstracted, there are things to see on the set, under the crackling of the room-tone, that are hot—or at least that's what I tell myself as I lean against a wall with my hand down the front of my pants trying to think past the denim overalls they have Lisa wear while she tugs her costar open.

Then it's time to ass-fuck Lisa. In white leg warmers, bent animalwise over cushions, she looks hungry and shakes her butt. My cock is skeptical. It is obvious our phrasebook English, which gives everything we say the pointless gravity of a child's first words, isn't going to help us any. Her blowjob, however, is articulate. It's from the patient school that painstakingly organizes all available skin to make it clear to the raw cock, in the language of nerves, that this other body knows all about how blind, hairless, and desperate for attention it is, and how that is *really* alright with it, and how all the details are going to be taken care of very soon and it should just relax.

So everything is good *there*. The next job is to white the footnote of Mikki and her lost luggage and her car and crying and crushed face looking at my blowjob out from the bottom edge of my consciousness—and also Cassandra crouching, just inches away, staring politely off like someone waiting for a friend to zip herself into an unnecessarily complicated dress to go someplace she (Cassandra) had had to be convinced to go to in the first place, then all the other stubbled Italians and Spaniards standing and perched around the loft throwing glances at each other over the edges of their idle devices; to basically cut off all empathy with the collective weight of all the expensive alien boredom.

The way blood moves in a body—and how it acts when it gets to where it's going—is not something that can be reliably explained across the wall between the sexes. I'll just say this—there's the time when the blood shows up in your cock and takes a look around, and there's the time when it decides to sign the lease. These times are not far apart, and they look identical to the outside observer, but they are distinct, and the one does not necessarily follow from the other.

The world has been reduced to the two of us and the blood is where the blood should be, and she lifts her face and smiles her baker's half smile again.

"Just a little more and we're good," I say, trying to work some kind of compliment into my voice.

And then the warm black alien neon in her eyes flickers and goes and she looks . . . like what? Like I have small, sticking meat crumbs on my face, and know it, and am refusing—in my foreign language—to brush them away.

Then one eye shrinks, and her head bends around and she looks back and forth and over her shoulder and then over at Cassandra with a questioning sideways look and Cassandra shrugs her tattooed shoulder at her, like Hey, it's okay.

But it's not okay, this is trouble.

The facts on Lisa's face are the kind that speak to your DNA—the protohuman part that lived in packs and hid from the dark and thinks anything orange is edible. This part of you spends its days in a lonely bend of the central nervous system, and it feeds on chemical substitutes and is flattered and fooled constantly, but when it comes to fucking it always has its say and although it can't read books or bicycles, it can read power and eyes. On rare occasions it sees in them things that are alarming enough that it peels itself out of its smothering haze and makes decisions the rest of you is not wired to resist. And now, here, it is saying: No good will come of mating with this female and you should not have come here.

A creeping, subtracting shadow steps into me, and down, and gobbles me up.

The line of thinking in the wet-lipped head suspended over my crotch is totally clear. *I am sucking the cock, the sucking is no longer being filmed, I am therefore sucking the cock because there is no Viagra in the cock so I have to suck it so it's hard so we do anal so I get paid for anal, if it is hard and it is not being filmed there is no reason to keep sucking on it. Wait . . . I should keep sucking? Fuck.*

Let's say you want, very badly, to play Ping Pong and there is someone on the other side of the net who is ready to play with you. The person serves, you hit it back, someone scores—Ping Pong happens. But then, when it's your serve, suddenly your opponent's features wither, and every time you hit the ball, she just snaps her paddle contemptuously at it and doesn't seem to care where it lands, or else, with a patronizing smile, hits it wherever you ask her to hit it.

It would make you not want to play Ping Pong.

It would make you feel bad about making this person play Ping Pong with you. It would make you feel bad for wanting to play Ping Pong.

No matter what nonsexual designs I had about the situation—to help out Cassandra, or get another movie under my belt, or get paid—they don't matter.

So that's it for me. There is no scene at all.

°°°°°°°°°

Sometimes, the female talent does not really want to have sex with you.

Sometimes, you can't tell whether the female talent wants to have sex with you and also there's some other simultaneous distraction like temperatures so extreme that any mammal would think twice about having normal sex in such circumstances, much less porno sex.

Sometimes a dog is taking a shit a few feet from you during the scene.

These may seem like good and humanly understandable excuses to not be in the mood to have sex. I have had all of them and occasionally used some of them. But, then again, good luck with your excuses. Because this is porno, and there will *always* be something that looks like an excuse. This is the job: show up and have sex under excusably bad conditions with somebody who could be anybody. If you can't do this, you shouldn't be doing this. You have no business in this business.

If I were in this business, if my money came from this business, I would be out of the business. I should get this out of the way as soon as possible: I very often suck at this job. Especially on features with big crews, where sucking would really matter. What makes it onto the finished film usually looks good enough, and occasionally was, but make no mistake—there are many more reliable porn guys than me. Hire them.

The worst part for me is, until I chose this, I had nothing to do with excuses. I am of the no-excuse school of making paintings and I am also, thus far, of the no-excuse school of private sex—I can afford to be; I'm still young.

But on porn sets I find myself wanting excuses. I might have gone my whole life without excuses, but then I chose this detour. And even if they are okay, these excuses, the thing to do really, the dignified thing to do, the professional thing, the thing that would display maximum self-knowledge, would be to just walk away when you see the trouble coming—just go, "Look, there's *this* and there's *this* and I apologize but now you have time to book someone else." And I haven't done that yet.

⊙⊙⊙⊙⊙⊙⊙⊙⊙

The script had to be rewritten, which is okay because it had started out making even less sense than the porn-usual. In the beginning, since there were no remotely "alt" porn girls they could hire, they'd convinced Claire LeJense to fly in from Germany to play a main character who never has sex. Now I—who they'd gone out of their way to get—am not fucking anybody either, but they still want me to stick around and do things in the movie. Over lunch at a basement-like restaurant whose English menu offers "meat gutters," "pulpy small to the plate," and "sepia iron," the director rewrites my character into a sort of ghost or recurring nightmare. He is nice to me, and I tell him I'll stick around and do whatever nonsex thing he needs me to do, because I guess I owe him and what else am I going to do in Barcelona for two days, and I probably signed something somewhere along the line.

The last day of shooting is long, with sex scenes cobbled together to make up for my scene and a handful of other scenes lost to disorganization, bad luck, or drug haze. Behind the camera it's a typical bohemian Babel: me and Claire and a bald costume girl from Morocco and local Spanish PAs, and some producer from LA and actresses from all over the right-hand side of the map. In front of the camera it is exactly *Italian Porno*. If the Italian American Anti-Defamation League ever got ahold of this movie it would drive it out to the causeway and fill it with lead.

It's all done on a scorched balcony where we watch Lisa and a new girl pivot around two broad, black-haired, Ray-Banned jocks the same color as the sun, which hangs over the angles of the mazy city like a sign over traffic, telling the entire planet to turn slower and slower. Shirtless and tattooed, talking to the talent, the director looks like a pile of sticky buns between padded headphones. People keep saying *"vafanculo"* and (better) *"porco dio!"* When clothed, the porn guys wear white linen with leather wrist thongs dotted with gold studs and sprouting beaded twists—obeying coolness rules of some foreign and totally other sexual order.

Even Claire seems reduced and pinched—in a room in the back of the villa overlooking the set, peering out onto the patio at this oily sex barbecue, smoking nervously, a blanket drawn up on her knees. She's just a girl in a green sweater shaking her head and Not Sure About This at All. Her usually drawn-on eyebrows are completely missing, which is somehow the worst sign yet.

It gets dark. I do something naked for the camera for five minutes and feel stupid. They take Claire off to shoot something late-night.

Cassandra asks if I want to get dinner with her and her people. I say great, awesome, get me out of here get me out of here.

Everyone at the restaurant and everyone I'm with knows and grabs and loves everyone else. The owners are some ex-squatmates of someone, gone pro. Their restaurant is on a curve across from a high stained wall, and they specialize in fish. The bellies of the saucers are heaped with viscous, overlapping wet. I don't want to have to tell anyone that I don't like fish, but they keep saying, "Here try this" and "Here try this," and they translate and narrate the choices and even though I tell them it's okay, I know that *ragù* means *sauce* and *pasta* means *noodle*, I am not allowed to hide in my menu and it wouldn't have mattered anyway. There is fish and fish eggs and fish parts and slimes. And scales and eyes set in dirty gold dead rings. Try it, it's Italian. So then I say it. I say I don't like fish.

"We can go somewhere else," says Cassandra.

"No, it's cool, it's okay, whatever."

"I *hate* that!" Cassandra says. "'*Whatever*'—when I *eat*, I want to *sit* and *talk* and eat good food and drink for hours and just go all night—what else *is* there? I can't just *eat*, I have to take *time* and *eat* and *love* the food and the people and everything."

An old blonde from the art department explains that Italians like to eat food that they like, and that I wouldn't understand but it is because it's their culture. A makeup girl explains that she also likes to eat food.

When Italians *do* explain things, using English, it's sometimes like the words are fat, squealing pets covered in engine oil, which they grab and lift and show to you like proud parents, grinning. Look, look, here is what I'm saying, get it? Eat! Food! Love!

I say okay.

I don't say that I feel disgusting and pathetic and stupid and stupid and I'm still adjusting to self-loathing and so would like to eat my bread and be ignored and they should all go fuck themselves and let me forget I ever came to this place with creepy whores and fish.

We finish eating.

They buy cocaine and the dealer offers me weird teacups I'd been staring at. I climb down an elevator shaft to get the makeup girl's keys after she accidentally drops them into it and starts crying. I sleep in a room in a hive of studios that another of Cassandra's exes is letting her use—behind a storefront policed by an ugly dog—and in the morning I follow directions to a bus station in a big plaza.

Inside, past the strip-lit room-tone ticket counters and pastry shops, there is a squat Internet machine, and I buy a Coke (I don't really like Coke, but it's hard to get anything else) so I can get coins for it. As the departure clock counts down, I write the longest letter I can to Candy, telling her how I want to get far away from Barcelona and then curl into a ball and drink Dr. Pepper. I think about how it would be to drink a Dr. Pepper again, and, for the first time I can remember since I was a kid, I cry. I put my head against a standing computer monitor in an empty mall in an empty bus station in the morning in Barcelona and I cry because I am imagining the taste of Dr. Pepper.

Leaving in the bus, on an expressway, while local fascists demonstrate with red and gold banners on the TVs, we pass an isolated building, chalk-white and bloated, seemingly uninhabited, and shaped like a corncob, all alone. Unbelieveable and extreme, it hulks over the ant stream of cars speeding past, massive, from a future or planet built on a different scale. There is nothing like it in America and I have no idea what this giant building is. It must be famous, some famous building. Jesus, I think—and keep thinking all the way to London—I don't know anything. I don't know anything. Why do they let me out in the world to do things? I don't know anything.

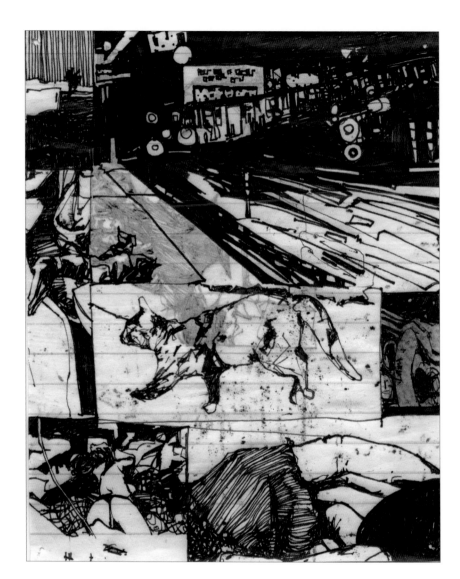

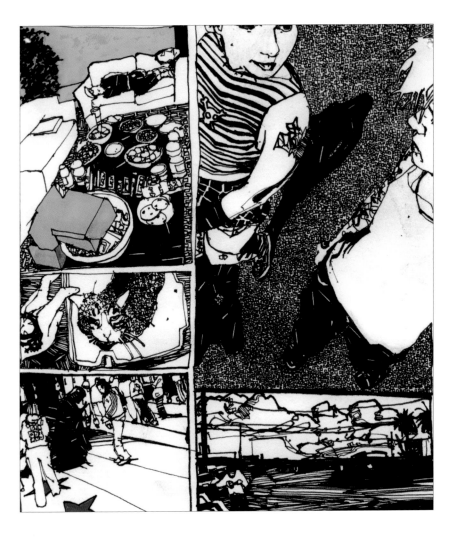

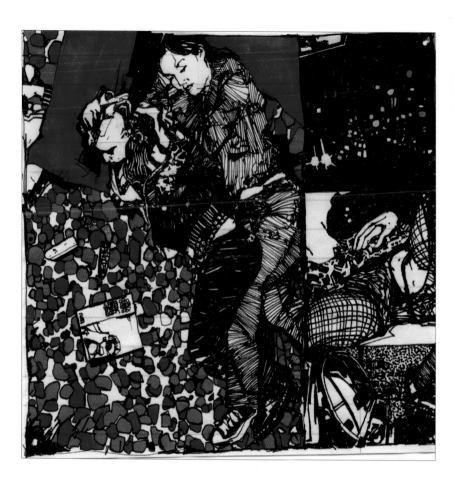

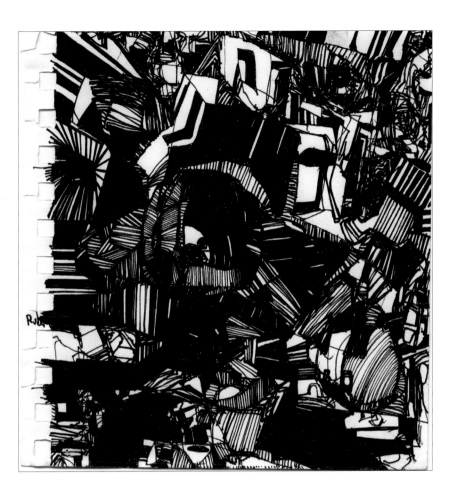

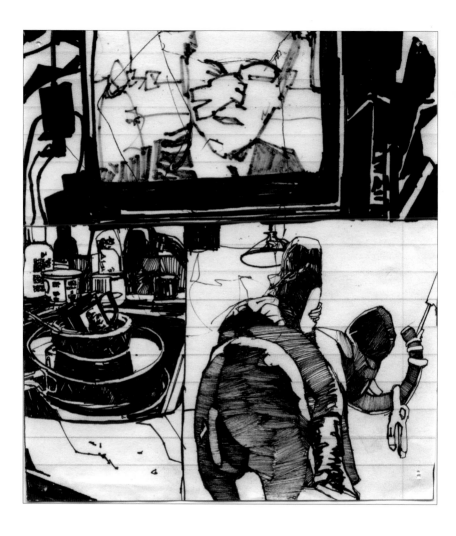

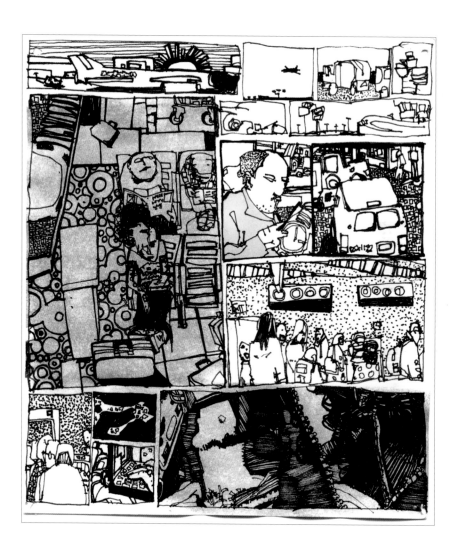

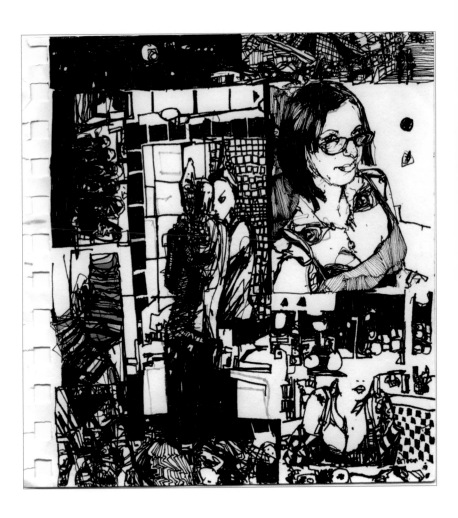

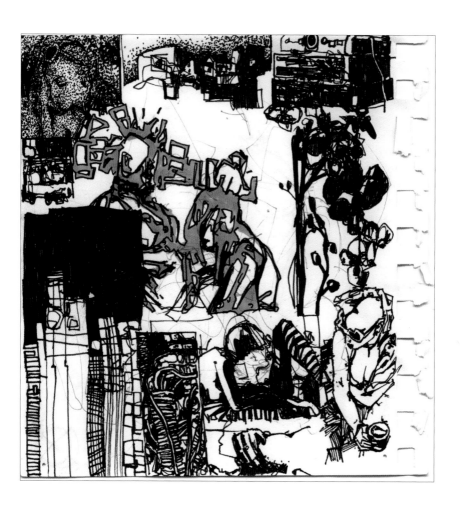

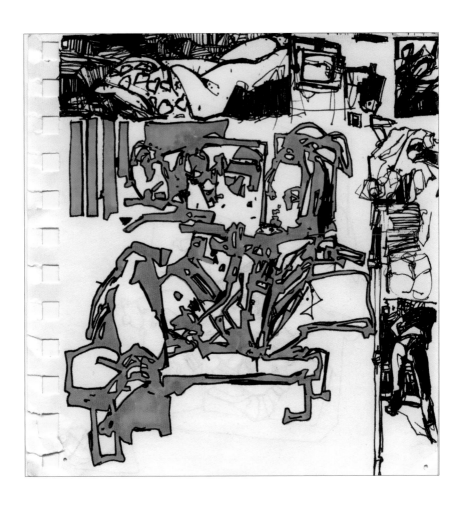

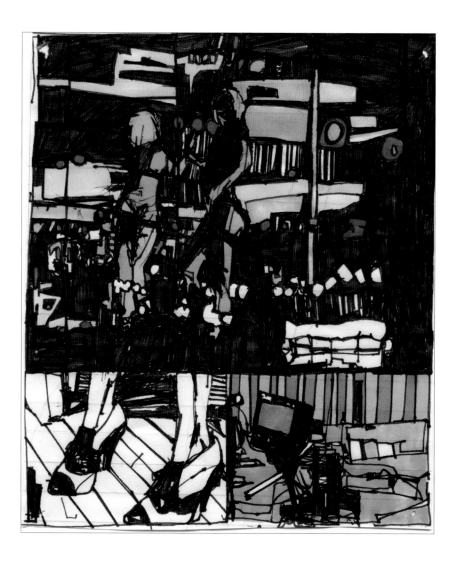

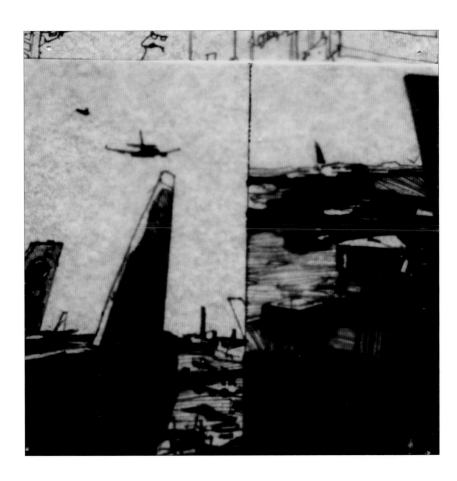

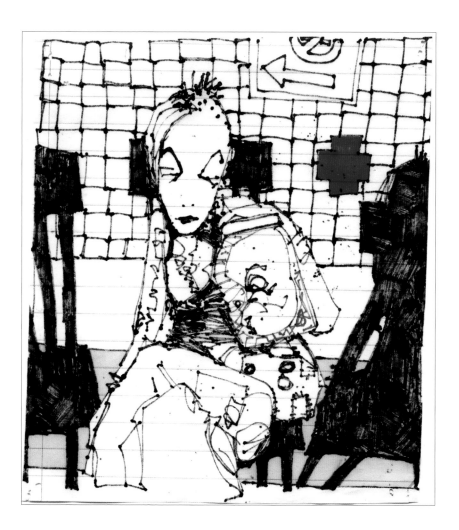

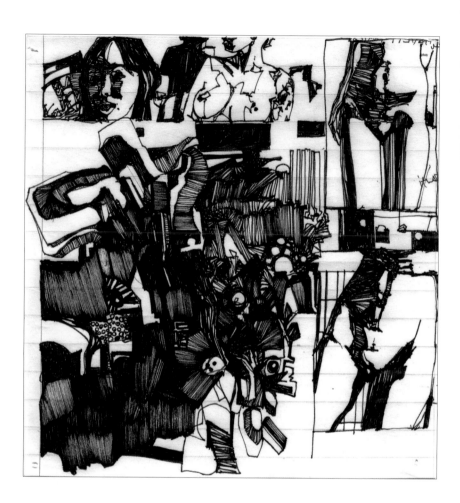

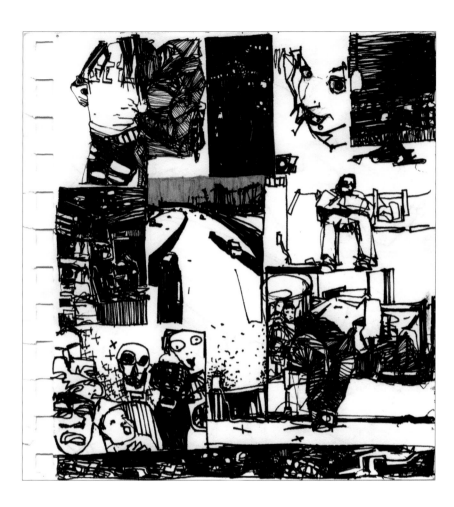

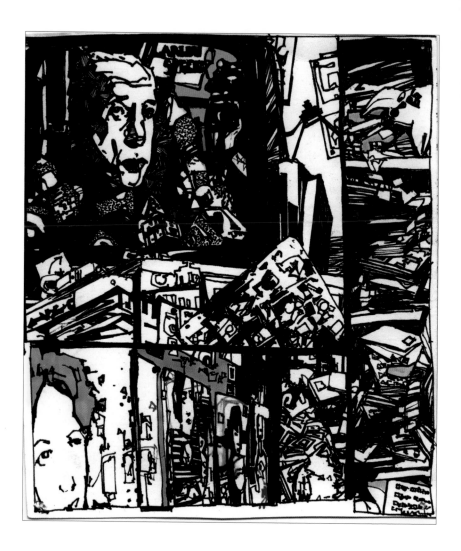

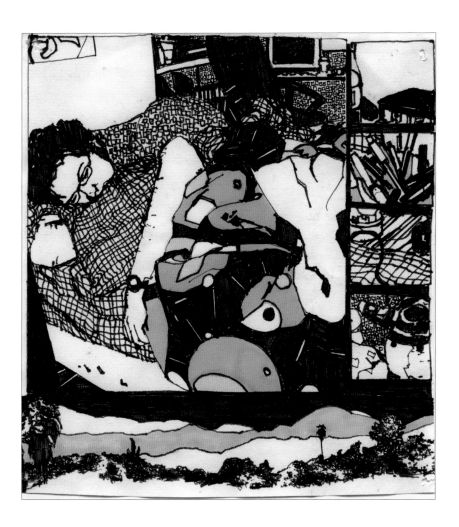

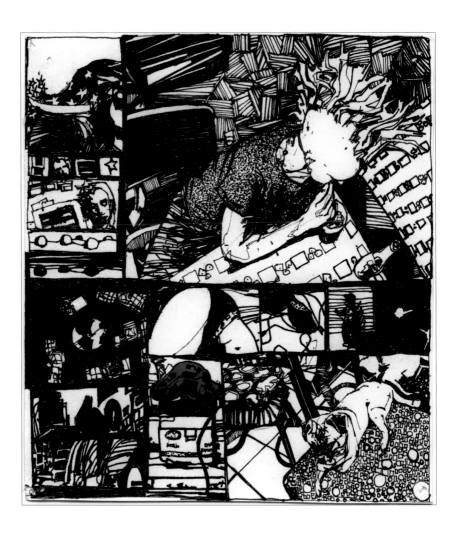

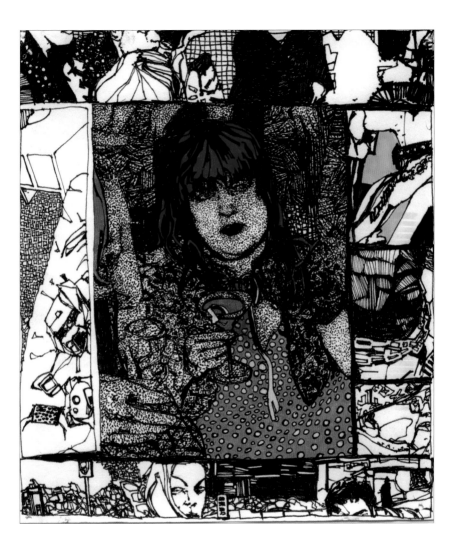

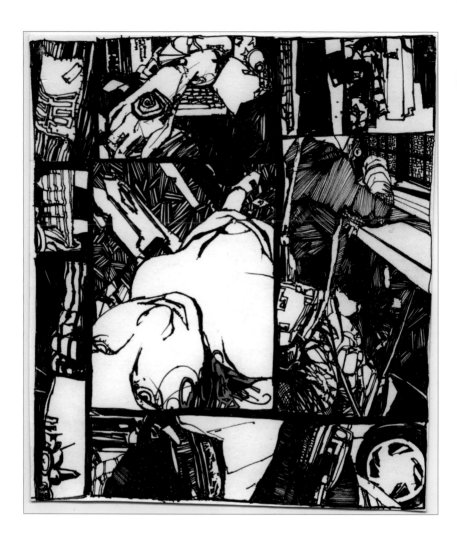

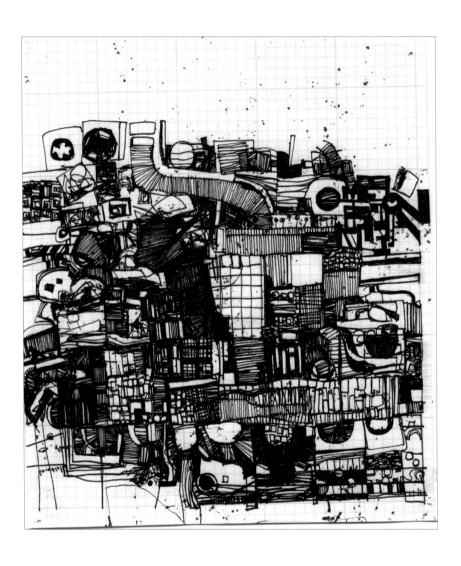

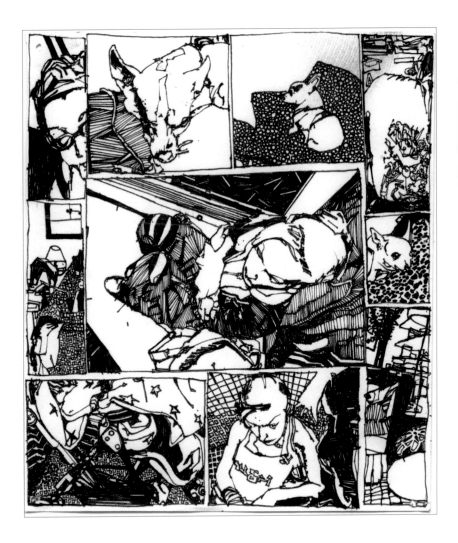

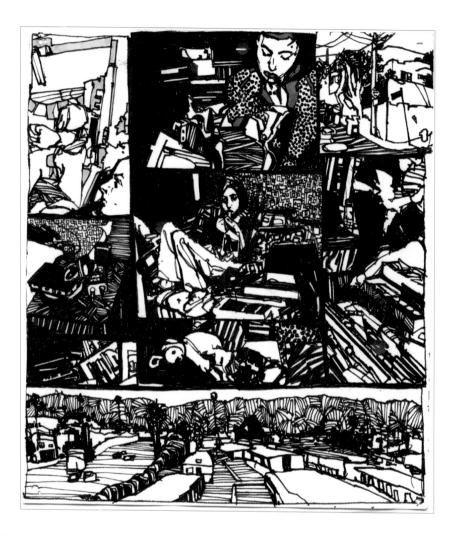

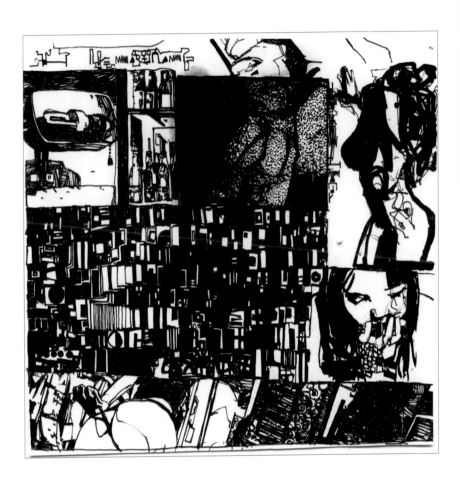

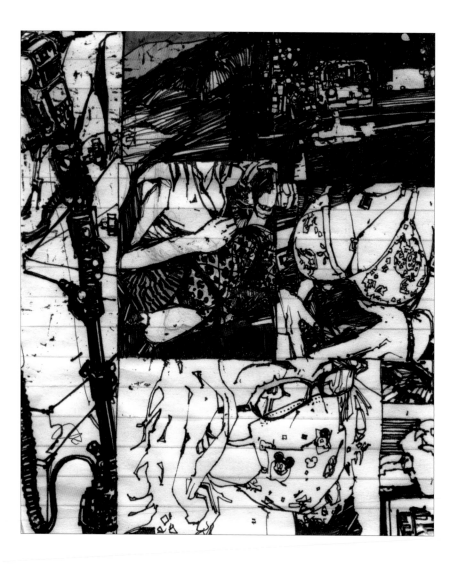

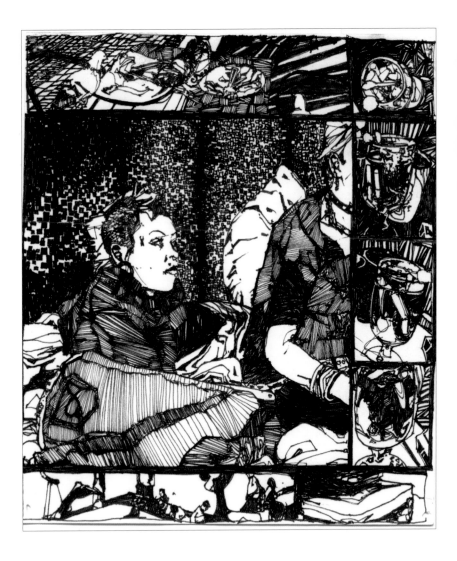

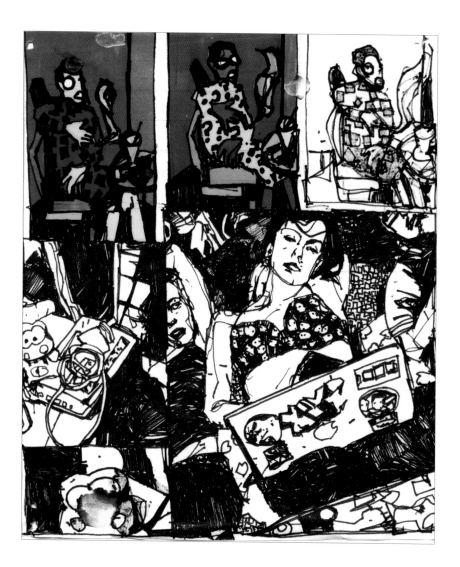

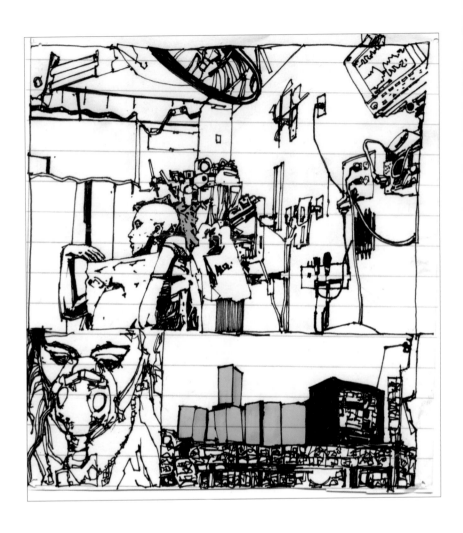

# A Few Brief Things I Should Say before We Get Started Talking about Porn Again

**In London,** I almost get arrested, someone steals one of my drawings, and the DJ the gallery hires plays old music all night, but the paintings get sold and a Lithuanian model gives me something for my face and *Laughter in the Dark* to read on the plane. I remember that—although, at least according to whatever philosophy is going on in my teeth and my face, the trip is a literally unprecedented disaster—it is really not at all actually that bad to be me.

I know that. I would just like to stop for a moment in my book and let you know that I know that. It gets much worse than being me. I get to America and Candy fixes everything instantly by being there and Candy. There isn't much to say there—happiness writing white and all that. And writing in white-out.

So enough about me. Let's talk about everyone else.

∘∘∘∘∘∘∘∘∘

For Christmas, my art dealer in New York sends me this book—*Glitter and Doom: German Portraits from the 1920s*. It's a hardcover book of terrible paintings from Berlin just before the Nazis, and the ink smells faintly like mayonnaise.

In it, there are addicts, cynics, sexual deviants, amputees, whores, artists, and art dealers, all dramatically deformed. The style at the time was called "new objectivity" and called on artists to use the dowdiest and most traditional painting techniques available to depict everyone in Berlin as a flabby grotesque caught stunned in a pose like a shot goose.

It's almost possible to see the paintings as radical and fascinating in their attempt to create an order that aggressively promotes the drab, the ugly, and the half-assed—since we're all so bored with an order that *passively* promotes the drab, the ugly, and the half-assed—that is, until you see the casual or posed black-and-white photos of each subject, usually posted on the page opposite each painted portrait in the book. The photos inspire genuine artistic awe. Here are real mutants, done in the colors of bones and the city, more awful in every way and more memorable than sofalike muddling from bad painters.

When you turn through the museum-white book and see these photos in the lower left of the even-numbered pages it is like looking at the half-assedness of *God*—who molds fresh wrecks and new freaks every day and sets them walking around on the earth with the rest of us.

And then you reel further at the extent of anti-Providence when you remember that, in the Berlin that made these paintings, *these* people—these wizened chain-smokers and bloats, the hideous addicts, cynics, amputees, whores, artists, and occasionally even art dealers—*were the good guys.*

°°°°°°°°°

Expressionism never really caught on in America. Americans are so bad at disguising themselves that it's tough for them to think of anything hidden to express. American addicts, cynics, whores, and bloats go around in T-shirts saying "Addict," "Cynic," "Whore," and "Bloat." Americans are all Expressionists.

You know as soon as you land. After all the connecting flights, canned Bloody Marys, time changes, and in-and-out window-seat snoozing, it can be easy to lose track of which connection you're in the middle of, but you always know when you've landed in America because when you walk into the airport they yell at you.

This is not a show of hostility or even impatience; they yell at you when you land in America because they—the badged blue-suits—don't want to be there doing their job where they yell at people who just landed for eight hours a day. Also, they are Americans, and so they believe it is important that you *know* this.

In European airports they don't yell at you. At least not until you've actually done something wrong, and even then they'll generally have been *chasing* you for some time before they start yelling at you. At some point after the Bourbon Restoration, Europeans all agreed that certain things were going to be kept *private* so that they could stop fighting with each other all the time. They agreed to suppress the public expression of all their differences of race, creed, and class except during soccer games and world wars. This was done for the sake of keeping things running smoothly and not ruining all their wonderful buildings. Sex was very much included—the porn company I worked for in Barcelona was called "Secret."

In Europe, they had kings and their names were King Something and they did everything they could all the time to remind you that they thought they were better than you and they lived in castles called Castle Something that everyone knew had alligators all around them that would eat you if you tried to go in them and empires called the Something Empire that ran your country for you and God spoke through a man in a big pointy stone house who made you kiss his ring. Meanwhile, on the other hand, most people would pretend to be nice to each other.

Here, it is all reversed. The people don't bother to pretend to be nice, but the men in charge do, and the companies that own them do, and the churches do, too. In America, power smiles like a hostess. The man in the seat next to you will eagerly and immediately tell you everything that makes him alien to you, while the airline will pretend it is your best friend.

If we want to look at people living in America, we will need a different thing.

## Cartoons about Pain

### God and Candy Crushed

have always had a strange relationship.

One morning, Candy puts a free video up on her site where she eats Sunday Dark's pussy and also Sunday Dark eats Candy's pussy.

A few thousand people all over the world watch it. Many, presumably, masturbate.

At exactly the same time, a pastor at Grace Community Church in Sun Valley, California, demonstrates, using passages from Romans 1 and 2, that girls eating each other's hot pussies will make God turn away and entirely forsake not only the eaters of pussy themselves, but the entire United States of America.

A few million people all over the world listen to it. Whether any of them masturbate is unclear.

In America in 2008, neither the sermon's intolerance nor its popularity is remarkable. It is, however, interesting for its intellectual coherence and rigor. The very strange and very normal Reverend John MacArthur of Grace Community Church is a learned man, an engaging speaker, and a good writer—he has a memorable phrase of his own toward the end of the sermon: "Nobody times nothing equals everything."

He uses it to make fun of the idea that there's no First Cause, that all of this—the world, the sky, America, California, the airport, Candy Crushed—could have come together by no hand at all, but, hearing it, I think it also describes the mathematics of love very beautifully: you are nobody and you are nothing, and then you are everything.

When I get back from my trip and land in America, they yell at me, like they yell at everybody; I wait in a line; I say to a guy at a desk that I'm someone who went somewhere for some reason, and they look through my stuff and I say it again, and then I see Candy, and the math happens, and then there are no other things.

Candy.

Candy:

In the winter, Candy is chosen for the lead roles in two movies. In both, she plays a patient. One is Osbie's next film, called *Medical*. In the other, she is cast as a celebrity from the future who, with a psychiatrist, visits her own various personalities (who fuck). The working title is *Shades of Romona*, which is—on an aesthetic, descriptive, and commercial level—the worst-ever title for a porno movie, or possibly anything, ever. The lead for *Shades* is recast after Candy's first scene because the producer lets someone smoke somewhere inside and she has an asthma attack. Taking care of her, I had to pass up a scene with the Heart twins, but reports from the set suggest they'd been difficult and anorexic and I hadn't missed much.

Well, lots of people have asthma. They have drugs for that, right, and those plastic periscope things you squeeze in your mouth? And they work very well unless you're Candy and have other, genuinely novel and frequently undiagnosable problems and also quickly develop, early in life, new and extra conditions due to all the steroids and amphetamines they have to give you to fix the ones you were born with. Candy is in a lot of pain often.

The outside of Candy, though, is an obscene, insane extreme of exquisite, annihilating perfection. So maybe to God it all evens out.

When she first moved in, Candy and I used to lie in bed all day and play Star Wars: Battlefront and read books. We read a book by a Yale prof named Harold Bloom (I never took his class). Bloom's idea is that if there is a God he is a jerk.

Whether or not he exists or is good, it is unarguable that God is a terrible influence on the lives of a great many porn stars. Everything else aside, any lingering belief in any spiritual ideas—that is, any philosophy that holds that there is some form of justice or appropriateness to the distribution of pain and reward in human affairs—is bound to work havoc on the mind and self-esteem of someone who has endured any real suffering.

Religion is not something I really ever expected to have to think about. Art and religion had a big fight in the '80s and by the time I came around they weren't speaking to each other. But once I started hanging out with people other than just painters and punks, I started noticing it again, everywhere.

If, in any context, someone starts talking about someone and says, "His parents were very religious," you won't necessarily know what they're about to say next. But if someone tells you, "*Her* parents were very religious," you get ready to hear roughly the same things you'd get ready to hear if they'd just said, "Her parents were meth heads."

It doesn't really matter what the religion is. It's not a secret that the majority of the practical work of *any* large religion is the sexual regulation of women. You have to get them to make as many babies as possible, then you have to get either them or the men to hang out with the babies and teach them the religion. Any faith that doesn't advocate this behavior, over the centuries, shrinks. It's basic Darwin.

Or, as the 2008 Democratic candidate for president put it, with his uniquely tentative charm, "I think faith and guidance can help fortify a young woman's sense of self, a young man's sense of responsibility, and a sense of reverence that all young people should have for the act of sexual intimacy."

Characteristically blurry, he doesn't say at what age people should stop having a reverence for the act of sexual intimacy or what they should use to get rid of it.

Candy had *faith and guidance* when she was a young person, and her main impression at the time was that it was hot.

The large Jesus on the large crucifix in the small Catholic school in Quebec was hot; Lot's daughters raping him were hot; *surely, therefore, I will gather all your lovers with whom you took pleasure, all those you loved, and all those you hated; I will gather them from all around against you and will uncover your nakedness to them, that they may see all your nakedness* was hot.

This is a common response to a Catholic education, at least in women, perhaps because Catholic aesthetics evolved during an age before birth control. During the Counter-Reformation, you decided Ezekiel 16:37 was hot and the next thing you knew you had quintuplets.

The careers Candy considered when she was very young—*very* young—in an indecisive rotation—were comic-book artist, nun that secretly had sex, painter in New York, stripper.

Candy liked, and still does, the George Perez run on *Wonder Woman*. She particularly likes the image on the back of the first issue where Hercules is standing over Wonder Woman and she's naked with a chain around her neck.

Wonder Woman was created by William Moulton Marston. He believed that women were going to eventually use sex to take over the world. He had no problem with that. He lived with his girlfriend and his wife, was a professor at Tufts University, and invented a key element of the modern-day polygraph test. He also invented Wonder Woman's arch nemesis, The Cheetah, who Candy also likes very much.

Marston didn't need the money, he wrote *Wonder Woman* comics because he *wanted* to. While it is unknown whether Moulton Marston hoped to inspire a sense of reverence in young people for the act of sexual intimacy, it *was* his avowed aim to inspire a sense of reverence in young people for the act of being tied up.

Wonder Woman's own religion is unclear: she definitely believes in Greek gods, but is also always fighting them.

The Cheetah worships Urtzkartaga, plant god of darkest Africa.

Candy herself is more the product of accident than design. Even before Candy's dad—who only has half a stomach—started working in toxic-waste disposal, the Crushed family gene pool was brackish with actual mutants: she has deformed, blind, palsied, and premature relatives—one with a hole in his heart and an extra aorta—and a Nazi in the family. And on the quiet edge of the pool there's Candy, crackling and fizzing, synthetic and irregularly assembled: one eye green, one eye blue, five-zero, feet that fit only heels designed by pedophiles, tits that fit in bras from only one company on earth, a useless third ear that had to be surgically removed, myopic, with a face like a fragile, depraved little doll. The doctors never thought she would live.

The Cheetah's curse was she would go from being aggressive, exotic, excitable, very attractive, and wearing either nothing at all or a skintight outfit with heels to being an ordinary human wearing glasses in more or less constant pain.

Because of Candy and her problems with health and pain, I now know all about hospitals. Now, whenever I carry Candy in through double doors to a waiting room, I know all about the foreplay and triage, the hard-to-get of the important machines (the fingertip heart-rate monitor just can't get past dark nail polish), their weakness for impatient and passionate letters full of numbers and preexisting conditions (How do I remember them? Acronym: A COMA CAMPUS), and, when it all comes together, their humming adjustable vinyl beds. She has a fantastic pain resume. I have seen her double up and cry and not move and not know what it is and not have anyone else be able to tell her either. It is not a thing you want to see.

In addition to *Wonder Woman* comics, Candy also likes Jean-Paul Sartre, who did not believe in any god, but would appear to approve of the Curse of Urtzkartaga, having said:

"Suffering is justified as soon as it becomes the raw material of beauty."

I have to think about that every morning since it's tattooed on the back of Candy's neck.

It's in looping cursive, center-justified right down the top of her spine—in that seeping aqua that tattooists pass off as black—through "is" "it" "material" and "beauty."

These back-of-neck tattoos girls get these days, they're not innocuous—certainly not in the case of Natalia Dionni's Wally, who felt he had to wake up to "Property of Wally" every morning—but also not with Claire, who leaves anyone lucky enough to take her home and unlucky enough to wake up first staring at "intelligence, awareness, creativity" and trying to figure out why they have to look at *that* before they've had breakfast. What *is* that about, Claire?

Like Candy, and a great many girls in the Industry, Claire spent some time when she was young in a psych ward, then got over it.

You can't *see* a tattoo on the back of your neck, and it isn't the kind of place you get a tattoo that's supposed to make you hotter. The back-of-neck tattoo seems like a kind of mantra, some lesson meant to be learned by osmosis. Or a broadcast to people you can't see.

On her neck, Grace Domaine has cheetah spots. She also has a tattoo on her (otherwise bare) arm that just says "Self." I ask her if this is so she doesn't forget her self. She says it is.

Once, when she had a master, he told her to burn all her paintings. She did it. There was no physical threat implied—that was just the way they did things, for years. People are more different than alike.

Candy's parents used to give her resigned, colorfully tragic books written especially for children with diseases that were going to kill them before they were old enough to understand what death was. She grew up anyway, but new bad things kept happening.

What I know about exactly how bad it was to go through these things and have them leave parts of themselves in you I only know from times in the middle of the night, when she wakes up from dreams. She is very bad at sleeping.

What little she says generally involves being chased, unbelievable animals and monsters—"a long, flat scorpion"—and, often, abandonment. There is a particularly awful, tasteless, repeating one, which starts with her hiding under a table with babies. The babies are stuffed and then sewn into the stomach of another baby, like a C-section reversed. Which is alive and which is a corpse—the entombed children or the child who was used as a tomb—is different on different nights.

Thinking about all the things that had happened to her made Candy unafraid to die. She kept thinking she would die; she kept not dying. At some point, she decided to make the kinds of decisions people make when they know they might die at any moment and when they know there will be nothing after that. And when they really believe it.

⊙⊙⊙⊙⊙⊙⊙⊙⊙

Osbie and his girlfriend or ex-girlfriend have a Christmas party and it rains on and off all day. The sky looks like a very old person's linen closet and it turns the whole landscape under the Hollywood sign black. Osbie, dressed in a Victorian waistcoat with a silver pocket watch and pin-striped vest, runs a scavenger hunt for thrift-store bric-a-brac and cheap liquor in a public park built around a Frank Lloyd Wright house. As for me, my shoes are caked with loamy mud from looking for things I'm not finding on a sheer hillside on the east end of the park opposite a fenced-in section of parking lot where a gutted van is beached next to a toolshed's yard scattered with jerry-built furniture and piles of rusting electronics. I do poorly, worse than anyone else. Since it's getting dark, Osbie's girl has sent him out to show me where the last few prizes are. I try to blame my upbringing:

"Even though I grew up in DC, I never did do that White House Lawn Easter Egg Hunt."

"You know how NORAD used to see Santa Claus every Christmas?" says Osbie.

Santa Claus as we know him was first drawn by the cartoonist Thomas Nast. The same goes for the Republican elephant, the Democratic donkey, and Uncle Sam's beard, and also the buck-toothed Chinaman, the immigrant-as-ape, and familiar versions of a great many corrupt political bosses, landlords, and clergymen. You would not want to live in a Thomas Nast cartoon.

I tell Osbie I didn't know the NORAD thing.

"Well, every year it was on the radio. They'd interrupt whatever was going on, on Christmas Eve, like an emergency, and say, 'Hey this is the NORAD satellite defense and there's this unidentified object and we don't know what it is,' and they'd track it and then after a few hours—oh—it's fucking Santa Claus. There's one in the tree."

"Jesus, right fucking there. I suck."

"Used to scare the shit out of me when I was a kid. Ruined Christmas. I thought there was going to be a nuclear war. There's one in the rain gutter."

Political forces beyond Osbie's control are set on ruining *this* Christmas for him, too.

This is partially just incidental: it's just best to deliver eviction notices on Christmas Eve. It makes it much more difficult for anyone protesting their eviction to file the necessary papers on time. Most lawyers and government offices are unavailable on Christmas and for weeks afterward.

Ever since Christmas was invented, of course, landowners worldwide have experimented with ways of ruining it, and such sport is, this year, the avowed policy of the Korean Methodist Church at 4101 Rosewood Avenue in Los Angeles. Osbie, along with everyone else on his block, is going to be forcibly relocated because the church wants a bigger parking lot. After months of visiting offices to avoid losing the small half house he grew up in, Osbie finds that all the city officials familiar with the case agree that the process is entirely legal and unethical.

Local and federal laws pertaining to the kicking of Mexicans out of rent-controlled real estate that's too good for them have changed considerably since they were first discovered living in Los Angeles over two hundred years ago—evolving gradually from early musket-based initiatives to current policies that clearly state that the victims must be told well before the *actual* eviction notices are delivered and must be moved into homes of roughly equal value. Nevertheless, Osbie has intimations that this will mean some ex-half-unit twisted into the guts of some part of town that's just as bad but harder to get to. The situation wastes a lot of time, does nothing for his general temperament and sense of well-being, and also means he doesn't help me build a robot. I change the subject:

"Hey, do you know what a 'frogged coat' is?"

"No."

"Y'know, sometimes people are wearing a fancy outfit in a book and they have a 'frogged coat.' I wish I knew . . . "

"Wait—you know those buttons on Chinese clothes that aren't actually buttons, they're just little pieces of rope that go together?"

"Okay, yeah."

"That's a 'frog.'"

What Osbie has hidden are actually envelopes with numbers on them, and we go back to Osbie's girlfriend or ex-girlfriend's house and redeem them for actual things with corresponding numbers. I trade what I win for a wrought-iron spiked ball on a chain. Someone else gets a movie about Gumby.

Some business gets done. The only other Industry people at the scavenger hunt are Juan Beak and his wife, Millie Peres, who is massive and gorgeous in a way where all of her moves whenever she moves and it is impossible to look over at her tits, strapped just barely into the top of her red corset and jammed up against each other like bloated, boneless twins in a loveseat, without wanting to squeeze yourself in up against them and pop white-hot all over their bouncy, featureless faces.

I text Candy asking if she wants me to ask Millie if she wants to do a content trade and she says "yes." And I ask Millie and she says "yes." Millie explains to Juan that "content trade" means she'll have sex with Candy and film it and Millie will get footage for her Web site and Candy will get footage for *her* Web site (which I don't get why she has to explain because Juan's been directing porn for like *how* long now?). Then I tell Millie how we'd done a content trade with Gina Giles the night before and afterward, at Sharkey's, I was filming Gina eating a vegetarian burrito and Gina'd said how her boyfriend had loved the part of Millie's Web site where she has all the food she eats on there and how it made him all hot and Gina said it was because he was a pervert. After Juan and Millie leave, Osbie talks about how on Halloween Juan had kept taking out his balls and also wanted Osbie to take his balls out but Osbie didn't want to.

When I get home, Suzanne and Candy want to watch porn.

Suzanne had just ordered it off the Web and Candy keeps feeling and turning the porn box while talking about other things. Meanwhile, Suzanne is swinging the spiked ball and chain and repeatedly coming very close to hurting herself because she is about like a matchstick with skin and it is heavier than her. Finally Candy says we should watch the porn even though she has a stomach flu—so then we three watch it.

Candy and Suzanne don't like to watch mainstream porn. They also don't like to watch alt-porn. What they like, and what they are hoping *Angel Blade: Punish* is, is porn where schoolgirls are raped, with tentacles, by monsters. ("Change Parental Control temporarily to level 8?" If schoolgirl tentacle rape is level 8, how can whatever level 10 is even be legal?)

These films are generally Japanese and are generally cartoons, and the plots, being free from the budgetary restrictions of normal porno films, often involve the annihilation of entire nations, planets, or levels of reality—or the threat thereof. Despite a surprisingly large amount of the three thirty-minute episodes collectively sold in the United States as *Angel Blade: Punish* being given over to dialogue, the premise of the show is never actually established, though it is explained almost immediately that it takes place in a version of our future where the earth as we know it has been rendered uninhabitable to humans and we now all live in impossible cities that float on cones of land, which look like inverted volcanoes, and that appear digital and futuristic at a distance but look exactly like contemporary Japanese buildings when characters are standing near or in them.

The exception, of course, is the villains' lair, which looks—rather in the tradition of villains' lairs—less like any architecture than like the inside of a metal animal, decorated with linked cables, blinking rectangles, and platforms covered in panels for characters to stand on and from which uncomfortably shaped pieces of symmetrical metal ominously emerge.

The film begins with two quivering women in this lair, one with pink hair and an eye patch, and one with purple hair and goat horns, shackled to machines that penetrate them while they tremble and moan, "Please forgive us, Phantom Lady!" Candy liked both of these girls very much in the first part of the series (called, simply, *Angel Blade*), but in this sequence, both the girl's snatches and the devices that fuck them are disappointingly underanimated and poorly rendered. It emerges that the inscrutable Phantom Lady, who has unnerving breasts the size of large dogs that pass her waist and strikingly unattractive headgear, still has, for reasons left entirely unclear, plans to rape or cause the rape of young girls throughout the city, particularly at the university level. Why one shy girl, Moena, plans to oppose this scheme, and why she hopes to accomplish this by turning at intervals into the costumed Angel Blade, and why this requires passing through a short but genuinely erotic sequence wherein the modestly endowed Moena spins on a pulsing pink background while a fetish outfit materializes on every part of her body except her tits, ass, and the lips of her snatch—and these parts all expand in spasmic lurches and then quiver wetly to a standstill in the gleaming void once she is fully and totally transformed—are all left, likewise, unclear. What is clear is that Candy and Suzanne sit on the bed craving for her only to fail, and to know ruin, and to be fucked by demons.

Japanese culture is indeed very intriguing, but the West is by no means silent on these matters:

According to the Catholic and Orthodox Bibles, the demon of lust is Asmodai. The Talmud explains that he was a son of Adam, by the succubus Naamah, who, along with Eisheth Zenumin, Agrah Bah Mahlat, and, of course, Lilith, comprise the four Angels of Prostitution.

Naamah means "pleasant."

In the movie, the screen pans over Moena's aunt—wrists bound, breasts likewise dog-sized—about to be raped by Phantom Lady's daughter. To do it, the daughter will grow a cock from her slit. As Milton put it, demons "Can either Sex assume, or both; so soft And uncompounded is thir Essence pure."

For her part, the hermaphroditic demon says, "Come on, I'll give you lots of juice!"

Suzanne says, "I had breasts like that once."

Essentially boobless, Suzanne was rigged at one point with colossal dog-sized breasts containing tubes for fake lactation by a site that catered to unusual tastes. Not Pomeranians, either—like labradors.

"What were they made of?"

"Silicone."

"That must have been expensive."

"They had access to it somehow—they were custom-made—they were huge. I couldn't walk or I'd fall on them."

Imagine a feminine stick figure with long black hair falling face-first into a bulbous pair of pork dumplings like couch cushions attached to her chest, triggering a gush of synthetic milk. "Did you get footage of that?"

Meanwhile Moena's aunt seems to be, against her better judgment, beginning to enjoy getting tit-raped by Phantom

Lady's daughter. The aunt's ridiculous boobs are agreeable enough in extreme close-up—each pushed tightly to the clear mirror face of its twin—and the nipples are stylishly done and the daughter has a cute, sick little voice. Though in all ways freaks, they are not monsters, however, and the girls grow restless.

It is, on paper, if not in emotional pitch, a lot like the scenes Suzanne's fans love most. It looks as much like rape as possible, while subtle details of piping and trim suggest maybe it isn't. In this scene, the aunt gets raped and then seems (as in Sergio Leone films) to change her mind halfway through. In Suzanne's films it always looks the other way around. She is like fear made flesh, and she clutches at herself as if any movement will crack all her bones like porcelain, an eggshell girl in an unknowable hard-walled planet of danger and fat cock. You will never hear anyone say, "Will you please tie me up and fuck me," less convincingly, while still *possibly* meaning it, or see cocks sucked with eyes so hopeless and drowned.

When Angel Blade and her friend Angel Ender end up thigh-deep in purple syrup, things begin to look promising again, but the creatures that emerge are anonymous and relatively well-behaved and have the hollow look of gingerbread men and limit themselves to holding the Angels in place while the villains look at a throbbing globe and the episode ends in an enigmatic stalemate. The closing credits sequence starts over the show's torchy J-pop theme song: "We're moving forward from here / An Angel flies away into the cold breeze / Thousands of lights are shining bright / I hope the light reaches you so let's jump out / Ah. Destroy the world / I want to penetrate it now / Don't stop, don't give up, let me know / If you never turn me now, are we shining? / Punish severely with Angel Heart / I will power any god, I will challenge any fight, loneliness speeds up / expose all the hypocrites / Now that you're here let's fight, Angel Blade."

When the next episode starts and is totally forgettable, Suzanne says she's hungry and goes into the kitchen. There is a lot of talking, fighting, bikinis, and straight sex, and more credits with yet another, different, theme song—also insane ("Another storm passes by / Many flower buds pop open").

The last episode on the disk opens with Moena walking though a forest and stumbling on an immense web stretched across a path, where all her friends are snared and bent into poses with their wrists and ankles trapped and their backs arched and their legs held apart, convulsing with terror while, in the center, a busty female spider-centaur threatens Moena while simultaneously violating all her prisoners at once with the screwlike limbs protruding from the needle tips of her terrible legs. We pause it and tell Suzanne there is a spider monster and she rushes in from the kitchen.

"Did I miss the spider monster?"

"I rewound it."

"She's so cool!"

"Yay! Spider monster!"

"I kinda think it might turn out to be a dream sequence."

It does. Moena awakes, drenched but all alone. We wait for the spider monster to come back, but it doesn't. There are some mutants with spider faces, but they aren't any good and don't really do anything and it seems like the spider monster was just a prophetic metaphor for them and we watch the rest of the episode on fast forward. Then there's homework:

Suzanne has actually quit the Industry and is trying to get her English degree—which, for convoluted economic and academic reasons, means, in her case, taking one class at a time for a while. Her dangerous parents, who insist she get a B average in the fall semester or else be cut off, are paying for that one class—a class on Thomas Pynchon. She is tied in a financial knot of long standing, and the only job she feels she can do that pays well enough to get her out of it without help is having sex with people she doesn't want to for money.

The deal, as it seems to Suzanne, is: move back home, be a hooker, or understand Thomas Pynchon.

So a project that winter is helping Suzanne with papers. Hers is a narrow, disordered, and panicking world and it has almost killed her more than once. She sets about, in her very serious, very frightened way, trying to grasp and write about characters who are either aimless and barely motivated or harrowingly and pointlessly obsessed, and plots that are not plots at all, and an author who, in general, has less respect for proper cause and effect than any novelist born.

In her papers, the ideas make sense but wind in spirals— sentences repeat, conjunctions and whole words are missing. She is constantly distracted:

"I have to reorganize the fridge."

"Great, that'll waste some time."

"But it's impossible to *do* anything in it."

"What were you planning on *doing* in the fridge?"

"Reorganizing it."

"So you're gonna reorganize the fridge because you can't do *things* in the fridge and the *thing* you wanna do is reorganize it."

"Yeah."

"Awesome."

I remind her how she asked me to help write a paper so she won't have to be a hooker.

"Yeah," she says, "well I read it and it's how nothing's connected and things don't make sense and there's no narrative and then I start to feel like my life is that way and nothing makes sense and I can't . . . and I just . . . and the dishes are . . . " and then she cries.

All this—fragments, drifting, disintegrated stories—is very big back at my real job, in the art business. Cause-and-effect abuse, the nonlinear, what they call "the Postmodern Condition." To hear them talk, everyone is like Suzanne, so soft and uncompounded is their Essence, and any influence—even *art*—barrels through them like a baseball through a mirror, leaving them shattered and prone and numbly reflecting it or its opposite.

Jimmy Walker, "The Night Mayor of New York," once torpedoed a censorship motion by saying, " I have never yet heard of a girl being ruined by a book." I would like to agree with him, but now I know that there are some people so fragile and so *postmodern* that ideas can hollow them out like a poison.

I wonder, for example, about Tina DiVine, whose favorite author is Kurt Vonnegut (not that it came up on our date, it's just "So it goes" is tattooed on her arm, so it comes up in her interviews)—which seems unfortunate. Although he was a very good writer, his stories tend to emphasize the essential decency of simple people who lead quiet lives full of simple enthusiasms and children, and they dispense the kind of humanistic wisdom that would play hell with the self-esteem of someone with the ambitions of a GSP contract girl. She might've been a saner person if her favorite author were Dorothy Parker or Irvine Welsh.

Suzanne's dad is likewise a postmodern reader. He spends his time reading stuff like

*Instead of imagining yourself caressing the silky thigh of some gorgeous blonde, realize that you are actually stroking the leg*

*of an eight-foot spider that sits patiently still, with poisonous fangs bared, just waiting for precisely the right moment to tear you to shreds, then carry what's left of your mutilated body and soul down to the abyss of hell . . .*

*Beware of Asmodeus and his kingdom of spiders.*

on Catholic antipornography Web sites. And then he believes it.

As for Suzanne, I try to point out the missing stuff in her papers and do the typos and repetitions, but I avoid talking to her about the actual ideas. Even if the empty space I create amounts to half the required page count, she doesn't need more influences.

And she's dying for them—anyone's ideas but her own. In the middle of all the mental thrashing and literal dishwashing she does while trying to convince herself to write a paper, she'll say things like, "Well there's a book of essays I want to read before I start on *Mason and Dixon* but they don't have it at the library and it's seventy dollars."

"Suzanne, you know, you ever play Scrabble?"

"Yeah."

"Well I did, too. And I would sit with all my fucked letters on my little slidey thing and after my turn, instead of looking for words to make there on the board with my letters, I'd *wait* for the other two or three people to go and hope that they'd put down something I could stick my letters onto. And I always *lost*. Get it?"

"Yeah."

# Barely Legal Whores Get Gang-Fucked

**Sometimes,** in the Industry, you see things that you really wish you hadn't.

If it's a certain kind of very independent girl, she'll shrug it off, like "Hey, it didn't turn out that well—but I have no regrets, and it's good for business." But it can be hard to watch someone you know being sincerely degraded—dressed up so she'll look half her age, ganged up on and treated like a whore, and edited so she'll intentionally sound like an idiot—even if you know she made a lot of money off it.

Like when Tasha Rey does *The Tyra Banks Show*.

It begins, as I assume is usual, with Tyra in front of a large blue screen featuring her own first name gleaming on an unconvincing computer-generated medallion.

Tyra says how, when she was in high school, her friends got jobs working in fast food, or at corporate chain clothing stores—like the kind that sell the sweater-vest-and-puffy-shirt combination Tyra is wearing. Tyra doesn't say how it was an all-girl Catholic prep school called Immaculate Heart that held its graduations at the Hollywood Bowl and that, when she was there, her own job was being a runway model.

Tyra says, "But today, you wouldn't believe the lengths that some teenagers are going to to make *money*."

Tyra doesn't say why she made *Halloween: Resurrection*.

Tyra shows some footage of Tasha Rey combing her hair and packing a bag and reading a book. It doesn't show which book.

Tyra says that, as a teenager, Tasha was *sexually active*.

There are no statistics available on how many girls at Immaculate Heart High were *sexually active*.

In a voice-over, Tyra says that Tasha, in school, was "bombarded" by pornographic images while Tyra shows footage of Tasha, seminude in pearls, eye-fucking the camera.

Tasha says that, in school, far from having porn dropped on or launched at her in a military setting, she actually looked for porn online and stole it from her friends. This is in a shot where Tasha is driving and looking very sleazy and blurry in wraparound sunglasses and lighting that erases her jaw and in a from-below, up-the-nose angle that everyone in television, film, or photography will tell you is the shot you use to make someone look ugly and morally bankrupt.

There is no footage of Tyra Banks from that angle, not in the show or anywhere else, even in that part of *Coyote Ugly* when she's dripping wet and doing a pole dance on the bar where it would be the most appropriate shot to accurately represent the point of view of the shrieking drunks she was supposed to be dancing for.

Tasha talks about the ways she likes to have sex. She is still in the horrible driving shot, where she is looking not at the cameraman, who must be sitting in the well of the passenger seat, but straight out the windshield. It makes her look creepily detached from the very many deviant sex acts and perversions she's describing.

But actually it is good because when you're driving you have to look not at the camera but straight out the windshield or you'll kill yourself and everyone in the car and possibly other people or animals.

There is a Godard-ian edit and Tasha says how much money she makes. It's unclear whether this is in response to a question someone off camera asked or whether this is something Tasha feels personally is important to communicate to the audience of *The Tyra Banks Show*.

Tasha says how she has to take some days off if she gets an infection and at the word *infection* there is a sort of doom-lite keyboard-where-a-guitar-should-be brake screech in the soundtrack and a sinister fade into a makeup room.

"Although the money is seductive, this young woman struggles with the trappings of her pornographic life," goes Tyra.

Tasha says something unrelated while getting her makeup done.

As the interview proper begins, Tyra says that Tasha looks like a middle-school student, but does not say that when Tasha walked into the studio, Tyra told Tasha she looked too old because, in her natural habitat, Tasha has almost intimidatingly extreme and sleek Francophile-fashion-model-on-cell-phone-with-agent-with-whom-she-is-none-too-pleased-this-morning style and so Tyra had her people put Tasha in a shapeless rubber-ball-pink shirt, and clueless-attempt-at-cute earrings, and bruised-peach makeup and iron her long, dark, shampoo-commercial hair into a flat playground slide awkwardly semitwisting around her neck so that she would—in the same daytime-TV hotlit-high-contrast glare that makes Tyra's own face seem like a rusting bone mask—look like a middle school student. Who smoked.

Tasha talks about movies where they want her to be like a little girl: "I don't do it though—you know—you wear the clothes, you wear the wardrobe, but I try to change that, I don't want to portray that, that's not me." The camera pans back to show the Gap jeans and rube-ishly awkward flat brown slippers Tyra asked the wardrobe people to put on Tasha.

There is a cut to the nearly all-female audience looking like they are watching a live appendectomy being performed on an unanesthetized kitten after having been told that, if they move at all, the kitten will be impaled on fence spikes and then incinerated.

Then Tasha tells the famous Asking-to-Be-Punched story, and a pall falls over what we can see of the room and an atmosphere takes over the broadcast that is rare, and funny, and disturbing in every essential way. It comes from the sequence where Tasha's small, roving, lash-shaded, and knowing eyes move easily, almost self-deprecatingly (I'm such a *freak*) across the crowd while she tells this story about how totally deviant she is, but then her whole face tightens as she realizes, in the middle, that she's talking to someone with no sense of humor and we notice too, since all this is intercut with the paralyzed, lip-lifted, triangular slab of inert judgment that is Tyra Banks's face and the edge-of-tears, speechless, butterfly-wing flickering of eyelids out in the audience.

Those who enjoy whatever private pleasure is to be gained from receiving physical pain publicly would appear not to overlap at all with those who enjoy whatever private pleasure is to be gained from inflicting shame collectively.

The idea that you could be playing a different game with your life than them and yet still be playing it with a full deck is totally alien to this audience.

Have you ever watched strangers play cards? It takes patience to figure out whether they have fifty-two, and whether the game is poker or rummy or bullshit. There is a cultural scar so wide and raw here that information can't cross it.

There are parts of Tasha's face that always seem like they're squirming to do something cruel, around the lower lip and lower lids, under the sated stasis in the eyes, but her business sense keeps them still.

Tyra asks Tasha what she will do. Tasha says anything but children or animals.

Tyra asks about anal: "Anal sex? On *film? Every scene?*"

Tasha also has to explain to Tyra what a gang bang is. The five gyrating guys in wifebeaters and jeans deflowering the air behind a lone Tyra in Daisy Dukes and a bikini top in the "Shake Ya Booty" video did not explain it to her, apparently.

Tasha explains about fucking fifteen guys at once. This is something the audience can imagine, and they do, judging from a real or inserted rippling reaction shot of them imagining what it would be like to have sex with fifteen men at the same time. The audience girls look grave. One of them is hot. I'd fuck fifteen of her.

Tasha talks, twinklingly, about the always interesting experience of telling your mother you're doing porn. Pale and still peachy in her makeup, time after time, she smiles and tosses the ball of human interaction to Tyra, where it hits a null field, loses all inertia, and is sucked straight to the floor. *Thuck.* If the look Tyra Banks wears while receiving reality was a sound, the sound would be *thuck*. If Tasha is *very* lucky, she gets instead a cautious, queasy nod before the next queasily asked question.

Station break.

"Up next: a teenager *sucked* into the seductive world of *porn*." Tyra asks Tasha why there is something cold, hard, and distant about her and says she can't help thinking there is something that made her that way.

This, coming from Tyra Banks, is really, really, really, *really* funny.

Tyra asks about child sexual abuse.

Tasha says she wasn't sexually abused as a child.

Tyra says, "So you got into porn just *because?*"

Tasha says no, like she said before, she got into porn because of things she wanted to do that have to do with having sex.

Tyra says that it's a fact that a *lot* of women in porn have *issues* whether they want to admit them or *not* and then talks a lot more about how people *do* things for *reasons* and then cuts immediately to Tasha's boyfriend.

We see Guy, looking as if the camera just woke him up. He comes across like a dazed, blunt-headed mouth-breather in a collared shirt who doesn't realize that his unwavering, upright posture and attempts at eloquence and pruned facial hair only seem to exaggerate how unwholesome and hollow he is. That is, Guy comes across here like all boyfriends ever on daytime talk shows.*

---

* Although, presumably, his short performance here is his own fault, it is misleading. In actual life Guy's swagger and goatee suggest he is the kind of guy who knows *exactly* how unwholesome and hollow you think being a thirtysomething boyfriend of barely-legal-porn-star Tasha Rey is but, much more than that, suggest he is kind of exactly the kind of lazily cynical would-be-director boyfriend an extremely sleek Francophile-fashion-model-on-cell-phone-with-agent-with-whom-she-is-none-

Tasha's agent comes on and helps even less. He looks exactly like a shaved wombat in flared lapels that just ate a truck, and also exactly like sleaze.

The show tapers toward the next commercial break and Tyra asks Tasha to really sit down with herself and do some soul-searching and find out why she's really in this industry.

And Tasha says she knows why she's in this industry, which Tyra does not expect to have to respond to because she was planning on just saying all that and then just going straight to commercial, but then she has to respond to this or else redo it so they can reedit the whole bit, in which case the studio audience might realize how strange and manipulative that is, and so Tyra quickly says, "Yeah, okay," but Tasha hasn't told her a *real* reason, a "deep soul reason," and then, okay, commercial.

Presumably there are soulful and deep reasons for a seventeen-year-old wanting to be a rich and beautiful actress/model/celebrity who fucks pop stars, gives people tips about makeup, cuts records, shows up in people's music videos, and eventually has babies, but there are no possible deep soul reasons for an eighteen-year-old wanting to be a rich and beautiful actress/model/celebrity who fucks porn stars, gives people tips about sex, cuts records, shows up in slightly better music videos, and eventually has babies.

"We'll be right back," Tyra says, and gives the camera a Sir-would-you-mind-standing-*behind*-the-line? smile and then there is a shot of Tasha looking off into the audience with controlled hate.

---

too-pleased-this-morning-type girl would have if she chose true kinky-hipster love instead of marrying the first Mediterranean shipping magnate who offered to buy her an island. Also note that the collared shirt is *not* Guy's fault, as Tyra's wardrobe department provided both it and a pair of loafers to replace the Motorhead T-shirt and whatever likewise cliché-reinforcement-inappropriate shoes Guy showed up thinking he was going to wear on TV that day.

When the show comes back there's a segment about a fourteen-year-old prostitute.

I watch all this on YouTube—where the show is posted by whoever runs antipornographyactivist.blogspot.com. This entity claims that the (extremely involved) montage the show inserts after the commercial showing "Victoria" (the prostitute) wandering a city in a short skirt at night is misleading because Victoria was never a street prostitute and also that Tyra's people told the prostitute they'd blur her face out and didn't.

The (now) sixteen-year-old prostitute comes on the TV. Tyra does not ask her why she is cold or hard or distant, because she is feverish and quivering and gushing and looks essentially like a piece of confused cookie dough. Which isn't surprising because she is a sixteen-year-old prostitute and she's on TV.

Tyra interviews the little hooker with a measured condescenscion that stands in stark contrast to the measured condescenscion with which she interviewed Tasha (now in the front row of the audience next to her agent). With Tasha she kept herself coiled and steady-eyed—like if she asked the wrong question, Tasha would blink twice and turn her into a pervert. Her style with Victoria is that of an SVU cop wanting to know just exactly where she was when the bad men came and took her mother away.

Victoria is clearly totally fucked up, and not comfortable, and sad, and not very smart, so Tyra knows she isn't going to tell her anything everybody didn't already know when they saw the commercial for this afternoon's show, and that that makes for good TV. Victoria says she became a whore because she wanted money and then started doing cocaine and it was scary and she says she is upset and that no one should do what she does.

Something that at first seems to be a giant pencil in a sport coat but is actually a celebrity doctor comes on in order to tell everyone more things they know.

He frictionlessly offers a Freudian, or post-Freudian, "compulsion to repeat" theory for Victoria's behavior. He uses plural nouns enough that you can't tell if he's talking about Victoria and everyone else who's irrational and on drugs and greedy, or about Victoria and *Tasha*, who is keeping silent in the front row of the audience next to her agent.

Tyra says she's gotten in touch with an organization that will help Victoria and her family and that *antipornographyactivist* alleges did not actually help her as much as Tyra told Victoria it would. Tyra touches Victoria a lot, and while being touched, Victoria has exactly the expression the girl who gets raped while she's high has when she's in the elevator in the movie *Kids*.

After the commercial, Tyra says:

"Now, when she was a teenager, my next guest thought sex was an easy way to make money, but now at age twenty-five she knows how wrong she was."

Her next guest is a fat whore (spiritually speaking) and a fat ex-whore (physically speaking).

Tyra asks her to offer advice to Tasha and Victoria collectively. The fat whore says she *knows* these girls and she *is* these girls. While the fat whore is certainly large enough to be at least tripartite, a certain ambiguity remains. She may be following the Catholic philosopher Peter Geach, who argued that the mutual indwelling of the Holy Trinity can be understood if one assumes that all identity is relative to a chosen sortal term.

To illustrate her perichoresis, the fat whore tells a story about her path from stripper to cam girl to whore to porn star

that is teleologically similar in no way to the story of either of
the other guests because, she says, it's a slippery slope.

Rejecting both epistemic and pragmatic modes of argument, she says:

"It's a lifestyle. I mean, you drive a nice car, you live in a
nice house, you have tons of money, you can buy whatever
you want, but, but what does that get you in the end?" Okay—
sure—I see where you're going—you have material things but
you don't have integrity or self-respect or love or Jesus in your
life or something, right? No, actually, that's not where she's
going at all—next she says: "I don't have *any* of the things
from when I did that."

So it's bad to be a whore or a porn star *not* because there
are more important things than money, but because somehow the money, house, and car evaporate due to some form of
as-yet-undescribed economic attrition that attacks only money
made in the sex industry.

The fat whore has advice for Victoria: "Money and material
things can be gone (snap) like that."

Victoria cries a lot and nods.

The fat whore has advice for Tasha—oh wait, no, she says
it is, but it's questions. The first question has a false premise,
which Tasha points out. The question also brings up the fact
that Tasha licked a toilet seat in a movie, which Tasha then
points out was her own idea because it was her movie. The fat
whore says, "Then, well, I have a question for you."

Examining the shrapnel in the wake of the rhetorical train
wreck that is the second question, you can clearly pick out
cars labeled *aren't-your-fans-horrible-masturbators? porn-is-a-
bad-example-to-somebody,* and *your-movies-make-people-think-
things-about-you-that-aren't-true,* but by the time the traditional
verbal-question-mark-followed-by-pause-to-receive-answer

is actually delivered, the fat whore is basically asking whether Tasha would like to be in an abusive relationship. Tasha says no.

Tyra goes on for a tigerish paragraph about how she—Tyra—can't judge Tasha or tell her what to do because she hasn't lived Tasha's life, but that the fat whore can because the fat whore used to have the same job Tasha has and is now seven years older than Tasha. Tyra does not then invite Nina Hartley on to give advice to the fat whore.

The fat whore then says that all that anal sex will destroy Tasha's butt. Tasha tries to say out loud that doctors servicing the world's many homosexuals have not reported this to be so, but she is interrupted by the celebrity doctor in the suit and also Tyra, who both agree about her butt based on unstated evidence. When they're done gang-interrupting her, the conversation has finally pinwheeled over to the point where Tasha realizes she has to explain to Tyra that, other than being white and a woman and once having had the same job, none of the things in the fat whore's life resemble things in Tasha's.

The fat whore says, "Your pimp is sitting right next to you."

This shifts cameras and attention to Tasha's obviously unsavory agent Jack Wiegler, whose silk-framed bald spot everyone in the studio audience has been eyeing queasily throughout the show, and so it gets the show's first full-blooded-Orc-horde-Nuremberg-pecking-party-vintage-daytime-talk-show-We-Will-Drive-Them-into-the-Sea roar of approval.

Commercial.

Tyra, having finally realized where her points are going to get scored, tacks Wiegler-ward. Is he a pimp? Wiegler points out that Tasha does what Tasha wants to do. The fat whore points out the fact that Tasha makes Wiegler a lot of money because of all the sick shit Tasha does. Wiegler fudges and lies and argues with the fat whore and sounds generally governmental.

The fat whore keeps bringing up how much money the agent makes. Tyra talks about how "seductive" the money in porn is.

Tasha's main crime appears to be talking about some other thing besides money. When she makes arguments that reference some nonmoney standard, no one else seems to believe or even hear her. The idea that *sex* might be "seductive" doesn't seem to occur to Tyra, which is sad because what you see in a Tyra Banks music video is a woman licking a fist-sized microphone who is going to make a lot of money off the fact that her only talent is she makes you want to fuck her.

The doctor says Tasha is like a heroin addict because she is trapped in self-destructive behavior that she says she wants to keep doing.

He says he sees porn stars on their knees begging him for help: "—and that's where this always goes. If it didn't, it could be a healthy behavior—who knows? The fact is it's destructive—if it were not destructive we wouldn't all be shaking our heads [saying], 'Why would someone put themselves in this position?'"

The audience applauds this provably inaccurate statement and its attached tautology.

"And Victoria wouldn't be crying the whole time," adds Tyra.

Victoria says it's because all her emotions came out. The fat whore tells her to love herself and that money isn't everything.

There's a commercial and then Tyra tells any teenager out there that there are other places to turn for validation and support than pornography and prostitutiton, because money that comes that easily has a lot of consequences, and then says that whatever money you make you will pay for emotionally and then she touches Victoria again.

There is not another *Tyra Banks Show* about Tasha when she wins Performer of the Year and announces she is leaving her agent to form her own agency. You get the definite feeling about Tyra, and the fat whore, and the doctor—and the audience—that they would not care that, if Tasha really did what she said she would and started her own agency that avoided agents and commisssions and therefore their desire to book you for *whatever*, this could be a major step in the practical prevention of violence toward—and exploitation of—women in the Industry. You get the definite feeling that this wouldn't matter to them and they would still think Tasha was missing the point.

The point is: they will not forgive her until she is ashamed.

# Year of
the Rat

**2008 begins** with an American diplomat getting shot through the neck and in the chest by parties unknown on his way home from a party at the British Embassy in Khartoum. "We do not know why this happened. All options are possible," says a spokesman for Sudan's foreign ministry—which is an unsettling thing to say in any context.

The next day, Candy puts up a video where she puts her foot in Gina Giles's pussy.

It is unusually ambitious for a five-minute porno movie where someone puts their foot in someone's pussy because it has Gina Giles in it and, of course, Gina Giles wants a movie where someone puts a foot in her pussy to be good.

Gina cares about the dark red walls being dark and red and being walls, and the spit-covered toenail polish looking like a glossy film, cataracted with suspended, small, live spit-bubbles—like a liquid universe on the toe that fucks her—and she cares about putting on a blindfold and Candy choking her with a belt and getting it all on film.

The video is popular. Other people appear to care, too.

It emerges on *Meet the Press* the night the movie goes up that former Arkansas governor and presidential candidate Mike Huckabee also cares, although he does admit to finding it all a bit overwhelming:

"It is now difficult to keep track of the vast array of publicly endorsed and institutionally supported aberrations, from homosexuality and pedophilia to sadomasochism and necrophilia."

The next day, in the first contest of the primaries, he comes in first. A man who blames the Columbine shootings on music and video games and pornography and who was on the board of a company that sells music and video games and pornography for nine years—and was named after the company's founder—comes in second. An actor who pretended to drive a red pickup truck so he could win a Senate seat comes in third. The guy who comes in fourth has seven houses, or eight—he's not sure.

In some circles, this is all big news, but porn people sleep very late, and they generally don't start a new year until the AVNs, and they're not 'til the twelfth. It would be nice if these larger forces would also ignore them, but that's not how it works. Even though she doesn't vote, Natasha Crash has a swimming pool that looks like a blighted salt marsh, mostly because of this subprime mortgage crisis. The pool man has not been coming around much lately.

"I have this shitty cold right now, and I have, like, no money, so I don't even know if I'm gonna have the money to go to AVN yet, but I'm planning on it, I mean, I don't know if I told you but I quit porn . . . "

"Yeah, you said," I say.

"Well, I mean, I'm still gonna do solo stuff and stuff for my site and Candy's site and, like, my friends and stuff but it's just too much work and not enough money and I just wanna fuck my boyfriend—I have a new boyfriend—and, like, he didn't even say anything but even before that, I got raped and . . . "

"Yeah, you said, by some guy pretending to be a cop . . . "

"Yeah, he was big and ugly and pretending like he was tryin' to be a cop and, anyway, I'm over it."

"Yeah."

"I mean, but the thing is, if I get Best Girl-Girl, then all these people are gonna want me to do scenes and . . . "

"Well maybe you can just pick the good stuff you wanna do."

"Maybe, people are gonna be offering a lot of money and it's gonna be tempting."

"Yeah."

"I don't know—I'm supposed to be modeling in a runway show for Tera Patrick's lingerie line but it's like two hundred dollars, which is like, whatever, like, did you read Belladonna's blog? She quit, she's just doing solo. Because there's, like, a lot of health risks now, like I heard from someone in LA that hepatitis B is going around and all these people had to get retested but they were okay, but y'know, I guess nothing should be tempting me that's putting my health in danger, y'know?"

"Yeah, you sound like you're in bad shape."

"Well, I guess I'm gonna watch the Steelers game and maybe that'll make me feel better."

Via e-mail, Cassandra Maniace reports that no matter what they may have said, nobody in charge of the Barcelona movie liked me at all, ever since that first e-mail where all I wanted to know was who I was fucking. They considered this rude. She also says that, since I got her keys out of the elevator shaft, the makeup girl and everyone else had started calling me Monkey Boy.

Natasha does go to Vegas, but doesn't win Best Girl-Girl.

The Steelers lose that night, but go 10-6 and win their division only to lose to the Jaguars in the playoffs.

Nevada has a primary coming up, and Hillary and Obama are both in town during the awards, but I don't see either of them because I have to spend that Friday night in Las Vegas on a radio show opposite a man who dresses like Nikki Sixx, wears a diamond-studded belt buckle that says "Godard," and paints cocktail olives with arms for a living—one of which hangs in the officers' lounge at the Pentagon.

On a similar theme, Tasha Rey's boyfriend goes around the AVNs in a T-shirt with the Danzig skull logo on it but with the word "Herzog" where it should say "Danzig."

That weekend, Herzog is stiffed at the Golden Globes, and Godard doesn't have anything out, but at the AVNs, their fan Tasha wins Performer of the Year—proving you don't have to be a blonde with big tits to get respect in the business as long as you drink mad cum and get hit and clearly like it.

Tasha has a look of levelheadedness about her that is rare to see in the Mandalay Bay at any time of year—and will definitely be better off when she retires than Jenna Jameson, who turns up at the ceremony looking, by all accounts, like a dessicated strip of bacon, makes a cryptic speech about her business and family arrangements that most people don't get, and, weeks later, goes on to endorse Hillary Clinton.

Also cryptic is the relationship between the owner of Nevada's most famous whorehouse and his "good friend"— bow-tied, right-wing, cable news tele-pundit Dwight Eisenhower. "Is he a customer?" I ask the big pimp after dinner at the Venetian.

"That's not something Dennis can discuss," says the guy to his left. As for Eisenhower, he is on the record as preferring that whores be in houses, because when they're not: "They make a mess, they snarl traffic." Which, I think we can all agree, is no good.

Meanwhile, Grace Domaine is up in the north end of a double suite having sex with everyone in sight and not getting paid for any of it. She calls it a "job," though, and takes it seriously: "Yeah, I agreed to be the orgynator." The word is awkward and ugly, but it means what it sounds like—she crawls around meowing and rubbing her face in people's crotches until they get comfortable with the idea of being naked in front of a room full of rubber and strangers with every sodomy in their eyes.

Natasha doesn't go:

"Is there gonna be crazy sex? I don't know if I wanna have crazy sex—I had crazy sex last night. I'm kinda tired, I just wanna eat. Plus I'm tryin' to fuck my ex-boyfriend."

Eisenhower isn't there either, but, this being Vegas, there are several sex clowns. One says she used to be a punk but decided that this was the *real* edge. They put on makeup and leather and noses and crash parties all over the city in an attempt to make people think about things in a new way. It didn't make a lot of sense to me, but I am not here to pass judgement on sex clowns.

Leopard skin is in at the awards this year, as it is every other year. Ella Revenge's coat is leopard, and so is her bag. She also has life-sized peacock feathers tattooed on her collarbones—suggesting she's a new combination-animal, like the hybrid and Jim Henson-ish statues standing sentry over the Mandalay Bay's valet stand and postapocalyptically quiet outer garden. Over dinner at the Mandalay, after the awards, Candy and I ask Ella if she wants to have sex with tentacles for Candy's site. She is the fifth person we've asked, and the first to say no, but she looks as if she might change her mind when we say we're going to use Tracy Stixx's hands for the close-ups.

Auspicia Clay is also there, wearing a fur with no pattern whatsoever. She isn't drinking, and Ella complains that no one is doing tequila shots with her. I tell her this is a problem that I can fix, and we drink. Then the waiter brings me a lemon cheesecake the size of a hockey puck and I make it into a face, with Piroulines for eyes and shards of star-patterned orange frosting for hair, and put it on a stick.

For the millionth time in my life I look away from the table and out at a lot of listless ordinary people on vacation, shuffling between one-armed bandits and indoor plants, and wonder if *any* of them were actually cut out for lives of baby shit and obedience. It is hard to imagine anything more fucked than them.

Since this time last year, Auspicia has managed to make her girl-boy-boy movie, but shooting with semi-amateurs in the dead of summer in New York has not left Auspicia hungry to shoot a new movie soon, and the *loaded*-gun version of Bella's fetish classic *Gunfucked* looks like it may never happen.

Godard was wrong when he said, "All you need for a movie is a gun and a girl"—you also need insurance.

Ella tells a story about how she was telling this new girl at the Circle Bar about how this guy over there had an enormous cock, and then the girl was saying how she'd never fucked a black guy, and then Ella said she went to the bathroom and when she came back they were fucking. It is a little difficult to picture people fucking at the Circle Bar in the dead center of one of the world's busiest casinos—but I keep trying.

Since there isn't a lot else to think about during the AVNs, one of the following realities is bound to hit you like a sickening stomach punch: how unbelievably much time people spend here having sex, or how excruciatingly *little* time people spend here having sex.

For example: right now Bella, Auspicia, and Candy are playing the Which-Porn-Girls-Are-Hot? game. This conversation takes place on a whole other plane from me—I've seen the least porn and pay the least attention to the porn news sites and am by far the least picky. I have to conceal my omnivorous approval—at least on a it's-the-thought-that-counts basis—of nearly everyone.

It is like those impenetrable circles girls form in school lunchrooms around thick fashion magazines, going page by page saying: "She's pretty," "I think she's pretty," "I don't," "Oh my G*od*, she's *gorgeous!*"

Their basic attitude—as they dissect the convention and the people in it—is that everything about sex and porn is really stupid, except the sex and porn that they like.

And this, again, is strikingly symmetrical to the way I feel about art.

I imagine what the AVNs would be like if I reacted the way I do to big art fairs in London and Miami and New York.

What would I be seeing? No-frills gonzo sites as cost-effective, time-efficient, loveless, and integrity-unintensive as minimalism? Extremist pornographers building an empire on the one idea they ever had as myopically as any conceptualist (quotes one scat-porn entrepreneur: "I don't have that much talent to compete with great artists—I chose shit to get to the fucking edge.")? Charmingly unprofessional amateur porn that all looks charmingly the same the way most charmingly naive neoexpressionist art looks charmingly like every other big charmingly muddy painting or charmingly tremble-knuckled drawing anyone ever accidentally made?

Okay, I get it now. We're snobs. Or just very serious. Professionals, anyway. And we despise unworthy competition with the bitterness of true professionals.

◦◦◦◦◦◦◦◦◦

Aside from Tasha's win, another piece of good news that emerges during the AVN weekend is that several FBI wiretaps were suspended because the bureau didn't pay its phone bills. This is nice because the FBI alleges that the organization I give all the spare money I make in porn to has possible terrorist ties and, according to an unsubstantiated report by a shoe-store owner in Kitchener, connections to Al Qaeda—thus meaning, under the current law, that everyone I've spoken to in the course of this book might be the subject of a wiretap.

A week after the AVNs, the student loan organization that Suzanne now gives all the spare money *she* makes in porn to, which in turn gives all the money it legally can to President G. W. Bush, announces that its marketing practices are being investigated by the New York State attorney general.

The same day, researchers in London discover that children don't like clowns.

"I had a dream about clowns—well actually it was a hallu-cination—with tiny heads and they had giant bodies and were on stilts, and they were coming out of big bubbles in the sky to crush me—I never took Wellbutrin after that," Suzanne says.

The guy who came in fourth in Iowa wins the next two primaries. He says he wouldn't mind if we were in Iraq a hundred more years. This is good news for the Industry, since it's hard to argue with U.S. foreign policy from a purely porno-graphic point of view:

Through whatever convenient means, maintaining or installing center-conservative governments around the third world—which dwell in, and support, traditionalist societies that are so obnoxious and oppressive to sexually aggressive women that they all want to leave and come *here*, but which, nevertheless, are just open enough, and friendly enough to the United States, that the women actually *can*—is good for business.

Even better, when parents from these countries move their families here, they occasionally bring their old ways of doing things with them.

Suzanne Lin's dad, for instance—like the caricature of every wave of educated, churchgoing new Americans since Mohicans and Mohawks first drew cruel pictograms of Jona-than Edwards creeping around Stockbridge with a candle and a spider moaning threats at anyone who would listen—is *awe-some* for the Industry.

When not secretly jerking off to Japanese girls and blondes on the Internet while his kids watch secretly through the door slats, this amateur painter, musician, and professional weapons designer spends his time praising the Lord, hitting children, ignoring people fucking his children, blaming the fucked for being fucked-with, and being generally a zealot and a fiend, and telling Suzanne she'll never be good at various non-fucking-related things she likes to do. On Christmas Eve, he used to write his children letters from the North Pole telling them how much more Santa Claus expected from them next year.

Saint Nicholas originally got famous by giving presents to three girls so they wouldn't have to become hookers.

Suzanne gets an A in her Pynchon class, and her dad welches on his promise to pay tuition and she goes into therapy.

Candy posts a video where she fucks Suzanne in a hotel whose manager was a six-foot-tall embezzler named Vlad.

The same morning, Huckabee—who wins the Republican caucus in Iowa—says that Suzanne fucking Candy isn't just like fucking dead bodies, it's also like bestiality—that is, like fucking all kinds of animals.

Earlier in the week, in Cornwall, an octopus fell in love with a Mr. Potato Head. "He's fascinated by it," said Matt Slater, of the Blue Reef Aquarium. "He attacks the net we use to fish the toy out every time we try to take it away."

Although it seems likely that Suzanne's father would prefer that she was a Mr. Potato Head, it is unknown whether Suzanne's father would want her to be *that* Mr. Potato Head. Also unknown is whether, if she were, he would prefer she be a contemporary Mr. Potato Head or an original-style Mr. Potato Head.

The original Mr. and Mrs. Potato Head toys were just a kit of artificial features meant to be stuck into a *real* potato. The plastic potato body was eventually introduced because of, among other things, the nightmarish things that happen to a Mr. or Mrs. Potato Head as it ages and the potato rots and dessicates leaving only a dark, shriveled core of organic parts from which the plastic characteristics that people have stuck on it poke out at wretched angles like spears from a carcass.

(There may be a lesson for parents here about what you should and shouldn't do to other living things.)

It's also true, however, that if Suzanne had been a potato, she would have been less likely to have been sexually molested as a child. However, if she had been, it would've been legal, unlike having sex with an octopus. Which, proving Mike Huckabee right, Suzanne says she would like to do.

It is a complex issue.

Another porn actress, known to engage in homosexual acts, says, "Yeah, well, one time I just really needed to get off and nothing was working—like nothing made me feel really *dirty*, and then but I had this *horse* porn Keith Knight gave me and, y'know . . . "

"Was it hot? Was it hot porn?"

"Well, it did the trick."

Meanwhile, the Department of Justice is trying to take down the guy who "chose shit to get to the edge" and also sold videos of people having sex with animals. The case eventually hits a speed bump, though, when the judge in the case has to recuse himself because of all the porn he has and then orders himself investigated for having pictures of sex fiends with animals and women painted to look like cows on his Web site.

Candy doesn't want to fuck a cow—she does, however, want to make a tentacle-sex movie. I ask Auspicia Clay if she knows anything about the legal consequences of going to Chinatown and buying a dead octopus and then fucking the octopus. She sends me a link to a news story about a Wisconsinite who shot a deer and then fucked it. Apparently, this is a legal gray area. His lawyer argued that once it was dead, it wasn't an animal anymore and so you could fuck it. Like, you can't fuck a cow, but you can fuck beef. Whatever else may be true, the law in free nations defends your right to put your dick in a hamburger in the privacy of your home.

The only time I was in Vlad the embezzler's room he said "I thought you were dead," and there was a man wearing a Darth Vader mask and meat all over the bed.

Things are this way. Apparently people are always trying to fuck animals.

# Useful Intelligence Gleaned from Simulated Drowning, Sexual Humiliation, and the Intentional Infliction of Bodily Harm

**On Groundhog Day,** no one tries to fuck the groundhog. However, as usual, a theme of repetition emerges:

In Los Angeles, Osbie almost gets killed by a UPS truck for the second time, and he has to again rewrite a script because he put in too much dialogue.

In Finland, scientists find yet another use for stem cells—by succesfully growing a jawbone in a man's stomach.

I tit-fuck Candy in the video posted that day, and tit-fuck her again the next day, and tit-fuck her regularly thereafter.

Punxsutawney Phil sees his shadow.

On Valentine's Day, former torture victim John McCain votes against a ban on simulated drowning. Some people approve of simulated drowning on the grounds that, often, useful intelligence is gained from it. Gina Giles approves of simulated drowning on the grounds that, often, it's hot. Suzanne approves of simulated drowning on similar grounds—plus Gina's paying her:

"There's a scene where you're floating in the bathtub and then Missy Ava pulls you out and wakes you up, and then there's the scene of Sunny and Ryan, and then there's the scene where Missy Ava ties you up and fucks you."

"You mean they cut out that whole water-bondage thing?"

"Well, they show you in the water, with your hands tied, and she pulls you out . . . "

"No, there was a whole scene where she put me underwater over and over and I was crying and I can't believe I went through all that for nothing."

"Yeah, that wasn't in there."

"She just kept *pushing* it and *pushing* it."

"Well, did you say 'stop'?"

"Well I'd never done it before and they asked me and I said, 'Okay' because I *wanted* to see—to see how much I could *take*."

"But you didn't like it. I mean, you're acting like you wish you hadn't done it."

"Well I started crying and so they just said okay, stop . . . "

"Yeah, but why didn't you say stop *before* you started crying?"

"Well, she should've *known* she was pushing too hard— she does that—she pushes really hard. She's a bottom but she plays a dom—and she used to *take* it really hard so she *pushes* really hard and part of being a dom is knowing to stop before you go too far."

"Yeah, but this is a *movie*, and Gina asked you to do something and you said yes and so she's gonna push until you say stop because she's like, 'I want this, will you do it?' and if you don't want to you've gotta say no."

"But in the BDSM scene—in the lifestyle, it's about trust, you know, the dom is supposed to *know* . . . "

"Yeah, but this isn't the BDSM scene, this is a *movie*, they're asking for something, if you can give it to them, you say yes and if you can't you say no. She would've been okay with that."

"But Gina knows me . . . ."

"Yeah, but you're putting Gina in this position, like, she has to be responsible for knowing what you want rather than you just saying it—it's a movie, it's a work situation, she's the boss, she's your friend, she doesn't wanna make you do something if you don't wanna do it, but you're asking her to know when you mean *no* even when you say *yes*."

"But—I was crying."

"But how come you didn't say 'stop' *before* you started crying?"

"Well sometimes you don't know . . . "

"You're saying you start crying before you realize you're not having fun?"

"Yeah, it's automatic, I mean—there's two kinds of crying—there's when you're sad and start crying and then there's when it's like suddenly the whole world is just going to end . . . "

ㅇㅇㅇㅇㅇㅇㅇㅇㅇ

Sometimes girls do things in movies that they shouldn't do. Sometimes it's because of money or drugs or shoes, sometimes there is a person holding a knife or who is much bigger than them in front of the door, but sometimes, even in the absence of all these inducements, the line gets crossed anyway.

Late one night in a Koreatown Denny's surrounded by, and mostly occupied by, pairs of crack addicts and lone mumblers, while I bite into a pie that will make me throw up later in the sink of the Standard Hotel, Osbie says, "There's this thing that happens about once a year, and people say it's an urban legend, but it isn't—it actually happens. Some guy is driving a truck stacked with four-inch drainpipe on a flatbed . . . "

"Okay . . . "

"And he crashes or he stops short for whatever reason and the pipes slide and they punch through the wall separating the flatbed from the cab of the truck and through the back of the driver's seat and through the truck driver's chest.

"And in every recorded case, every medical journal says the same thing: if the first EMT on the scene puts a coat over the drainpipe sticking out of the guy's chest—to hide it from him—and just says, 'It'll be okay, we're gonna take care of you, it'll all be fine,' while they cut him out and get him to the ICU, then they operate and the guy lives, but if the first EMT just gets there and goes, 'Jesus Christ, you've got a four-inch drainpipe sticking out of your chest!' then the truck driver goes into shock and dies. And this is how some of these girls are—they're just walking around with a fucking four-inch drainpipe sticking out of their chest and if you just never draw their attention to it, then nothing bad will happen just yet."

ooooooooo

There is not much arguing that needs to be done, to people who read books, against the sexual abuse of children. The body of pro-child-rape literature is admirably thin. However, every Drainpipe Girl I've ever met was also a victim of the *other* kind of child abuse, and this kind of child abuse still gets a lot of play in 2008. This is the school of parenting where parents imagine their child as a decorative status symbol and a child's life not actually as an existence being experienced by a fellow and self-aware mind but merely as a slow, monitored transformation into a pension plan or morality badge. This is the school where parents force pre-made ways of being into the child the way naïve, plastic eyes and fixed smiles are shoved through fresh, thin vegetable skin by the proud owner of a brand-new Mrs. Potato Head kit.

On his birthday, which comes during National Child Abuse Prevention Month, the leader of the world's oldest and largest institution, and great advocate of Potato Head parenting, Pope Benedict XVII, talks to a group of American bishops. He blames the Catholic Church's problem with child abuse on an environment where "pornography and violence can be viewed in so many homes through media widely available today."

The next day, Candy posts a video of herself being raped and molested by a demon with eight tentacles and the pope meets with five of the people who were raped or molested by Catholic priests whom he himself personally prevented police from investigating.

Candy, in an early cut of the movie, tries to fend off the demon by throwing a stuffed bear with stripes. It is not an effective tactic. What she should've done, according to the pope, is say the Prayer of St. Michael.

"The prayer is useful not only for priests but also for lay-people in helping to fight demons," says Vatican spokesman Father Gabriele Amorth, senior exorcist of the Diocese of Rome.

Church authorities are, however, conflicted about whether or not demon sperm is like that of ordinary men or is icy to the touch.

Candy maintains that the eight-armed demon's semen is not only "cold" but "gross."

It is made from a combination of one part Johnson's Soft-lotion to two parts Glow-in-the-Dark Slimy Ooze from Holly-wood Toys and Costumes on Hollywood Boulevard. The Ooze makes the mixture remarkably cohesive, and you can do a cum shot, screw it up, and then scoop all the goo up without leaving any behind and try again, which is good because as the goo tends to tremble gluily from the lotion pump as it comes out and overlap the edges of the tentacle tip as if it's just some stuff dangling down behind the monster's tentacle (which it is) rather than gushing (optically) from a fixed point at the tentacular apex, it has to be done several times and takes a steady hand. It's also good because it makes the whole thing go faster, which Candy likes because the goo is, as established, cold and gross.

Lots of people help make the monster. The very drainpipey Tracy Stixx helps make the tentacles, the cores of which are made of long cylinders of rolled cloth and the skin of which is made of condoms. She needs a lot of condoms—unlike Africa, which does not need a lot of condoms, at least according to the pope, who feels that condoms help cause "a breakdown in sexual morality."

Speaking of breakdowns in sexual morality, Tracy Stixx used to be a coked-up Craigslist hooker.

Tracy Stixx doesn't know where to buy condoms. You would think that perhaps one of the only advantages of having been a coked-up Craigslist hooker would be, when it was all over, at least you'd know where to get condoms. You'd be wrong. We tell her.

You would also think that being the incumbent party's candidate for the most powerful office in the world would mean you'd know that condoms are used for other things besides making tentacle monsters that fuck Candy Crushed, but you would also be wrong.

The day the video is posted, a reporter in Iowa asks John McCain, "Do you think contraceptives help stop the spread of HIV?" and, after pausing to think about it, or just pausing, he says, "You've stumped me."

This begins a long back and forth on the question—during which the candidate says he's "never gotten into these issues" over the course of his twenty-one years in the military, eighteen years in the Senate, and seventy-two years of having a cock—which goes until another reporter cuts in and asks him how fat a pig he once saw was.

○○○○○○○○○

When it comes to the unfamiliar issue of fucking, McCain says he defers to the judgment of Doctor and Senator Tom Coburn of Oklahoma. It is Tom Coburn's opinion that breakdowns in sexual morality come about because of the Gay Agenda. Other people will tell you breakdowns in sexual morality come about because of abuse.

So:

Sometimes you will see a porn star interview, or a blog, or some personal ad that a nonporn woman has posted somewhere, with someone who sounds like she's got her shit pretty much together, saying she likes to be choked or hit or spit on or tied up, or gag on cock.

There are a lot of people who will tell you these women are lying and will tell you that they pretend to have orgasms in private when guys choke them or tie them up for years and years and years because they are seeking some obscure form of approval whether or not the guys in question evince any opinion either way on choking or hitting or spitting or gagging or tying. And when these amateur psychiatrists are forced to concede the basic fact that all evidence suggests you can be about as sure certain sober girls like certain violent things as much as any person ever can be sure about what another person wants, then they say this:

*"Well it's probably just they were abused as children."*

As if being abused as a child means you're pretty much totally useless as a human being and you aren't actually entitled to your weird orgasms or, if you are, then you shouldn't tell anyone about them because it's all just so terribly toxic.

It is widely known that a disproportionate number of porn actresses suffered sexual abuse as a child or rape at a young age. Nothing I've heard while talking to girls in porn suggests this isn't true.

The pop-psychological explanation of this correlation is, roughly: people who go through insane *childhood* things related to sex later go on to do insane *adult* things related to sex.

There are three popular and slightly less woolly variants:

1. *Abusive parents who do insane sex things will, through the magic of heredity, produce children who do insane sex things.* Which is obviously wrong because many of the incidents of abuse are not actually committed by family members.

2. *People who grew up in families so deranged and/or neglectful that the children were allowed to suffer sexual abuse were clearly not raised properly and so are likely to fall into crime and crimelike vices.* Which is alright as far as it goes but doesn't explain why the correlation is specifically between *sexual abuse* and later porn stardom rather than *all kinds of abuse or neglect* and later porn stardom.

3. *Porn chicks just want love and attention, and an experience of sexual abuse accustoms them to expect love and attention to come in sexual form.* Which is directly contradicted by the behavior of those porn girls who enjoy their work at all, since they are totally capable of having regular love-and-attention-type relationships simultaneously with totally heartless fucks. In other words, the porn chicks who *like* their work act a lot like men. And not all men were abused as children.

Swiss-cheesy as they are, the pop-psychological explanations satisfy both the part of the population that wants to feel as though there must be something wrong with women who like to have sex all the time with lots of different people *and* the part of the population that feels as though there's something distinctly too-good-to-be-true about women who like to have sex all the time with lots of different people.

Although it may be good enough for the audiences of both Oprah and Howard Stern, the problem with the pop explanation, scientifically, is that it's painfully vague and, ethically, it's condescending. It can only explain women who are hypersexual *and* fucked up. Now there *are* lots of them, but not every girl who wants to fuck all day wants to because she is confused or desperate or has some kind of child-abuse genetic marker. Like most painfully vague and condescending explanations in psychology, the pop explanation of hypersexual women is Sigmund Freud's.

Forgive me for getting technical—this part probably won't be funny or hot—but we *are* talking about my friends here. Feel free to skip to the next chapter if you don't like science.

Basically, Freud believed in something called the *compulsion to repeat*—a desire to move toward earlier states of being. It is the basis of nearly all of Freud's ideas. Why do you want to fuck your mother? Because (depending on what year you asked him) either you're trying to crawl back into the womb or when you were a kid your parents fucked you. (Presumably Freud meant that organisms only feel compelled to repeat *intense* experiences—otherwise he'd need to explain why adults don't feel a compulsion to wear pajamas with feet and eat strained carrots.)

So where did this compulsion to repeat come from and why would animals have it? Freud, in his—already suspiciously titled—*Beyond the Pleasure Principle*, explains the origin of the compulsion by evoking the earliest and most primitive lifeform—our original single-celled ancestor—and saying that, shortly after it came into being:

"The tension which then arose in what had hitherto been an inanimate substance endeavored to cancel itself out. In this way the first instinct came into being: the instinct to return to the inanimate state."

Or, in other words, because the first organism on earth was fragile and died quickly—thus returning to its previous state—we all inherited from it the desire to return to earlier states.

The problem with this is it flies in the face of all later, and *earlier*, scientific discoveries about how evolution, brains, and biology in general work and, like most of Freud outside his observations that people think about sex a lot and occasionally have notions that aren't conscious, is now believed only by morons and literary critics.*

In fact, scientists before and after have tended to believe the opposite—they agree that the "returning to the inanimate state" is generally the last thing on most organisms' minds (even when they don't *have* minds) and that the only drive that unifies life—from bacteria and pond scum to polar bears and dogcatchers—is the drive to discover strategies by which to keep themselves animate as long as possible and help them make more things like themselves.

People will do any strange thing, of course, but science can explain this away as a random mutation. It only asks for an explanation when a lot of people all do the *same* strange thing after having the *same* strange experience. So without the compulsion to repeat how *do* we explain how people who are unwillingly fucked as kids become adults eager to fuck?

One explanation offered by many of the most articulate women in the sex industry is that it has to do with control. Approximately:

---

* Even Freudians admit that the "single-celled-organism" thing is laughable and one I know said that they generally assume that Freud was just unusually coked-up when he wrote that. Okay—but so then where *does* the compulsion to repeat come from?

*Once upon a time, something grisly happened to me, and I was not in control of it, but now I can revisit that same area of experience, only this time, I am in control.*

This does explain why so many of them have fetishes that seemingly exist in order to trigger the memory of the abusive situation (being hit, insulted, saying "daddy," etc.). There is something a little cloudy and incomplete here, however—it doesn't explain why revisiting that place in better circumstances would be pleasurable on anything but a *symbolic* level. After all, you aren't controlling the fuckwad who raped you— you're just controlling a similar situation. The idea that a person wants to have sex in a certain way primarily in order to prove a point about herself to herself seems a little distant from a bodily reality that creates an orgasm. Without more explanation, there's still a zone of Freudish voodoo here.

Another common explanation involves the violation of taboos—people allegedly always want what they can't have. Does that really explain why getting it should give them an orgasm? For some people, yes—and why?

Many women report that they like someone not because that someone is desirable or attractive so much as because he makes *the women themselves* feel desired and attractive. This makes biological sense. Your organism likes to hear that people want you and think you are pretty—this is survival-positive news—and it will reward you with endorphins for finding a situation in which this is the case, to encourage you to stay there.

Under these circumstances, it is not altogether unreasonable to see how a group of people could be neurologically wired to feel that if someone wants what you have *so much* that they are willing to cross, despite all of society telling them not to, the student-teacher line, or the parent-child line, or the human-rapist line, or the line between the hater and the object of their hate, then that person must want what you have a *hell* of a lot and that this would be—correspondingly—a hell of a turn-on.

Another thing about taboos can be gleaned from watching any nature special about baboons. There they all are on their rocks, staring off at a tree. The beta male creeps up and starts doing the alpha male's main baboon-squeeze. One of the other baboons notices and suddenly the alpha male and his crew are bounding through the grass to rip the beta's face apart.

There is probably a switch on some people's circuit boards that says: *If you're fucking someone against the rules, you'd better cum quick before somebody notices.*

Again, though, this is still largely in the subject's head and fits nicely in with the stereotype that sex for women is mostly mental—and doesn't really go very far in explaining why the taboos a woman likes to violate are so often specifically ones the woman associates with her abuse.

Candy Crushed has a very physical explanation, that, while contradicting neither the "control" nor the "taboo" ideas, seems to explain more people's behavior more clearly than either one by itself:

Our possible range of responses to small things is drawn from the library of our memories of big ones. That's why people who have had long lives are more likely to cry when they see something happen to someone in a movie than people with little experience of the world. It makes you think of something you saw.

The psychological damage caused by abuse is not so much the memory of the event as the emotional trace of it in the mind (some people have a hard time identifying what the bad thing was—but they know there is a *bad thing* there). It is an extremely *intense* experience. Ordinary events and experiences around or after it—for years and years—seem faded or gray in comparison, not worse, but less dominant. Quieter.

The future that's typically offered you by your parents and the rest of the characters in your environment—years of school, then years of work, etc.—seems not only to offer more of the same but also to avoid any mention of—or intersection with—the alternate and menacing plane on which the abuse took place. So the most powerful emotional marker in your mind is a distant and awful experience that was, to put it as simply as possible, bad. And everything good that happens after seems to happen on a lesser and grayer scale of magnitude. You get butt-fucked by your uncle and then, the next day, someone yells at you for losing your paste. Things that are supposed to make ordinary people happy or sad are molehills in the shadow of a morbid, thousand-mile-high monument to suffering and shame at the center of the city in the brain.

The abused person then not only wants to *not* be abused—but she *also* wants to try to set up experiences of pleasure that equal or exceed the mental and emotional peak of pain that, otherwise, will be the highest and clearest peak in the history of her feelings.

So she goes to the place the heavy bad thing came from—the sex place—and tries to see if there is a heavy good thing there, too. Because nothing else has that weight. You can't erase pain from life, but you *can* get enough pleasure that life seems worth living anyway.

So some people in the business—I think that's them.

There are some others, though, that are just totally fucked up.

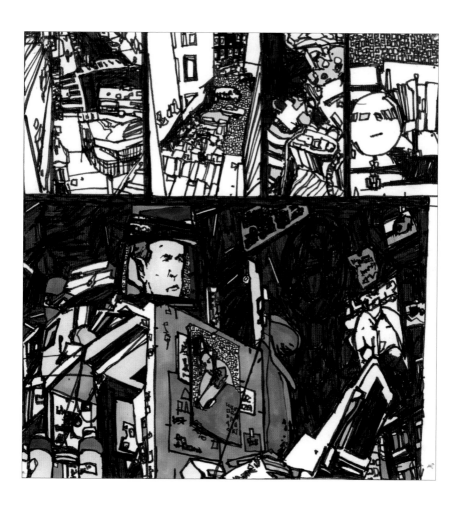

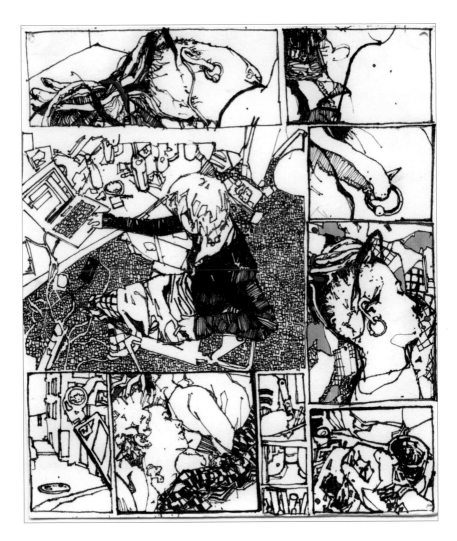

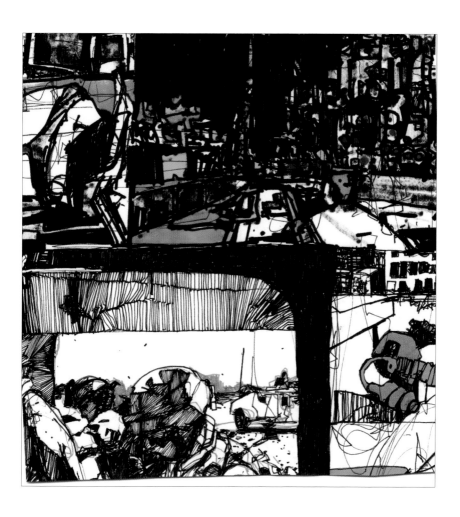

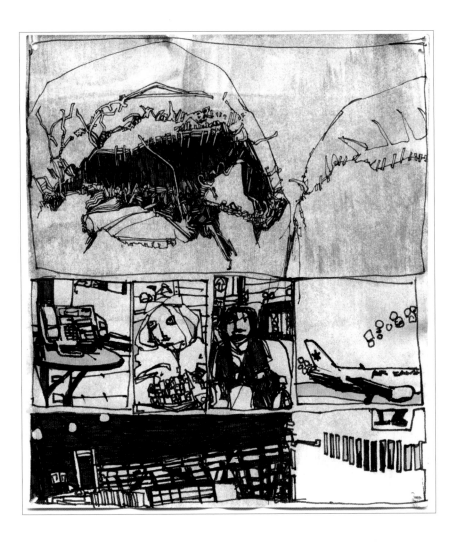

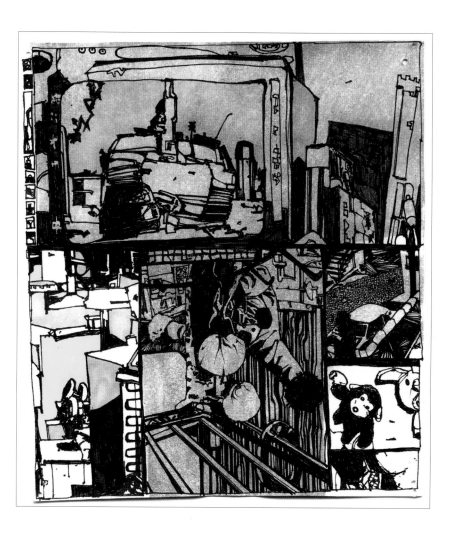

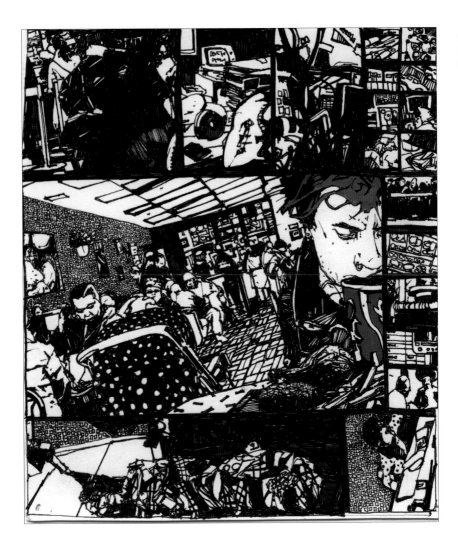

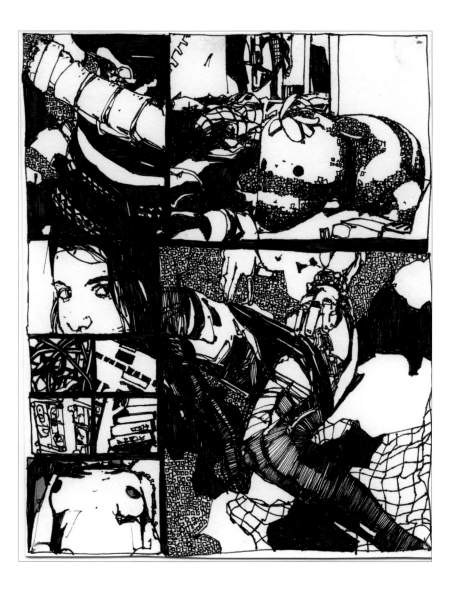

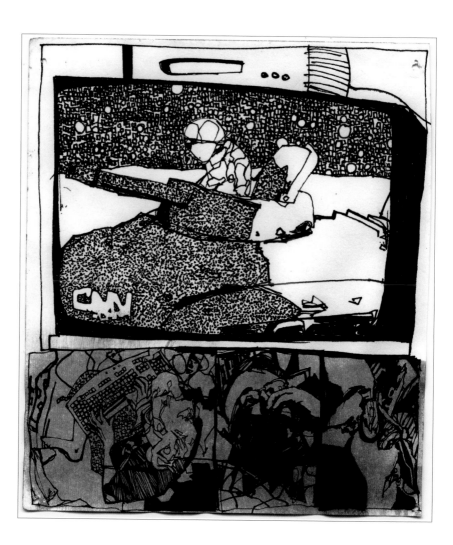

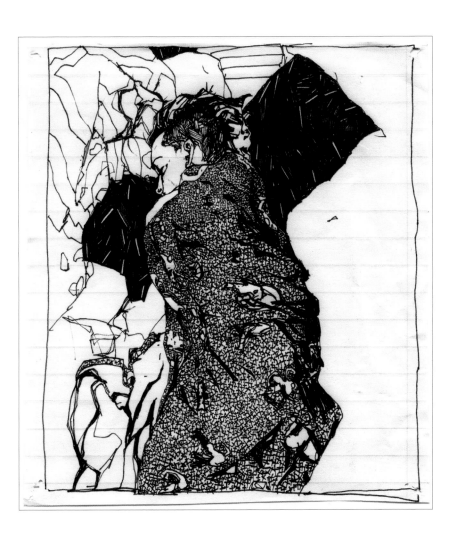

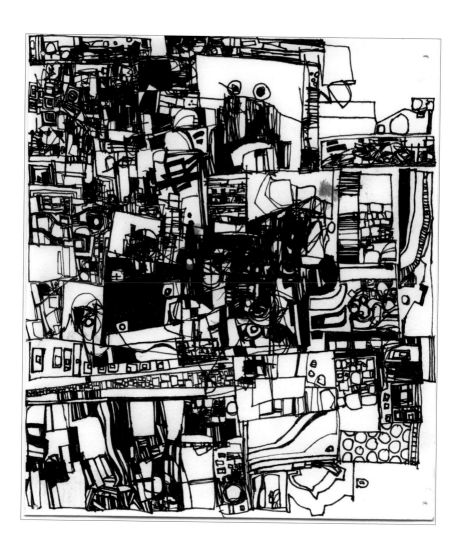

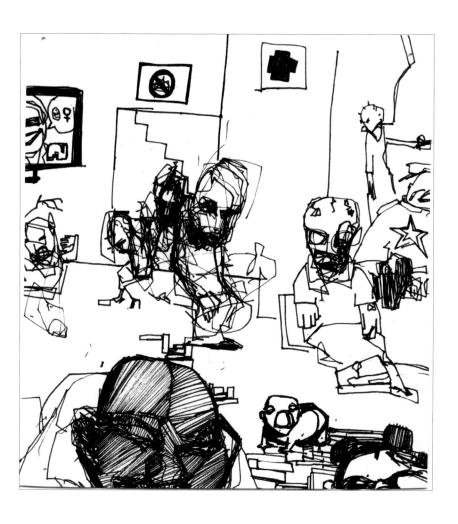

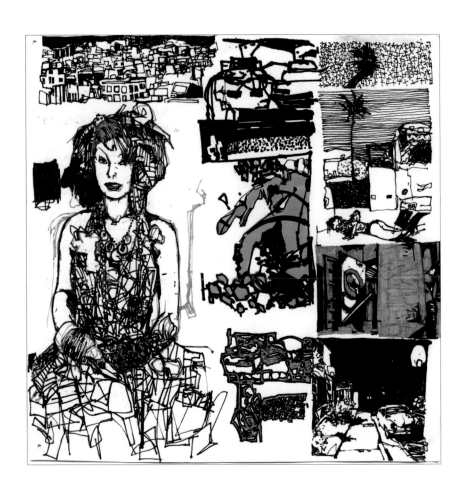

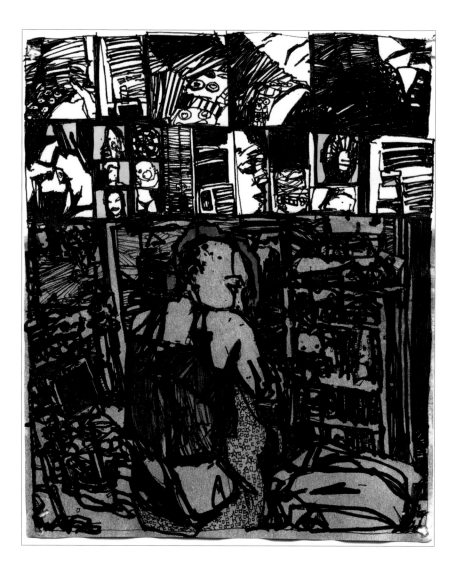

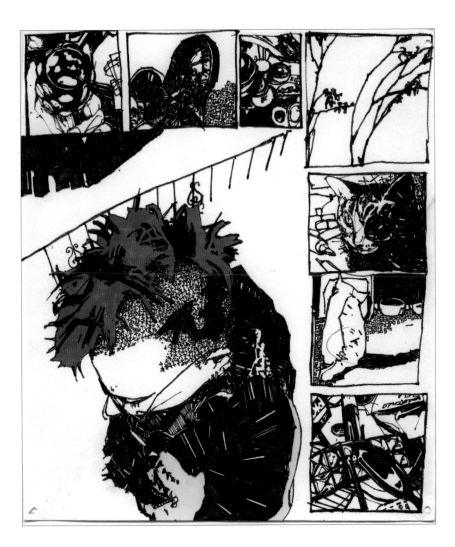

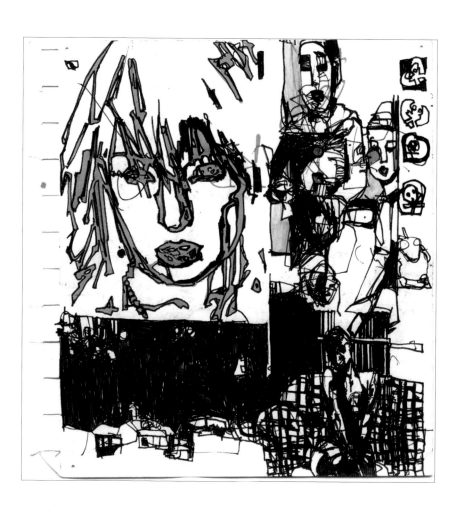

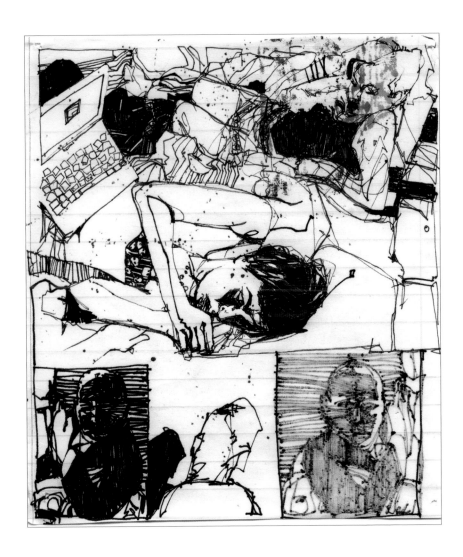

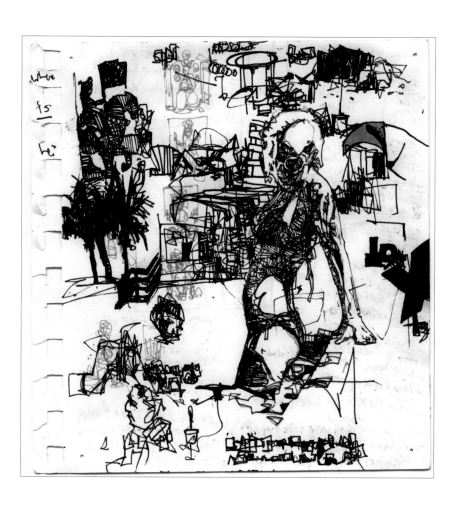

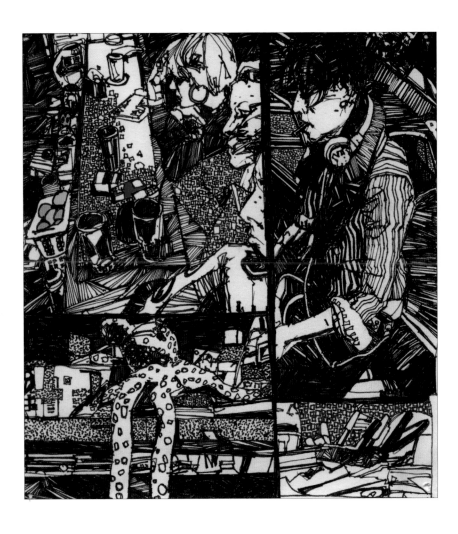

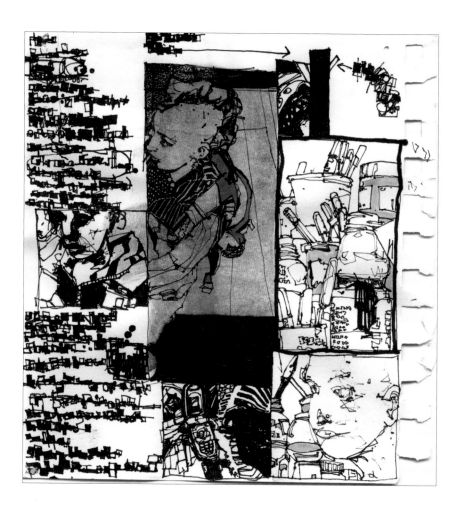

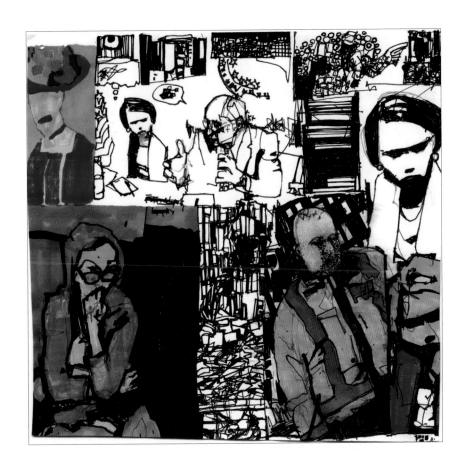

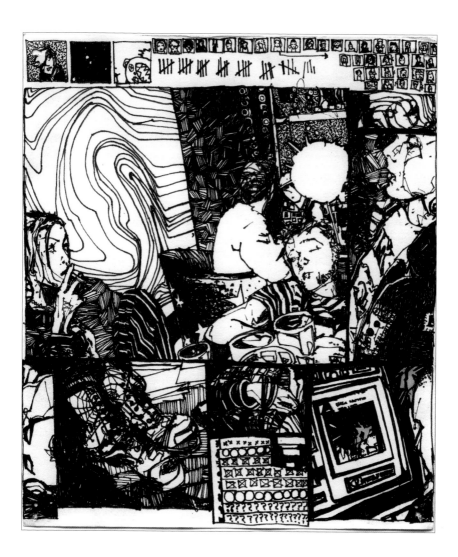

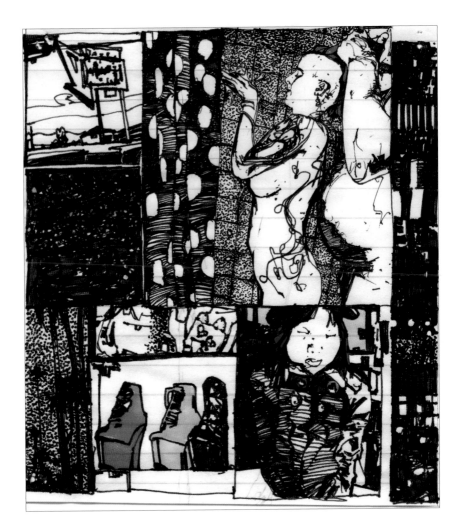

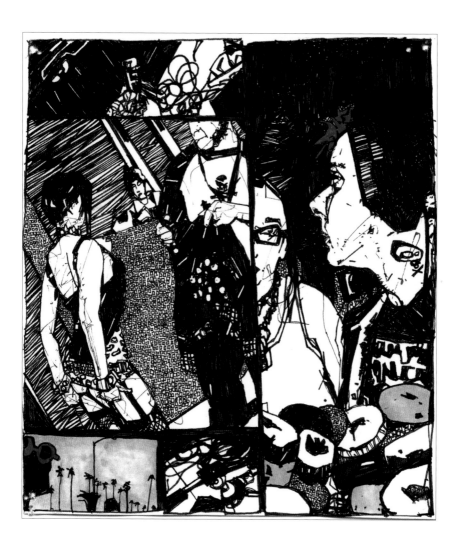

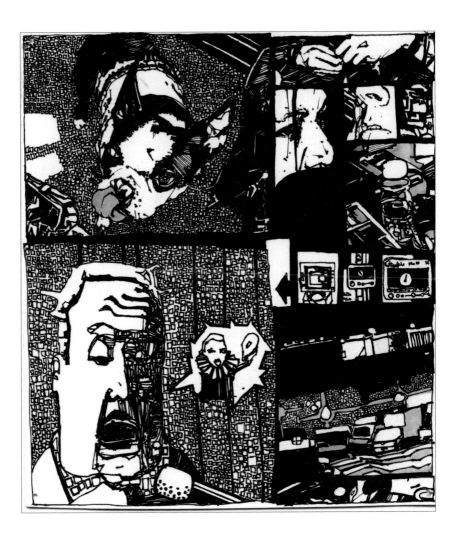

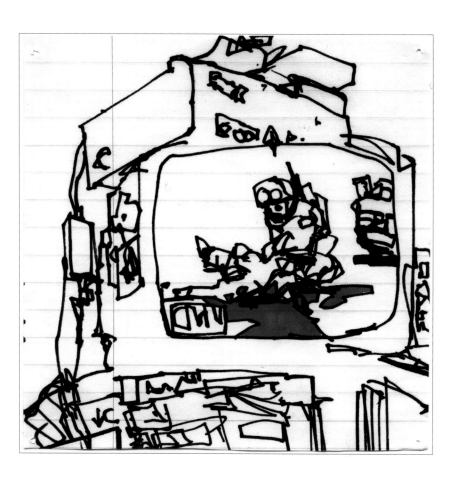

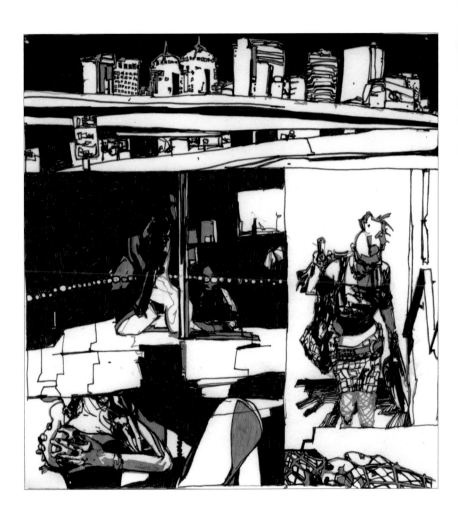

# Conversation I Have with Leom McFrei Just before Shooting MEDICAL

**L: "Yeah, it's just like—** on these other movies it's, like, heartbreaking, like the studios don't *get* him and things get fucked up and fucking Max Clamm was in there and I just feel like he never gets a chance to just, like, do his *thing*. I mean, I'm psyched, y'know, 'cause, like, you know I love Osbie, right, I've always like loved his stuff and this time he's really gonna get a chance to just do it and I'm totally behind him. It's gonna be good. I'm excited."

Z: "Yeah, it'll be good."

# Conversation I Have with Osbie Feel Just before Shooting MEDICAL

**O: "I don't want to get** too ambitious on this one—nothing crazy, no Hindu gods or robots, just a camera pointed at cute girls fucking and whatever. I'm gonna make it for Intensity-Alt, we give them an Intensity-Alt movie, nothing can go wrong. I mean, we get Candy's tits and Madeline's ass and some cameras—what else do you really need? It's porn. I'll just make it so easy nothing can go wrong."

Z: "Totally, totally."

# Conversation I Have with Osbie Just after Shooting MEDICAL

**O:** . . .

Z: "*Fuck*ing Jesus fuck."

O: "At a certain point I just started laughing, y'know . . . like it was just funny."

Z: . . .

O: . . .

Z: "Fucking . . . *fuck* . . . I don't know man, it's like—remember that time you said you felt like that headline in *The*

*Simpsons*—'Local Man Ruins Everything'? This reminded me of that time when Marge tries to start her own pretzel company and she ends up with her head on the kitchen table and she says to Bart and Lisa, 'Never, ever try. Aim *low*, kids, aim so low you can't possibly fail.'"

O: "Yeah . . . " and there is a long pause where you can see him looking off through the windshield into an infinity of things he could say and finding no reason to say any of them and then saying, "*The Simpsons* . . . sucks."

Z: . . .

O: . . .

# MEDICAL
## (part one)

**The script opens with me**
fucking Candy ("Lucy" in the movie) from behind.

Candy wears a wig that makes her hair look normal and my head and tattoos are cut out of the shot so it looks like she's fucking some other guy. It is like a window into an experimental reality created to demonstrate how the rules of our universe would have to be altered in order for Candy to get more work.

*"Once again,"* a voice-over says over this sex, *"she was look-ing down at a long trail of cum spurting onto dirty hotel sheets. The swirls and filigree of sperm always looked like Arabic writing, sometimes Sanskrit. She had always thought that if only she could learn to read that writing, she might know her entire future."*
Then: *Cut to black. Fade to Lucy's POV: Int. hospital room.*

Lucy/Candy/the camera sees failing paint and pipes turned leopardlike with wet rust and then pans over to a wall sten-ciled with the word *Medical*, which is the title (because Osbie knew *Necrotic Flesh Heralds the Godless Void* wasn't going to fly with Intensity), and then over to a pair of nurses stacking pickled fetuses. (The original script reads, *"Because fetuses are gross."* The revised script reads, *"Because fetuses are a source of ancillary protein."*)

The nurses are Slice 16—a narrow, leggy girl with bat tat-toos on her, who one female fan says she likes because "she has the most beautiful vagina I have ever seen, she has per-sonality, and I can relate to her" (which is the kind of baffling thing female porn fans say about porn girls a lot)—and Mad-eline Sharp, a curvy, dark-eyed, juicy-assed plum from Las Vegas, whose calendar the entire production has been sched-uled around, and whose appearance at the same place and the same time as Slice 16 is so difficult to arrange and is actually arranged for with such desperate skin-of-teeth ingenuity by Leom that Osbie forever decides that Leom is the finest pro-ducer on earth, and whose girl-girl scene with Slice is the cin-ematic, logistical, and erotic centerpiece of the whole *Medical* experience so far as Osbie is concerned.

Anyway, they have sex. Then there are two flashbacks to Candy/Lucy's life before ending up in the disturbing sex hos-pital: one where Suzanne Lin plays with a kitten while dressed like a witch and Lucy brings her cupcakes and then has sex and one where Lucy scams a girl in a car out of ten bucks by pretending she's having a miscarriage and is covered in blood and then has sex and has candy (small *c*) poured on her.

Osbie then appears as a doctor in the hospital, who is high or drunk and also bad. He tells Lucy that she is a drug addict and a sex addict and a lesbian, then Lucy stabs him in the head with a screwdriver and escapes and Carly Nixon and I pick her up in a car and have sex with her on a small wooden box, which is about as fun as or more fun than it sounds but more difficult.

Then the nurses reveal they are seeing this fucking on a little TV set that is scanning Lucy's brain[*] and they say that it's really contrived and that Lucy should write porn movies and then Ella Revenge gets suspended (really, actually) from flesh hooks over Lucy and gets fucked from behind by this guy Ash and splatters blood all over Lucy while the doctor whispers:

"Lately, I've been studying the connection between night terrors and seizures. They act on the same part of your brain,

---

[*] And there is also a footnote at the bottom of the original script:

> *Every emotion Lucy expresses is ambiguous. Is she really scared, or is she just faking it? Is it lust or just opportunity? Her lifetime of elaborate scams, coupled with the opportunistic nature of junkie day-to-day survival, have left her true motivations enigmatic even to herself. She has embraced the mind-set of a hive insect: capable of always putting the most sympathetic face forward, but never truly in touch with one's own desires. She would make an excellent spy, a sociopathic agent for shadow governments. She could trick herself into passing a polygraph test; "I suspect that you could blend into a crowd of no one if you had a mind to," as someone once said to me.*

Which doesn't happen because it's not even stage directions or dialogue and so why is it even there, and also the last part of which I thought was total bullshit except then I remembered that Osbie was supposed to hold a light stand on someone else's movie during a sex scene once and in the final cut of the scene you could clearly see him, full-body, crouched like a random light-stand-holding guy, in the lower left-hand corner of every long shot throughout all the sex so I guess he was right because at least whoever edited the film didn't notice him.

you see. A person having a night terror will be awake, conscious, for all intents and purposes, but paralyzed, unable to escape the experience. And it is a completely irrational experience, your mind is telling you so; you lie there paralyzed, unable to move, but you obsess over the terror. Like, your mind tells you something stupid, like: 'If the ghost in the air conditioner doesn't eat enough moths, my lungs will stop functioning.' Now you are awake, your conscious mind tells you that this is all irrational gibberish, but damned if every sense in your body hasn't jacked this up into a life-or-death struggle. Seizures, after all, are primarily a symptom of membrane depolarization. The only difference between an epileptic and a junkie is that an epileptic never had a choice."

# MEDICAL
## (part two)

**Osbie alleges this script**
was inspired by a drawing I did of Candy in a hospital bed
once while she was at Doctor's Medical Center in San Pablo,
which we ended up at around 2:00 A.M. one morning because
it was the closest place when she started having an asthma
attack her Salbutamol couldn't fix and which was like this:
    "What's your social security number?" "She doesn't have
one. Like it says on the form." "And your name is?" "Like it

says on the form." "And your address?" "Like it says on the form." "Do you have insurance?" "No. She's Canadian, like it says on the form." [Verbal essay on the various payment levels and what will be done to her if she fails to pay.] "*We'll pay it all in cash as soon as we're done, please hurry.*" "Heart rate's pretty high for Salbutamol. Are you sure there isn't anything *else* you wanna tell me about?" I want to tell you about going and fucking yourself, you condescending shitfuck—if you were five feet tall and trying to breathe through acutely asthmatic lungs and arthritic ribs buried under size FF tits and everyone you met seemed not to actually care if you kept living you might have kind of a fast heartbeat, too. "Okay, so I just paid this bill for three hundred bucks, but whenever I pay a hospital bill I get the same bill again in the mail after I paid it already, is that going to happen?" "You're going to get another bill from the doctor." "Um, well can I just pay that in cash now?" "That's a whole other department." "So what you're telling me is, I am going to get a bill sent to me from that doctor sitting right there, and I am not allowed to pay it now, and no one in the hospital can tell me how much it will be." "Yes." She looks around at her people as if, like, *duh!* "Can you call us a cab?" "Do you have any *money?*"

In the script, the hospital is depicted as a circus of rancid dilapidation and is ably, if a bit fussily, played in the film by a rotting, charming art deco ex-hospital in Culver City. Actually, the rooms and machines and pills of Doctor's Medical Center were clean and modern and kind and thanks to them Candy didn't die, and the rancidness of Doctor's Medical Center was strictly human. However, all things—including that this is how they act when you *can* pay and when there's no other patients in the emergency room, and how much money and time Osbie himself has spent watching people die in hospitals—considered, making the hospital *look* like a fuck-realm of evil neglect falls well within the rules of the expressionist tradition.

Anyway, so that's why Osbie made a movie about a hospital. He'll also tell you that the cupcakes are in there because girls like cupcakes, the flesh-hook scene was in there because Ella and Ash wanted to do it and it sounded fucked up, the Slice/Madeline scene is there because he really really wanted to see it, and the getting-scammed-out-of-ten-bucks-by-a-girl-pretending-to-have-a-miscarriage-and-covered-in-blood is in there because it once actually happened to Osbie.

# MEDICAL
## (part three)

**Lots of things once** actually happened to Osbie.

Once, at a friend's funeral, the family started smoking crack and weed in a car parked outside the South Central graveyard, and Osbie smoked it with them with the windows rolled up while some local children shot bottle rockets at the car. Once, Osbie found a kid in his Hollywood High stagecraft class murdered and hanging. Once, Osbie married the unwitting model for the character Roxy in the semipopular comic book *Gen 13*, who, in turn, was beloved by a comic-book-collecting junkie porn star who used to fuck Osbie. Once, there were distressing revelations about dead family members of Osbie's who were fairly distressing to begin with. Once, Osbie had a job on a *Star Trek* show, but not one of the good ones, and anyway he likes *Star Wars* not *Star Trek*. Once, Osbie walked onto a subway car where everyone was vomiting and crying because someone had just thrown himself on the tracks. Once, Osbie was dressed up like an RX-78-2 Gundam and fell unconscious while making out with a girl dressed like Strawberry Shortcake and when he woke up he was on a median strip and people were peeing on him. Once, Osbie was urged to take giant roaches from *Fear Factor* home with him. Once, Juan Beak swung his balls in Osbie's face. Once, Osbie was disgusted by the ocean. Once, Osbie had friends who kept selling their babies for speed. Once, Osbie went to Sea World and all the manatees did was suck each other's cocks.

Los Angeles is a sprawling ghost town crawling with the ghosts of things that happened to Osbie. Los Angeles happens to Osbie. And to everyone else in Los Angeles.

And everything that happened on the set of *Stagger Lee* happened to Osbie* and everything on *Far Gone And Out* (and everything *in Far Gone and Out*†) happened to Osbie, and everything on *Medical* happened to Osbie.

* Except the thing about the property guy giving marijuana to the developmentally disabled kid, because that turned out to be a lie. What actually happened was the guy had these homeless meth heads working for him cleaning up the warehouse. They left their works there and asked the property guy if they could have them back and he said, "No," so the meth heads told the cops they found a dead body in the warehouse and they came and searched the place and found a bag of pot, but it was no big deal because the property guy was actually worried about the truck pallet full of weed he was holding for a Very Well Known Los Angeles Street Gang Who Shall Remain Nameless and which the cops didn't notice at all.

† Except the elephant-head thing.

One night—before shooting starts—around 5:00 A.M., Suzanne calls from her car crying and tells me that "the worst thing" has just happened.

"The worst thing?"

"They found out."

"Your family? About the porn?"

"They said that . . . "

The theology involved was more complex than the threat, but it involved the staining of the family honor, and murder being acceptable in God's eyes under certain circumstances, and Suzanne being defective from birth. All of these ideas she seems to believe or not believe or repeat or question, like a true sub, depending on who is talking to her. The basic idea is that she would come to live with her family again, and not talk to any of her friends again, and then eventually the whole family would move back to Japan, and so she should go out in the car and think but if she drove away she was disowned, and that, most important, no one else was ever to know about this.

"You should come home, Suzanne."

"He said he saw something, he saw me in something, a clip, I don't know what it could've been—like, he said it was something with cum in it—but I don't think I have any creampies online but—and—and he saw *God* when he saw it."

"Okay. *That's crazy and you should drive away and come back to LA.*"

"But don't you think that's kind of a scary thing to see *God* in?"

"Listen to me, Suzanne, this is important. Are you listening?"

"Uh-huh."

"I think it's very important that you drive home now."

But she stays on the phone, crying and sifting through

meaningless arguments, unnoticed, on a street somewhere in Orange County.

"I think my battery's dying."

"Are you sure you don't want us to come get you?"

"No, I'll be okay. I'll just talk to them in the morning."

"Do you think you'll be okay?"

"I think I'll be okay . . . as long as that scarecrow doesn't come any closer."

"Scarecrow?"

"There's a scarecrow on the hill. When I look it moves closer."

"Suzanne. You're hallucinating and that isn't real."

"It's not real?"

"No, and I think you must be really tired."

"Yeah."

"You think so?"

"Yeah, I'm going to sleep."

"Okay, you sleep, but call again in the morning when you wake up so we know you're okay?"

"Okay."

So although, many months earlier, Suzanne was planning on *maybe* coming out of retirement just to do *Medical*, it's definitely not happening now. So the script is rewritten so that Lucy runs into her doppelgänger instead of bringing Suzanne cupcakes and sex.

Her doppelgänger is played by Dixie Rok because the first time Osbie ever saw Dixie Rok in real life it was with Candy in Las Vegas and Candy had a white shirt and a studded belt and a pink mohawk, and when Dixie Rok showed up she had a white shirt and a studded belt and a pink mohawk and they thought this was funny and then had sex.

Except in the movie they *don't* have sex because Intensity rejected that draft of the script because they wanted more boy-girl scenes in the movie and so then the camera follows Dixie Rok as she goes to have sex with a boy.

Except it isn't Dixie Rok because her cell never works right and because her car breaks down when she's visiting from Vegas and she's stranded in LA without Internet access and she needs money or she'll have to go to jail for a traffic viola- tion but she doesn't want to strip because she lives in Vegas and her mother was a stripper and her sister was a stripper so it's just such a cliché and she doesn't have enough for an AIM test and the last time anybody saw her she was having boy- friend issues and was cut up and covered in infected bruises at the Rite-Aid on Sunset and Gower.

So then, anyway, the least-tanned girl the agency could send over on a day's notice is written into the script interrupt- ing a *"handsome young junkie"* played by Nathan, who is play- ing a video game, except, when the camera moves, we see it's not a game but just a burned-out TV set with bits of glass and fire in it, even though he's got a controller and seems to think he's playing. Nathan looks more like the buff, blond, all- American kid they hire him to play on MILFattack.com than a junkie, but he's on the movie because everybody likes Nathan and would like to give him the opportunity to fuck a girl his own age once in a while and there's no time to be picky and also he's pretty good.

Except today he *isn't* good because today everything must go wrong because of the obvious sucking hex vortex created by having Tracy Stixx (see below) and Osbie on the same set at the same time.

Likewise: I completely fuck up the Zak-and-Candy sex scene by making everyone but Candy leave the room every five minutes while I get my hard-on back because there is an addict in the crew who—I know for an electronically recorded fact—constantly talks smack about Osbie and me whenever we aren't around; Slice 16 does not play Nurse Number Two and therefore participate in the entire-raison-d'être-for-the-whole-movie-nurse-on-nurse scene because Slice didn't get on her plane at JFK and is therefore replaced with the first nonblonde the agency could get on the phone on two hours' notice; the stabbing screwdriver is replaced with a stabbing pencil because it's hard to rig half a screwdriver sticking out of someone's head because screwdrivers are heavy; and ex-coke whore Tracy Stixx does not play the girl in the car who gets scammed out of ten dollars because she is the kind of girl around whom appliances break, ropes unravel, dogs attack, friends go mad, and the take-out guy gets lost and forgets the rice and the kind of girl who will, at the end of a long day, sometimes clap and hop up and down and say, "I didn't hit any parking meters today or poles or people!" and so no one really would want her driving near them anyway even if she didn't, on the day of shooting, have some eye infection, which blurs the vision in her right eye and forces her to stick to her original job of being a production assistant and so just basically wander around the set with medical gauze taped over one eye like a roaming goddess of bad luck. Also: Anna Queen replaces Carly Nixon because Carly Nixon has been lying on Nathan and Lacey McNeil's couch for months saying she can't work, Anna Queen's *mom* comes and hangs out while Anna is in makeup—which, yeah, no one can explain—and of course the cock-jinxing junkie cameraman is still around for that scene and the flesh-hook scene is canceled because Ash is arrested for a parole violation (assault)(framed)(apparently) and put in a supermax prison for three years, and the police confiscate all his money and also Ella's because she can't prove it's not his and because they think, with no evidence, that he's a drug dealer and a vampire-cult leader and they print that Ella does porn in the local paper along with her name and address and so everyone in the town she lives in hates her and she has to sell her house and move to another state, and when she drives up to the prison on the one day a month she can see him they tell her she can't come in because her skirt's too short. And the credit card company says they can't run the risk of doing billing for her site anymore. And someone sideswipes her car on the freeway and spins it around completely and totals the car.

So that's *Medical*.

# Death

**Because he is such a shy**
and private person, unexpectedly noticing Osbie Feel talking
to anyone he doesn't already know always feels like some sort
of reality mistake.

Even after the oxygen hisses in and you remember *everyone* has to go around getting things done even when you're
not around, the impression remains that Osbie must be *lying.*
Even if all he's saying to that waitress or hostess who's bend-

ing over him on the other side of the scrubbed window glass is "Oh, I'm fine, I'm just waiting for a friend," there is something about the weight of what's not said that makes it seem like a lie.

"Oh, here he is," he says (unconvincingly) as I walk into the House of Pies.

"How was Gina's party last night?" he asks—not wanting to get right to the point and accidentally aiming straight at it.

"It was alright. You know it was a black-eye beauty contest . . . yeah . . . well I saw the invite and I got all excited—any excuse to use fake blood, y'know—so I told Candy. And she said, well, if she's gonna have a black eye, then I should have one too—which I thought was alright since then, on our way over, people wouldn't think, like, I'd just domestically abused her. So we got there and we were early and just Leom and Shadrach Meshach and Janna are just standing outside and Leom's all, 'Hey, did you hear from Osbie?' And I say, 'No, is there some disaster?' And he says, 'Well, uh, yeah, um—why don't you walk with me?' And so I say, 'Okay'—and smile all goofy at everyone like, 'Oh great—what's this?' and go walking with him. And then so he shows me your text message like 'Hey I just attempted suicide this morning,' right? And so then I walk up to the corner and spend two hours outside trying to get you on the phone and I realize I'm in front of Popeye's on Hollywood Boulevard at midnight with a big black eye with blood running out of it and down my neck looking desperate on a cell phone and people keep looking at me—this one blonde just walked right past and just pointed and laughed. Like just *ha ha*. I thought about running up and kicking her but somehow I felt like because she obviously thought the eye was real but it wasn't that somehow that meant I secretly won, but I don't know . . . so yeah, that was the party . . . "

I once asked Osbie—I suppose in a vaguely why-not-get-out-and-embrace-life-and-try-new-things-type spirit—why he always ate here at the House of Pies and never went to Fred 62, across the street. He then world-wearily explained that whereas the House had always been here in this part of Los Angeles, Fred 62—with its Fred McMurray egg sandwich and its grilled Bukowski—was clearly a recent and interloping attempt to capitalize on diner chic brought in once the neighborhood had gotten trendy. He did admit to liking the boots the waitresses wore, however.

The House dates from the heroic and aerodynamic age of diner design, at least in its basic architecture and permanent fixtures, but it was obviously redecorated in weak pastels in the '80s and neglected ever since. The surfaces, like the staff, have become timid and ignorable. The owners, like the pale zigzags and thick spirals integrated into the booth cushions, might have come from something Greek or Mexican, but are now clearly neither. The nearly invisible pictures hanging there, done in tissue-box colors and matted on broad strips of slatey burgundy, show views of dense, seaside neighborhoods, empty of all commercial, animal, or human traffic—with the blue ocean sometimes explicit and sometimes implied—and would be striking in their airbrushed autism if there were any reason to look at them.

Osbie explains, in strictly local and logistical terms (they had him on a lot of medication, there was someone there he wanted to fight), why he hadn't gone to the party. Over his shoulder, the glazed strawberries of a white cake stare wetly up into the ceiling from under a glass dome. Candy won the beauty contest, but I don't mention that.

We jockey into a pattern, with him (deaf in one ear, and so probably loud enough to unnerve half the lunching seniors) laying out his unsurprising reasons (other than obvious recent—constant—stressors and precipitants) for trying to kill himself—namely, people very close to him who shouldn't be and who particularly don't like him being a porn director and a slut—and me trying to reassure my friend that I haven't taken his suicide attempt as a sign he's gone insane.

Performers in the adult-film industry often note that society unfairly pressures people not to behave like performers in the adult-film industry. Now, you will also hear, from the kind of people who automatically don't like this book, that society unfairly pressures people *to* behave like performers in the adult-film industry. Since they're both right, it's easy to see how this could create a problem for people who care what society is pressuring them to do. However, it can also be a problem for *smart* people, since sometimes society appears in your living room in the form of someone you care about, drunk, crying, and throwing sharp or heavy things.

Nearly everyone in the Industry faces Osbie's dilemma at least once, and it's never pretty. This is what strippers and porn starlets talk about when they're alone in the dressing room and are done talking piercing gauges and feminine hygiene: the wrong kind of love coming around again.

I'm not sure I can say Osbie actually *looks* any different than usual, but there is something dried and narrowed about him—perhaps having to do with the potential for a smile having deserted his face. The features seem to relax gratefully in the knowledge that at least one social obligation can be safely crossed off the calendar—at least for the length of *this* conversation.

He talks and I eat.

Gnarled and moist, the House's stunted hot dogs doze in their buns like the red cudgels of brutal children—but they are good. The fries, on the other hand, are terrible and there is no reason to order them. (At Fred 62, it's the opposite.)

The only other visible change in Osbie is that the joke-sized pimple that had dominated the tip of his nose during the shooting of *Medical* is gone. It is hard to say how long it'd been there—at least a month—since I always tried not to look at it. It was the kind of awful blimp that would've put anyone's face off its game—the first and most obvious step a cartoonist or special-effects artist would've used to make it clear to children that they were dealing with a twisted schemer, or a pity-worthy mole-person. Probably as inspired by its new absence as by anything else, I say:

"Well you know I don't want to be all sweetness and light here, but—y'know . . . "—I try to use my tone to explain how I know this is stupid— " . . . like, most people, they are in a bad way—but even if they weren't, they haven't got much immediate chance of getting *out* of their current, real-life, practical problem." I hold up one hand, like it's balancing a pizza. "And, psychologically, they haven't got anything that's their own—that they like to do—where they can park their mind" —I hold up another invisible pie— "I mean—and you've got *both*, so . . . it's bad but it doesn't have to stay bad. Y'know?"

Looking at my two raised hands, I realize I am not going to bring up the children of the Lobster Boy, Grady Stiles Jr.

"You're looking at all this rationally," Osbie says, "but I'm—well it sounds all emo and goth and it's not like this but this is the only way I can think of to put it right now, so: Your life is wonderful and everybody likes you and thinks you're great but I'm not like you." Okay, fine . . .

He twists in his booth. "There's something that's *always* been like that—I can't stand people, I can't handle people, I never have—there's something wrong there. There's a reason

I never look anyone in the eye. I don't ever want to be out
or to do things or . . . " I try to nod the most sympathetic
nod you can nod, without it becoming a nod that pretends
the nodder knows what he does not. He says, "I'll put it
like this—most people's memories go back to when they're
four or five—mine go back much further." Someone moves
across our daylight, holding a lime pie with an interesting,
five-way cutting wheel sunk up to the hilt in its meringue.
"My parents—we'd moved—we just moved into this house—
you know the house—and it was all bare wood floors. And
there was a marble—like a, like a regular glass marble, and
I dropped it and it rolled in between the floorboards. And I
spent hours—*hours*—trying to dig it out from the gap, *hours*,
like that marble was the whole world and it would just be over
if I didn't get it out. I've always been like this."

I try out that nod again.

I'd helped him move out of that house—he'd put me to
work smashing hundreds of unsold copies of *Darklands 3* one
by one with a crowbar so he could throw them away without
someone stealing them and eBaying them and driving down
the price of the rest of the copies.

I ask about his new shrink. He's alright, but the first thing
he told Osbie to do is join AA, but Osbie has a problem with
God. I make a totally halfhearted argument that I know people
who were in AA in New York and they say the whole admit-to-
a-higher-power thing is really just, y'know, a thing you say to
say things aren't in your control and then you just . . .

"Look, I've done it, I've been in and out a million times,
and . . . "

"I didn't know that."

"Well, you're not supposed to, it's *anonymous*."

He almost almost almost smiles.

"Yeah, but I always assume that nobody is unless they say they are because I know so many people who say they are that if even half of the ones who *don't* say they are actually *are*, then I'm like the only person in the world who's not in AA and it's like a secret tree house."

"Well anyway, even without the God thing, I *hate* twelve-step programs. Like the *people*. I just can't stand the whole thing—like, I was—I'm obviously not supposed to tell you, but I'm going to—I was at this meeting, over here, and Dwight Eisenhower was talking. And she was saying how she was with someone—she didn't say who it was, but it was obvious it was Dwight Eisenhower—anyway, they wake up one morning in bed and there's vomit all over them and they don't know whose it is. And he doesn't care, he's like okay, but she's— she's really affected, right, like, 'This is really . . . bad,' and she was up there and she said it and it was all really intense. It was, y'know, it was like that, like it's supposed to be. And then I see her a week later on some show—like a week later—and she's getting interviewed, on *Entertainment This Week* or whatever, there telling *the same exact story*—only it's like all funny now. It's just . . . I fucking hate it."

"Yeah, well, it's LA, y'know, movie people are . . . "

Movie people like Los Angeles and are like Los Angeles.

Los Angeles is the worst place to be depressed. The lack of seasons suppresses the basic death consciousness encoded in the brittle claws of fall leaves, cold iron railings, and sullen light stored in the empty streets of residential districts in older cities farther north and farther east. And the desert is carpeted in deco storefronts and vivacious young trees that refuse to reflect any reality but their owners'. "I'm tired," you say, listing across the city. "Whatever," says LA, in the language of some salmon-pink concrete abutment or pitiless lawn—or else it tries to convince you it's too busy to say anything at all.

"The other thing he said right away"—he's talking about the psychiatrist again—"was when I told him I did porn he said, 'Well do you feel like you should be in such a predatory industry?'"

The waitress hovers over that sentence and asks if we want anything else. I don't want mozzarella sticks, perhaps for the first time in my life. I ask for another hot dog.

Over new coffee, Osbie says, "The first thing they said when I got to the hospital—they ask you your occupation—'Porn? You should quit.' The desk people. It's not like they're going to believe me when I say the only good people I know are in porn."

Otherwise, the shrink is good. He says things to Osbie about himself that are exactly the things I say about him, and that I say because Osbie is always saying them to me about himself, and that everyone else who knows him says. They are, also and ridiculously, what tarot cards say about Osbie—at least according to the rather myopic six-cards-where-there-should-be-ten reading given in the first porno movie I did for him, a reading whose *predictive* reach clearly expired eighteen months earlier, and whose first card Waite suggests "is rather a card of temporary durance than of irretrievable bondage." So anyway, everyone is agreed about Osbie. About what he should do. Get away from bad people. What do you tell the man who knows everything? The only thing now is to go ahead and do it—and we are both embarrassedly conscious of playing along in rickety roles—all molasses and clichés.

I've done drawings with Osbie in them but none where he was really the subject—unless you count the series of pictures derived from the scene where he has sex with Madeline Sharp while wearing an elephant mask. I keep meaning to do one from a picture I took when we were on the useless Los Angeles subway together. It's from when his hair and mutton chops were growing wild in every direction and he was refusing to cut them on some I'm-going-to-let-them-grow-for-six-more-months-for-every-time-someone-says-I-should-cut-them policy. He was exhausted from going around wearing a double-breasted suit in the sun, and he had a bag with something in it, and he was looking at the floor, and it looked like him but different. It looked to me like maybe this was the way Osbie looked when he was alone.

Aside from the wretched and perennial problem presented by all Irish noses, the main thing, from a drawing point of view, is a fundamental disagreement between the eyes and the cheeks. The eyes, bowing to the weight of tradition, accurately reflect a clever inner man—pointlessly contained—an insomniac, and a pedestrian, but the cheeks—there is something *political* about Osbie's cheeks. Even without the sideburns, they would be cheeks from the Gilded Age, made for orating and broadcasting contrived passions, like the cheeks of Chester Arthur or Pancho Villa. His cheeks want to get out there and *do* something, but his eyes want to close, to go nowhere, and sleep.

ooooooooo

He was found half dead, completely out of his mind, behaving strangely, overdosed on sleeping pills, and he put his girlfriend or ex-girlfriend through one of those nights of trying to drag someone loved out of the gravity of a horrible, private, meaningless drug place. Sitting across from a friend who, but for a total coincidence, would be dead, you can't help but think what it would be like if they *were*, and the stupid significance everything would take on if they *had* died.

Trying to figure out how to write this book, I kept having irresponsible semifantasies that someone—anyone—would get murdered (instead of just assaulted, imprisoned, or raped). Then I could call it "Who Killed Tina DiVine?" or "Who Killed Max Clamm?" and all my observations about porn could be wrapped around that death and loaded with the sexy intensity of true crime. And then they'd plaster Sarah Silverman and Anne Hathaway in fake tattoos to play Tina and Candy for the movie.

It never occurred to me the victim might be Osbie. Because no one wants Osbie dead. Arrested, deported, evicted, defeated, ignored, ejected from the premises—sure. Yes. But no one who knows him intimately enough to have any intense feelings about Osbie dislikes him. No one would try to kill Osbie. But not no-*thing*.

No one would want that little black pig cowering in the stall on the set of *Stagger Lee* dead—but they do want their bacon. If it were instead called "*What* Killed Osbie Feel?" this book would have to be much fatter. I would've found it hard to think of any inanimate entity in Osbie's life that hadn't arguably been trying to kill him for years—drugs, Los Angeles, America, money, loneliness, social life, the law, successfully making porn, unsuccessfully making porn, love, lust, his house, his own constantly frustrated and immensely frustrating creativity, hope, hopelessness. If his girlfriend or ex-girlfriend hadn't happened to wander into just that room at just that moment I would be spinning out some crackpot theory right now.

And this goes for all the potentially dead—a list of names from this book I could reel off without even stopping to think—a list much easier to make than any list of potential murder victims—friends who could turn up dead tomorrow and I wouldn't let myself be surprised at all because of the wide range of forces that they tempt by existing. People who no person could possibly want dead but who exist under some lens that magnifies the burning apathy of the world of things. When death comes, it very often comes with eyes averted, and with interceding machinery.

⊚⊚⊚⊚⊚⊚⊚⊚⊚

Candy came from Canada, which, to Americans, is a joke place with snow and mooses. It is also boring.

After *Medical* we go there. We get in, after the usual excitement in the Suspicious-Looking Person Room—the customs guy takes my digital camera and looks at every single picture. The memory card is very large so it takes a long time.

"Have a lot of people been smuggling digital photos into Canada?"

"I'm just checking for illegal images."

"Illegal images?"

"Like child pornography."

He doesn't ask any questions. The thousands of images are, of course, mostly pornography. He goes fast. I suppose after working at customs for a few years, you get a knack for telling the difference between a seventeen-year-old on her hands and knees being fucked in the ass on an inch-by-inch-and-a-half screen and an eighteen-year-old on her hands and knees being fucked in the ass on an inch-by-inch-and-a-half screen.

We'd invited Osbie along and he comes in hours later; they look at him and send him to the Suspicious-Looking Person Room, where he tells them he's there to see me. I am Googled.

After reading about me, they then decide to do a criminal background check on Osbie. They find an old DUI, to which Osbie pled no contest, and on which the statute of limitations has expired. The person in charge of the Suspicious-Looking Person Room tells Osbie and all the other people working under her that technically she can use this to deport Osbie. The people under her, who are all Canadian and so are all drunk all the time, go, *Oh come on.*

Of course, maybe Canada is right. In addition to his DUI, Osbie has, after all, abused dangerous drugs. But then, so has the president . . . and the president before . . . and the president before that.

Bill Clinton said he didn't inhale and that's just politics— just like LBJ saying one of his opponents maybe fucked a pig, that's just democracy. Whatever, Bill. But now it's the zeros, and lying has entered a fascinating baroque period. G.W. Bush saying he did coke because he was stupid but then he found God and so then he wasn't stupid anymore and people believing it is creepy and bodes ill. And Obama, the most gifted political orator of our age, saying he did coke in order to "push questions of who I was out of my mind" and expecting to be believed, and *being* believed, is creepier and bodes iller. In 2012 I expect Osbie Feel will be elected president after saying he became a junkie because a flying turtle named Cyril Beeswater convinced him that shooting heroin was the only way to save the magical kingdom of Froompius.

For the time being, however, Canada assigns two very reluctant women to watch over Osbie in their small airport until his airline has another flight back to Los Angeles.

Candy's father picks me and her up at the airport, as usual, and, as usual, we head out on a turnpike that goes into the horizon.

When we drive in the summer, we drive between lots isolating one-storey branch headquarters of obscure companies with letters for names and open fields and trees and huge, green nothingness.

In the winter—which is long—the roadside is just endless banks of stacked white—gray-bellied and pitted by exhaust—inches from the motes and flaws of the fogged windows.

Over the hiss of heat or drone of the AC, we listen to Alice Cooper, or the racing bands of sustained static hum coming across the lonely traffic.

Candy's father is a narcoleptic—he is always falling asleep. He also has a small dreamcatcher hanging from the rearview mirror, and I used to wonder whether, if he were to fall asleep and crash and die, the dreamcatcher could be emptied out like a flight recorder's black box and you could see his last dream before dying. (Recently, I found out dreamcatchers are supposed to be a kind of protecting spider—their purpose is to keep nightmares *away* and make it so the sleeper only has good dreams. Knowing that, having one in *that* car just seems unsafe.)

"Is this where you hit that deer?" Candy'll ask, on a seemingly meaningless hairpin bend.

"No, but over there is where I hit that guy."

The guy had been drunk in the snow, Candy's dad tells us, drunk in the snow and wandering in the dark when he lurched in front of Mr. Crushed's car. But the guy didn't die.

Visiting Candy's family in Canada, I end up thinking a lot about death. Not usually violent death—usually the other kind. Canada isn't really violent. It's just *cold*—cold and quiet and white and endless and enormous. The towns and clusters of homes seem arbitrarily spread across the long, slow, white empty.

The beautiful thing about the night is, there is always the impression that, even if there's something there you can't see, there might be something there. There might be anything. In the white-daytime car-ride, on the other hand, you see nothing, and you know there's nothing.

While we sit in the car, thousands of Canadians and thousands of Americans and thousands of other people are watching Candy and Grace fuck me after having rolled around in ice cream and Twizzlers and Mike and Ikes on a new video posted that day.

"Each day, it seems, thousands of Americans are going about their daily rounds—dropping off the kids at school, driving to the office, flying to a business meeting, shopping at the mall, trying to stay on their diets—and they're coming to the realization that something is missing. They are deciding that their work, their possessions, their diversions, their sheer busyness, is not enough."

Obama said that, in one of his speeches about God, and in LA, while I was shopping with my basket at the 99-cent store near Sunset and Micheltorena for ice cream and Twizzlers and Mike and Ikes, I was thinking the same thing. What was missing was two girls rolling around in the candy and then fucking me.

Here's something everyone knows:

There is everything in the whole world and there is, in stark contrast to it, *death*, which is the time when there isn't everything in the world anymore.

John MacArthur of Grace Community Church in Sun Valley, California—who is, as we drive, telling his people that "the Word itself is the sea where Christ the pearl rests"—has some very clear ideas about death, and what he'll do until then, and even what he'll do after then.

All the people in all the cars all over the turnpike from the airport have got some ideas about death and are all driving somewhere to do something about them.

Alice Cooper on the speakers says he's eighteen and he doesn't know what he wants and he likes it.

I don't know if I believe him, and Candy's dad sings along.

°°°°°°°°°

Gina Giles calls Candy about Gina's next feature. Gina's decided she does not want Candy to do the interracial blowjob, but she does want her to do the blood orgy.

"Who are the other girls?" I ask.

"I don't know, I think Gina called me first."

"That makes sense. There's no point in making a movie without you in it because you're the best."

"But I guess no black cock for me."

"You gonna argue with Gina about black cock?"

"No, I mean, it's her movie and she's really excited about it, she should do it however she wants. I'll just text-message her."

"So you *are* going to argue with Gina about black cock?"

"No . . . she should do what she wants."

Gina calls back.

The blood orgy will be with Tasha Rey and, if she can get her, Christine Ice. Tasha and Candy have worked together before; the scenes are unpredictable—Tasha's eyes are greedy with dreams, and Candy's mismatched ones are greedy to see what you're greedy for. Candy wants to use real blood; Tasha Rey wants to use real blood—"like you could use pig's blood," they tell Gina. Gina is going to use lube and food coloring.

Gina wants to see blood, she doesn't care how it got there.

Candy is morbid. But, if anyone comes by a predilection for patterns of death's-heads in baby pink wearing big baby bows honestly, it is her. She is ready and inoculated.

And "Suffering is justified as soon as it becomes the raw material of beauty"?

This probably makes good sense to people who make their money printing French gibberish on the back of pretty girls' necks with a vibrating electric needle, but the rest of us can't be blamed for demanding proof. It'd be nice if we could do an experiment: do a life with *no suffering* and see how it works out.

When *I* was a child, my parents gave me books explaining how the Buddha said all of life is suffering (this was before they started giving me books explaining how the Buddha had great investment tips). This would seem to suggest, by extension—and rather conveniently for painters—that *life* becomes justified as soon as it becomes the raw material for beauty. But the Buddha is not someone I take much advice from.

The longest and most involved songs on the subject are generally by doom-metal bands. Candy likes doom. She also likes your heavier industrial products, anything featuring women shrieking, as well as death metal and grindcore. Especially that band Death.

It is tedious to go into technical details, but some people may not know the difference between *grind* and *death*—the extremist's choice in music for the last twenty years of the last century—and *doom*, which suddenly became very big in underground music in the zeros. It's easy, really:

Doom can be as simple as grind, or as complicated as death, only it's slow.

Doom comes from the Anglo-Saxon word meaning "law" or "judgment."

Parties interested in doom should investigate Grief, Neurosis, Winter, and Sleep.

The *shortest* punk song on the subject of suffering (or any subject) is by Napalm Death, and I reprint the full lyrics here, as they are cogent and relevant:

*You suffer . . .*
*But why?*

Maybe I'll get it on the back of my neck.

# Mailbag

**Outside professional stuff**
and hate mail, my mail tends to fall into a few categories: art
students with questions; men who self-consciously announce
that they are eccentric and that they like my art; women who
solemnly, tentatively write that they are artists—or "just"
something else—a hairdresser or broker or mother—and like
my work; and the porn mail, which from the guys is generally
in a yo-bro-you-think-you-can-hook-me-up-type key and from

the women generally follows a line of "Oh my God, I hope it's not creepy to say this but . . . " Also, outside hate mail and fan mail, there is a considerable percentage of abstract expressionist mail whose approval/hostility valence is impossible to measure, like a woman who says she is an art student and here is a painting she did of me sucking on balls and how she'll see me at my next opening and wouldn't like to fuck me and is a leopard, or a guy who said he read an article where I said I gave up painting completely and went into porno for the money and how he thought this was dumb and how he's a "serious money/power guy" and has a big cock and owns a building and would like me to draw something on the side of it for him.

Candy's mail is generally less strange, evasive, embarrassed, and sexually dimorphic. It usually begins with some sort of straightforwardly appreciative message—"You have an amazing butt!" or "My boyfriend and I watch your porn every week!" and then goes on to ask some semiconversational, preflirtational question like "What are you doing this weekend?" "What kind of music do you like?" "What does that tattoo say?"

Well, you know what that tattoo says and you know what kind of music Candy likes, so now what is Candy doing this weekend?

So far, she is asleep.

Candy is blonde today, and asleep in her two white socks and sun-shot lace underwear, shoved face-first into a blue snowdrift of bedding, ass up, little lacquered fingers all askew, (blackpinkblackpinkblack) under a picture window where the bright ink of the day fades into a pale powder clinging to the chaotic and green crowns of one more postcard line of hundred-foot palms anchored in a cityscape-horizon long shot drained of foreground distraction by a block-long parking lot.

It is exactly the kind of moment they were hoping to get when they invented Los Angeles. "We'll need a blonde, and a butt, and the sun, and palms, and dreams . . . "

Let's hope she's having a good dream, and never mind that the palms are all full of rats, and the sky is the most poisonous sky in America, and that the parking lot is a Mormon church parking lot and that Mormons are the driving force behind the state's Defense of Marriage Initiative this year, and that they think that the prophet Joseph Smith was once hit in the head by a five-hundred-pound toad who knocked him fifty feet, and that there are thirteen million of them (Mormons—not toads).

If Candy is having a bad dream, she will come up out of unconsciousness rueful and resigned, as if she is just getting off a day at the office the likes of which no one here could possibly understand.

I have an interview to do. Someone's writing an article—it's a phone thing. I check my mail.

"Hey, hi. Yeah, well enough . . . " They want to slaughter six thousand wild horses—the government—it says on MSNBC.

"Wait, what? . . . Yeah, I guess, shoot . . . "

*Inbox (0) Junk (15)*

"Not so much—I mean, I was at the police station—and the cop there sees I have tattoos and he points to his bicep and he starts explaining like what he wants to do is he'll get a yin-yang here and the ocean here"—*Slate: Should we eat insects?*—"and then around it's like the universe, and then he wants a tear dropping down into the water—and it's like, y'know, usually you see a cop and think, 'Well at least he's not a hippie,' and then usually when you see a hippie you think, 'Well at least he's not a *cop*' . . . yeah, the full package."

I'm shaving. Our new bathroom mirror makes it look like we have two of everything, two silver razors, two blue razors, two toothpastes, two cans of Gillette Series Gel with their bald black-domed cyclops heads spattered with a sky-colored web of foam, two aerosol cans of Candy's Giga Hold in radioactive yellow.

But, the interviewer wants to know, do I think there is a stigma against tattooed performers in the adult industry?

"I don't know about a 'stigma.' I think maybe just a lot of people don't like it."

"And what about," she asks, "being *in* the adult industry—a lot of people, in my experience—I mean how many people just won't even talk to you because you're in the Industry? I mean, I did porn for a few years and there were just so many people that were just like, 'What?' I mean, all kinds of people that just didn't even want to talk to me or have anything to do with me anymore . . . "

"Yeah—maybe so . . . " I open a window and think about it: friends' boyfriends and girlfriends, some Yalies and secretaries and neighbors, people's bosses, half of Candy's family, half of my family. "It's pretty great, isn't it?"

The morning air is good, and belongs to us as much as them.

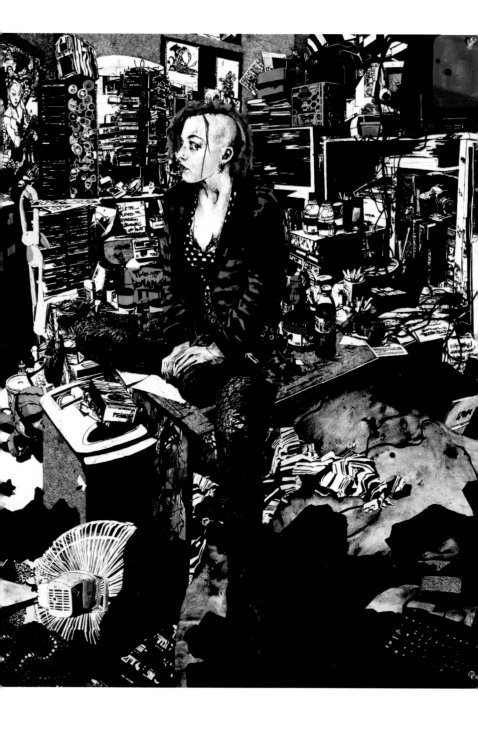

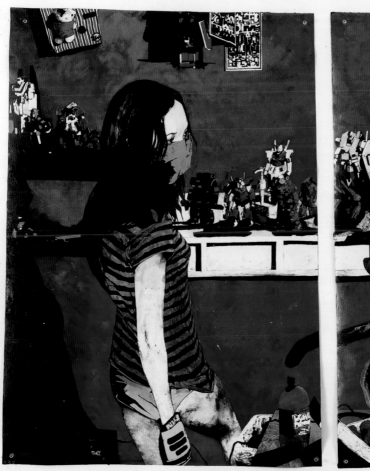
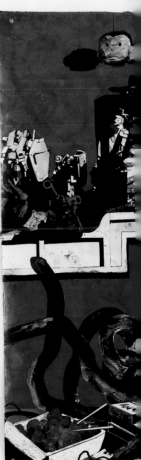

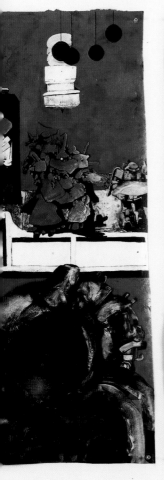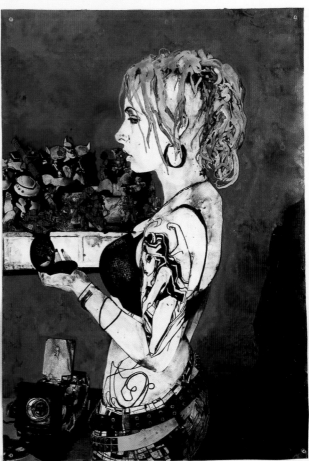

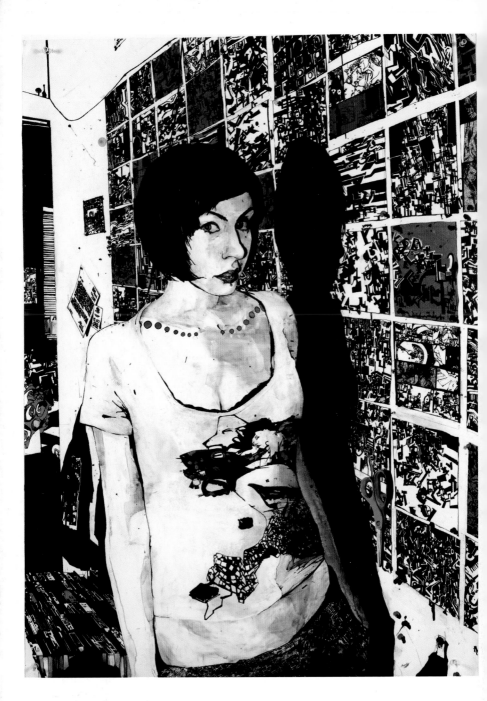

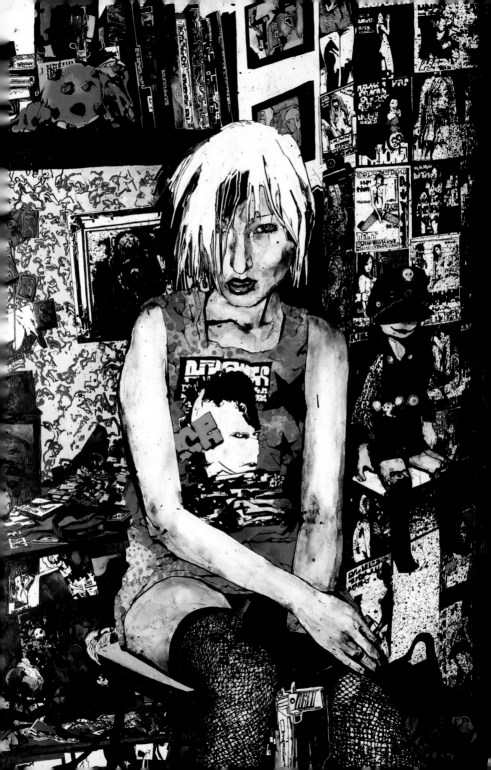

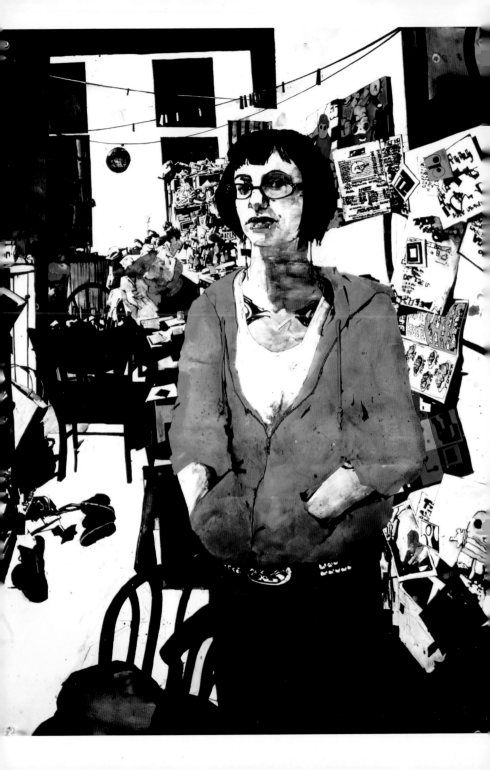

# Technical notes on the artwork

**The drawings** were done in ink on paper using whatever pen was around, usually a Uniball Vision Micro or Pigma Micron. The paintings are acrylic paint.

Although there are no photos, there are two images that are derived from drawings that have been transferred and altered in a chemical darkroom using a process called contact printing. It brings out the texture of the paper and the color in the ink and makes the drawings blurry in an interesting way.

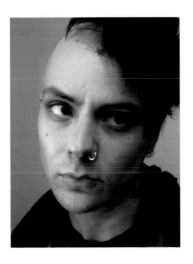

Zak Smith's paintings and drawings are held in many major public and private collections worldwide, including the Museum of Modern Art and the Whitney Museum of American Art. His other books include *Zak Smith: Pictures Of Girls*, and *Pictures Showing What Happens on Each Page of Thomas Pynchon's Novel Gravity's Rainbow*. This is his first book with writing in it. He lives and works in Los Angeles.